Book 1: allegorical co...

all is not as it seer...
operates on two levels
1) what it 'looks' like
2) what it means

Red Cross →

strays from path
yet his...
due to self deception
ie. → believes Una is unfaithful
→ believes that Duessa is Una
→ comfortable in house of pride ○
→ proud of defeating Sans joy ○

→ when Duessa ...he, T, he switched
think → R/c's self deception =
she's talking about him

Self-deception → Byrd
more connection

Una   pilgrimage

Duessa

THE STRUCTURE OF
ALLEGORY IN
The Faerie Queene

Oxford University Press, Amen House, London E.C.4

GLASGOW   NEW YORK   TORONTO   MELBOURNE   WELLINGTON
BOMBAY   CALCUTTA   MADRAS   KARACHI   KUALA LUMPUR
CAPE TOWN   IBADAN   NAIROBI   ACCRA

THE STRUCTURE OF ALLEGORY IN
The Faerie Queene

BY

A. C. HAMILTON

OXFORD
AT THE CLARENDON PRESS
1961

TO MARY

PREFACE

My interest in Spenser began over twelve years ago in a graduate seminar under Northrop Frye. While writing under the stimulus of his teaching since that time, my very considerable debt to him has only increased. At times I wonder whether I can even say with Touchstone that anything of worth in this 'ill-favoured thing' is my own. While at Toronto I was greatly influenced, as a generation of students have been, by A. S. P. Woodhouse: like Coleridge by Kant we have all been held 'as with a giant's hand'. Through the generosity of the Canadian Defence Department I was able to continue my study of Spenser at Cambridge where my dissertation on *The Faerie Queene* was written under the supervision of E. M. W. Tillyard. Whatever clarity of expression or strength of argument this present study possesses, it owes all to him. Yet in acknowledging my debt to Frye, Woodhouse, and Tillyard I am only too aware that I may seem to echo the boast of Chaos in *Paradise Lost*: 'havoc and spoil and ruin are my gain'.

Since my dissertation was accepted at Cambridge in 1953, it has been thoroughly revised and extended. During this stage of writing my constant mentor has been D. C. Allen. Through my struggle to meet his exacting critical standards some parts of this work have appeared as articles, and for permission to use them I have to thank the editors of *ELH*, *Modern Language Notes*, *PMLA*, *The Review of English Studies*, and *Comparative Literature*. Also I have to thank the Graduate School of the University of Washington for relieving me of two months of summer-school teaching to complete my research.

For their conversation and encouragement I owe a debt to Arthur Barker and J. Max Patrick, and to my colleagues at the University of Washington, chiefly to Arnold Stein, Brents Stirling, James W. Hall, and David C. Fowler.

My greatest debt is acknowledged in the dedication.

A. C. H.

CONTENTS

I

The Nature of Spenser's Allegory

> Beare with me gentle Poet, though I conceiue not aright of
> thy purpose, or be too inquisitiue into the intent of thy
> obliuion: for, how euer my coniecture may misse the
> cushion, yet shal my speech sauour of friendship, though
> it be not alied to iudgement.   NASHE

I

WHEN *The Faerie Queene* first appeared in 1590 Spenser disclosed
the general intention and meaning of his 'continued Allegory, or
darke conceit' in a letter to Ralegh which he appended to the poem
in order to avoid 'gealous opinions and misconstructions, as also
for your better light in reading therof'. From its reception by his
age there seemed little to fear either from misconstruction or
failure to construe his allegory. 'Should the challenge of deepe
conceit be intruded by any forrainer, to bring our English wits to
the touchstone of Art, I would preferre diuine Master *Spencer*,
the miracle of wit, to bandie line by line for my life, in the honour
of England, against Spaine, Fraunce, Italy, and all the world.'[1]
In these terms Nashe had already extolled the '*Virgil* of England',
and the age agreed. That 'hearers hong vpon his melting tong, /
While sweetly of his Faiery Queene he song', is praise we would

---

[1] Preface to Green's *Menaphon, Works*, ed. McKerrow (London, 1910), iii. 323.
The references given below to Spenser's contemporary reputation may be found in
F. I. Carpenter, *A Reference Guide to Edmund Spenser* (Chicago, 1923), pp. 229 f., and
D. F. Atkinson, *Edmund Spenser, A Bibliographical Supplement* (Baltimore, 1937),
pp. 166 f. My references are from the following sources: 'The Returne from Parnassus', in *Elizabethan Critical Essays*, ed. G. Gregory Smith (Oxford, 1904), ii. 400,
Richard Barnfield, Poems, 1594–1598, ed. Arber (English Scholar's Library, 1882),
p. 118; *Du Bartas, His Deuine Weekes and Workes*, trans. Sylvester (London, 1633),
p. 81; *Works of Drayton*, ed. Hebel (Oxford, 1932), iii. 228; *Works of Gabriel Harvey*,
ed. Grosart (London, 1884), i. 217; *Poems of Henry More*, ed. Grosart (London, 1878),
p. 4; *The Collected Poems of Joseph Hall*, ed. A. Davenport (Liverpool, 1949), p. 16;
Ben Jonson, ed. Herford & Simpson (Oxford, 1925–52), viii. 263; *Poems and Letters of
Marvell*, ed. H. M. Margoliouth (Oxford, 1927), i. 186; The Columbia Edition of
The Works of John Milton (1931–40), iv. 311.

expect. But the age found more to praise in the poem's dark conceit which Barnfield found 'as passing all Conceit, needs no defence'. Sylvester saluted 'our mysterious ELFINE Oracle, / Deep, morall, grave, Inventions miracle'; and Drayton honoured the 'grave morrall *Spencer*' whom he found more fit than any since Homer 'to set downe boldly, bravely to invent, / In all high knowledge, surely excellent.' Such praise was given not only by friends, such as Gabriel Harvey who called him 'a deuine Poet indeede', and disciples such as Henry More who found his poem 'as richly fraught with divine Morality as Phansy', but even by Joseph Hall's satiric muse:

> let no rebell *Satyre* dare traduce
> Th'eternall *Legends* of thy *Faery Muse*,
> Renowmed *Spencer*: whome no earthly wight
> Dares once to emulate, much lesse dares despight.

His poetical supremacy extends from Ben Jonson's praise of his 'noble booke' to Marvell's respect for 'the learn'd Bard' and Milton's tribute to 'our sage and serious Poet *Spencer*'. He inspired a worthy band of disciples in his own age and served as midwife to major English poets, such as Milton, who acknowledged that he was his 'original', and Cowley, whom he made a poet.[1] The early praise given by Nashe extends into the middle of the seventeenth century: to Sir Kenelm Digby Spenser's learned works alone provided ample testimony 'that our Northerne climate may giue life to as well tempered a braine and to as rich a minde as where the sunne shineth fairest. When j reade him me thinkes our country needeth not to enuy either Greece, Rome or Tuscany; for if affection deceiue me not very much, their poets excell in nothing but he is admirable in the same; and in this he is the more admirable, that what perfections they haue seuerally, you may find all in him alone.'[2] One who first appeared anonymously in *The Shepheardes Calender* as 'our new Poete', the successor to the 'old Poete' Chaucer, thus became 'England's Arch-Poet'.[3] Harvey was right when he quipped that Spenser was 'HOBGOBLIN runne

---

[1] Dryden records Milton's remark to him in the Preface to the *Fables*, in *Essays*, ed. W. P. Ker (Oxford, 1900), ii. 247. For Cowley's statement, see his essay 'Of Myself' in *Essays and Plays*, ed. A. R. Waller (Cambridge, 1906), pp. 457–8.

[2] 'Concerning Spencer', in E. W. Bligh, *Sir Kenelm Digby and his Venetia* (London, 1932), p. 277.

[3] His title in the 1611 edition of his poems.

away with the Garland from APOLLO.'[1] For he is the English
Virgil, and his poem created 'this our golden age'. But

> wicked Time that all good thoughts doth waste,
> And workes of noblest wits to nought out weare,
> That famous moniment hath quite defaste,
> And robd the world of threasure endlesse deare,
> The which mote haue enriched all vs heare.[2]

'Who knowes not *Colin Clout?*' is not the rhetorical question it
was once; and the modern reader is haunted by that vast disparity
between the poet in his own age and what he has become in ours.

That 'huge heroicke magnanimity' with which he projected his
poem in 1580, a time when the English Parnassus was barren, was
tempered ten years later by an awareness that allegory was not
'the vse of these dayes'. 'To some I know this Methode will seeme
displeasaunt,' he writes to Ralegh, 'which had rather haue good
discipline deliuered plainly in way of precepts, or sermoned at
large, as they vse, then thus clowdily enwrapped in Allegoricall
deuises. But such, me seeme, should be satisfide with the vse of
these dayes, seeing all things accounted by their showes, and
nothing esteemed of, that is not delightfull and pleasing to commune sence.' When allegory declined in favour, his supremacy
too declined. The transition is seen in Rymer who allows that
Spenser 'had a large spirit, a sharp judgment, and a *Genius* for
Heroic Poesie, perhaps above any that ever writ since *Virgil*', but
complains that 'it was the vice of those Times to affect super-
stitiously the *Allegory*; and nothing would then be currant without a mystical meaning'.[3] By the mid-century Henry Reynolds is
almost alone when he denounces his age which sees poetry as 'a
superficiall meere outside of Sence . . . neuer looking farther into

---

[1] 'A Gallant Familiar Letter', in *Elizabethan Critical Essays*, ed. Gregory Smith, i.
116.

[2] *Spenser's Faerie Queene*, ed. J. C. Smith (Oxford, 1909), IV. ii. 33. This edition is
cited throughout.

[3] Preface to Rapin, in *Critical Essays of the Seventeenth Century*, ed. Spingarn
(Oxford, 1908), ii. 167, 168. Cf. Sir Richard Blackmore's reproof: '*Ariosto* and
Spencer, however *great Wits*, not observing this judicious Conduct of *Virgil* [whose
poem all along contains a double sense], nor attending to any sober Rules, are hurried
on with a *boundless, impetuous* Fancy over Hill and Dale, till they are both lost in a
Wood of Allegories,—Allegories so *wild, unnatural*, and *extravagant*, as greatly dis-
please the Reader. This way of writing mightily offends in this Age; and 'tis a
wonder how it came to please in any.' Preface to *Prince Arthur* (1695), in *Critical
Essays*, ed. Spingarn, iii. 238.

those their golden fictions for any higher sence, or any thing diuiner in them infoulded & hid from the vulgar, but lulled with the meruellous expression & artfull contexture of their fables'.[1] Metaphors mark the change nicely: Dryden sees Milton as Spenser's 'son', and his master; but to Pope he was 'like a mistress, whose faults we see, but love her with them all'.[2] Even that love is gone when Addison, who speaks for the new age, allows that Spenser 'in ancient tales amus'd a barb'rous age',

> But now the mystick tale, that pleas'd of yore,
> Can charm an understanding age no more;
> The long-spun allegories fulsom grow,
> While the dull moral lyes too plain below.[3]

When the poem did please again in the nineteenth century, it was enjoyed without being understood. Abraham Cowley, standing at the watershed which divides Spenser's world from our own, records how he was 'infinitely delighted with the Stories of the Knights, and Giants, and Monsters, and brave Houses, which I found every where there', but explains parenthetically that as he was not twelve years old 'my understanding had little to do with all this'.[4] The child's response satisfied future readers. When Warton defended the poem against the neo-classical age which read it merely to catalogue defects, he did so as it 'engages the affections the feelings of the heart, rather than the cold approbation of the head'.[5] Such a response informs Wordsworth's praise of 'sweet Spenser, moving through his clouded heaven / With the moon's beauty and the moon's soft pace.'[6] Suffused with this romantic moonlight, the poem was read in the age of Romanticism; but in such light its allegory could not be understood. It was either ignored, as by Hazlitt who urges readers that 'if they do not meddle with the allegory, the allegory will not meddle with them'; or hardly allowed to exist, as by Leigh Hunt when he claims that the poem is 'but one part allegory, and nine parts beauty and enjoyment'; or where it exists, rejected for being rudely distracting, as by Lowell: 'we may fairly leave the allegory on one side

---

[1] *Mythomystes* (1632), in *Critical Essays*, ed. Spingarn, i. 142, 149.
[2] Letter to Hughes, in *Works*, ed. Elwin & Courthope (London, 1886), x. 120.
[3] 'An Account of the Greatest English Poets' (1694), *Miscellaneous Works* ed. A. C. Guthkelch (London, 1914), i. 32.
[4] Essay XI, in *Essays and Plays*, ed. Waller, p. 457.
[5] *Observations on the Fairy Queen of Spenser*, 1752 (London, 1762), i. 16.
[6] *Prelude*, iii. 280–1.

... the true use of him is as a gallery of pictures which we visit as the mood takes us, and where we spend an hour or two at a time, long enough to sweeten our perceptions, not so long as to cloy them. ... So entirely are beauty and delight in it the native element of Spenser, that, whenever in the "Faery Queen" you come suddenly on the moral, it gives you a shock of unpleasant surprise, a kind of grit, as when one's teeth close on a bit of gravel in a dish of strawberries and cream.'[1] It is surely a major irony in the history of literary taste that the poet whom Nashe considered 'the *Sum* *tot*' of whatsoeuer can be said of sharpe inuention and schollership'[2] became a dreamer, that the poem whose end is to move the reader to virtuous action became a Bower of Bliss where the reader is lulled asleep as Acrasia's victim. Yet such a metaphor dominates romantic criticism. It appears in Lowell's observation that 'to read him puts one in the condition of revery, a state of mind in which our thoughts and feelings float motionless', and is used most effectively in Hazlitt's account of the poem's music: 'the undulations are infinite, like those of the waves of the sea: but the effect is still the same, lulling the senses into a deep oblivion of the jarring noises of the world, from which we have no wish to be ever recalled'.[3]

More recently, in reacting against this romantic indulgence in the poem's sensuous surface, Spenser's critics have urged us to seek the hidden allegorical significance. In effect they echo the poet's cry on seeing Acrasia's victim asleep: 'O horrible enchantment, that him so did blend.' Though the poem's fiction affords delight, it is only a veil which we must rend to reveal the hidden allegorical truth. This modern critical approach derives from Dowden's reply to Lowell in 1882, in an essay significantly entitled 'Spenser as Poet and Teacher'. In the eighty years since this essay modern criticism has transformed *The Faerie Queene* from merely pretty poetry into a serious poem. Now we are well aware of the philosophical ideas, the moral concepts, and the contemporary allusions hidden under the poem's surface. To rephrase

---

[1] Hazlitt, *Lectures on the English Poets* (London, 1818), p. 74; Hunt, *Imagination and Fancy* (London, 1844), p. 73; Lowell, *Among My Books, Second Series* (Boston, 1876), pp. 177, 184.   [2] *Works*, ed. McKerrow, iii. 108.

[3] *Lectures on the English Poets*, p. 85. Cf. Coleridge: 'the poet has placed you in a dream, a charmed sleep, and you neither wish, nor have the power, to inquire where you are, or how you got there'. *Lectures and Notes on Shakspere*, collected by T. Ashe (London, 1885), p. 514.

Warton, we defend the poem as it 'engages the cold approbation of the head, rather than the affections the feelings of the heart'.

Yet our modern criticism inherits a fatal dichotomy between poet and thinker. The romantic reader's response to the poem's surface was not wrong, only incomplete; and the same is true of the modern reader who focuses instead upon the allegorical meaning. Spenser should accommodate both kinds of readers, as he did in his own day when 'hearers hong vpon his melting tong', while Jonson would have him 'read for his matter'. Moreover, in our schizophrenic image of Spenser, poet and thinker conflict. There is, for example, the classic crux of Guyon's destruction of the Bower of Bliss where, in Legouis' words, the poet's 'innate voluptuousness is in constant antagonism with his earnest protestant, almost puritanical creed'.[1] It is true that modern historical criticism can partly resolve this crux by pointing to the parallel controversy in *Paradise Lost* where Satan's heroical stature has also been interpreted as a conflict between the poet and thinker. Both controversies are sustained by modern romantic humanism, and both fail to place the poems in their original framework of Christian belief. In Satan the heroic virtues are defiled by their possessor and by the destructive ends to which they are applied; and in Acrasia sensual pleasure is defiled by its giver and beauty perverted by its end which is to embower the knight in a hell of unsatisfied desire. As Christians we are meant to respond to Satan's magnificence and Acrasia's beauty with the cry: 'lead us not into temptation'. Our response must be that of St. Augustine who, though he had wept for dead Dido because she killed herself for love, as the convert asks 'what is more miserable then a wretch not pitying of himselfe, and lamenting *Dido's* death, which was caused by louing of *Aeneas*; and not lamenting his owne death,

---

[1] *Spenser* (London, 1926), p. 137. Cf. Sir Herbert Grierson: 'It is not only Guyon but the reader whose moral alertness is lulled by stanzas such as these [he quotes the song which Guyon hears in the Bower], and their tone is that which predominates in one's memory of *The Faerie Queene*. I know that Milton and Professor de Selincourt assure us that in the description of the Bower of Bliss the poet displays the charm of the sensuous in order to emphasise the stern morality which destroys the Bower. But this is not quite relevant. The senses have their legitimate claims. There is no virtue in the mere destruction of the beautiful. The moralist must convince us that the sacrifice is required in the interest of what is a higher and more enduring good, that the sensuous yields place to the spiritual. It is this Spenser fails to do imaginatively, whatever doctrine one may extract intellectually from the allegory.' *Cross Currents in English Literature of the XVIIth Century* (London, 1929), p. 54.

which is caused by not louing thee, O Lord.'[1] When the poems are placed within their Christian framework, the reader may see that, as Milton shows Satan being steadily degraded until the final horror of his serpentine form, Spenser shows the successive degradation of the Bower. As we move with Guyon from that outer Eden which is guarded by Pleasure's porter, to come to the spacious plain whose porch reveals the figure of Excess, and then into a paradise where the naked damsels tempt all strangers to secret lust, and finally to the centre where the sleeping knight, forgetful of all virtuous actions, lies enshrouded by Acrasia, at this point the final horror of the Bower breaks into the poem: 'O horrible enchantment, that him so did blend.' The Bower has, in effect, destroyed itself. But the parallel with Milton and the resolution in terms of the historical background take Spenser's reader only so far. The delight which the poet seeks to arouse in his description of the Bower is as insistent as the final moral teaching of its perversion. Man's delight in beauty and in the pleasures of the senses have never been so severely tested as by the rejection given in Guyon's act of destroying the Bower. And by the same token the historical framework of Christian belief has never been so severely tested as by the enormous delight which the Bower evokes. That background, it becomes clear, is not a norm determining our response, but is itself being manipulated by the poet.

Behind this dichotomy of poet and thinker is the problem of the poem's form. If the poem is a literal surface which delights while obscuring allegorical levels of meaning, we must read by translating. We must render the poetic image into philosophical idea, historical example, and moral precept, and read the poem not in its own language but in another which is given by philosophy, history, and ethics. Yet how may we fit the thought into a poem which ostensibly seeks to delight, when our method of reading has destroyed the literal surface which alone can determine our understanding? Unless the poem means what it says, that is unless it is what it appears to be, it is like Duessa whose borrowed beauty disguises her reality. I may illustrate this problem by the interpretation which we have come to accept for Book I. F. M. Padelford has discovered a spiritual and political allegory, specifically the growth in grace of a Christian gentleman

[1] *Confessions* (London, 1620), pp. 33–34.

and the events of the English Reformation.[1] Thus the episode of
the Red Cross Knight's sojourn in the house of Pride where he
defeats Sansjoy who is then conveyed to hell to be cured of his
wounds, is translated into spiritual terms as the Christian gentleman being tempted by joylessness: 'Sansjoy is . . . the joylessness
which finds nothing in life engaging and satisfying. . . . Very
properly Sansjoy is banished to Pluto's realm, for the essence of
the spiritual life is joy.'[2] It is translated also into political terms:
'the execution of More was the chiefest of the crimes for which
Reginald Pole excoriated his royal cousin, and Sansjoy can hardly
be other than this fearless and austere Cardinal. . . . Again, the
mysterious way in which Sansjoy is snatched away from his
adversary, and the vain efforts of the Red Cross Knight to discover
him, find a close counterpart in Pole's hurried departure from
England at the summons of Rome, and the baffled efforts of the
enfuriated Henry to recover him.'[3] These two kinds of meaning
are unrelated and entirely distinct from the literal meaning. The
assumption behind this interpretation of the poem's form is that
the allegory is an allegory 'of' a spiritual state or Reformation history, that it may be understood by substituting for the characters
terms drawn from another frame of reference and then by rendering the action into this framework. Inevitably within such a closed
system and with a choice of references, interpretations conflict.
Readers remain lost within a Wandering Wood 'so many pathes,
so many turnings seene, / That which of them to take, in diuerse
doubt they been.' It is true that some medieval allegories respond
to such reading by substitution, translation, and addition: as in
the moral reading of *The Castle of Perseverance*, the allegory of love
in *The Flower and the Leaf*, and the psychological reading of the
Romance of the Rose. Only *The Faerie Queene* will not yield: not to
any one, or to their sum.

Can such a reading ever satisfy? By destroying the literal meaning it destroys the reader's response. The intense delight aroused
by Spenser's rendering of the traditional descent into hell bears
no relation to the understanding which it is said to yield, other
than sugar-coating to a pill. The reader feels, and rightly, that he
has been betrayed into a response which is irrelevant, sterile, and

---

[1] *The Works of Edmund Spenser, A Variorum Edition*, ed. Greenlaw, Osgood, and
Padelford (Baltimore, 1932), i. 431.
[2] Ibid., p. 436.   [3] Ibid., p. 468.

meaningless. Nothing given on the literal level may be taken to mean that the essence of the spiritual life is joy, or that Cardinal Pole was forced to make a hurried trip to Rome. Such interpretation must leave the literal level to flee ever farther from the poem towards the 'something' which the poem is an allegory of. For there is the rest of the continued allegory to be fitted into the Procrustean background. The reader is left to wander in a wilderness where Spenser may have been, but without his imaginative powers to return.

Of the two kinds of interpretation which are generally accepted, the moral or spiritual and the historical, the latter satisfies least. Identification of characters in the poem with certain historical figures fetches the wildest interpretations—subtle, logical, and beyond all imagination. Any other identification serves as well, for each is highly selective. What may logically fit one episode twists and stretches the others upon the rack of the reader's own dark conceit. Why not allow Book I to be an allegory of modern Russian Communism? The Red Cross Knight stands for the working class armed with the Marxist faith: naturally his colour is red, and his cross refers to the *crossed* hammer and sickle. Una is clearly the spirit of Communism. The opening battle against Error refers to the Revolution. That monster's books and papers which she spews at the knight refer to the flood of Trotskyite writings, and her death marks the first triumph of the oppressed peasant class (the knight is *Georgos*, one brought up in ploughman's state). The scattered brood who feed upon Error's body represents the landed kulaks who used the time of distress to get rich; and the account of their swollen bellies 'with fulnesse burst,/ And bowels gushing forth' shows what rightly happened to them. But the knight is then separated from Una by the wiles of Archimago who stands for the hypocrisy of the *bourgeoisie*. Though he is able to defeat Sansfoy, who is lack of faith in Marxism, he becomes the willing tool of Duessa, the Church of Rome, which is in league with the Western imperialists—her father is an emperor who 'the wide *West* vnder his rule has, / And high hath set his throne, where *Tiberis* doth pas'. She leads the knight to the house of Pride which is the modern capitalist world—hence the gold on the roof, the weak foundations, the general corruption, and the masses chained in the dungeon. Here the knight is attacked by Sansjoy, obviously referring to the misery of the working class under capitalism, and betrayed into the hands of Orgoglio who is the U.S.A. After he is rescued by Arthur, the agent of the Comintern, he enters the house of Penance, where he repents his deviationism, is trained in the Marxist dialectic, and sees a vision of the future classless society—note the mingling of angels (probably a pun on Engels) and men. Finally he overthrows the dragon of Capitalism in order to free mankind from its chains. Or again, if historical allusion is everywhere embedded in the poem, why not see that Spenser refers to Shakespeare as his rival poet in Book II where Cymochles exclaims over the fallen hero : 'yet gold all is not, that doth golden seeme, / Ne all good knights, that *shake well speare* and shield.' That first line is repeated in *The Merchant of Venice*; the pun on the dramatist's name is common—to Jonson 'he seemes to shake a lance'; and Shakespeare had been accused of seeming to be what he was not by Green who was a friend of Nashe who was Spenser's close friend. Since Spenser had declared his ambition to 'reare the Muse on stately stage' and wrote nine comedies, it is only natural that he would regard Shakespeare as his rival. This kind of interpretation is all too easy if only, to adapt Dr. Johnson's phrase, one will abandon the poem to it.

Does a moral or spiritual interpretation satisfy? Necessarily it reduces the poem from poetic image to moral concept, and abandons the unique particularity of the work itself for an amorphous and abstract background. All too often a moral reading yields platitudes which the poet need never have laboured to conceal. Though 'the essence of the spiritual life is joy' may be meaningful within some theological framework, how much does it illuminate Spenser's episode? To recall for a moment that image in its particularity: its occasion when the knight returns from Lucifera's processional to be challenged by the wrathful Sansjoy who seeks revenge for the death of Sansfoy; the fierce encounter on the following morning during which the two knights display equal strength until with Duessa's intercession, 'thine the shield, and I, and all', which the Red Cross Knight takes as addressed to himself, his quickening faith defeats Sansjoy; Duessa's meeting with ancestral Night with her thrilling revelation of the battle between the children of Day and the sons of Night; the superbly rendered description of Duessa's descent into hell with Night and the wounded Sansjoy; the story of the reluctant Aesculapius, how he has suffered from the anger of the gods, how Night persuades him and how he agrees to heal the dying Sansjoy. How much of this unique image is satisfied by our moral reading that 'very properly Sansjoy [the joylessness which finds nothing in life engaging and satisfying] is banished to Pluto's realm, for the essence of the spiritual life is joy'? How does this allow for the fact that Sansjoy passes the night 'in ioy and iollity, / Feasting and courting both in bowre and hall' or the fact that he is not banished at all? But these questions are slight compared to that which asks what the poem becomes through such reading. Is this the morality which More found divine? 'Inventions miracle'? The 'conceit as passing all Conceit'? Or the poet's profound learning everywhere praised by his contemporaries?

Somewhere we have gone wrong. Unless, of course, Spenser's age was deceived. Either that, or he was betrayed by a romantic imagination into so elaborately disguising moral doctrine in his poem, or he failed to realize any unifying argument throughout the poem. No one has put forward the first possibility, though our present understanding offers little support for the high praise given him by his own age, and the second is implicit in the response of readers during the nineteenth century. The third possibility, that the poem lacks any unifying argument to sustain a continued allegory, is generally accepted today. We have Josephine Waters Bennett's classic study of *The Evolution of 'The Faerie Queene'*[1] which argues that the poem lacks unity because the poet's plans changed during its writing. By accepting her conclusions we have come as close as possible to totally reversing the judgement of Spenser's contemporaries. We are asked to regard the poem ('a Poem as richly fraught with divine Morality as Phansy') as 'a thoroughly experimental piece of writing', to hear the poet ('hearers hong vpon his melting tong, / While sweetly of his Faiery Queene he song') as 'smooth of tongue and subtle in his tale as his own Guile', and from this new point of view to praise him ('the *Virgil* of England', 'our only living *Homer*') as 'a rational and a not incompetent workman'.[2] This approach takes the life of the poem leaving dry bones that do not sing; but the reader must protest '*e pur si muove!*'.

Spenser himself believed that he was never astray in the poem. At the beginning of its last canto, he writes:

[1] Chicago, 1942.   [2] Bennett, pp. 3–4, v, 253.

> Like as a ship, that through the Ocean wyde
> Directs her course vnto one certaine cost,
> Is met of many a counter winde and tyde,
> With which her winged speed is let and crost,
> And she her selfe in stormie surges tost;
> Yet making many a borde, and many a bay,
> Still winneth way, ne hath her compasse lost:
> Right so it fares with me in this long way,
> Whose course is often stayd, yet neuer is astray.

Perhaps we are astray: the fault is not in the poem but in ourselves, in our reading.

My own approach to the allegory of *The Faerie Queene* involves a simple yet radical re-orientation. In this study I shall focus upon the image itself, rather than seek the idea hidden behind the image. In the letter to Ralegh Spenser writes: 'I labour to pourtraict in Arthure, before he was king, the image of a braue knight, perfected in the twelue priuate morall vertues, as Aristotle hath deuised, the which is the purpose of these first twelue bookes.' From this I assume that he labours to reveal his meaning, not to conceal it: to reveal as clearly as the matter and form of his allegory will allow. Further, what he labours to express is an image rather than moral ideas. These may inform and sustain the image, but the image itself is primary. If it points *beyond* itself, as it certainly does, it first points insistently to itself. Accordingly, the structure of meaning which is usually considered to lie behind the image, I find to lie within the image, being defined by it. When the reader unfolds the image to reveal its inherent meaning, he reveals what it says rather than what it implies. The term 'allegory' suggests that one thing is said while another is meant; but it need not follow that the poem does not mean what it says. Its allegory is not like Duessa, then, but like Una who 'did seeme such, as she was' when she is crowned as a maiden Queen: where appearance and reality, that is what the poem says and what it means, are the same. My approach, then, is to focus upon the literal level in its depth.

My approach cannot claim to involve any new understanding of the nature of allegory. I claim no more than a change of focus in our reading. My quarrel with modern criticism is that by turning all too quickly to allegorical levels of meaning, it short-circuits the poem, so that the meaning which is offered to our understanding (to switch metaphors) sells the poem short. Despairing of the complicated puzzle which has been made of the poem, many readers respond: 'I read Spenser because I enjoy him, and don't pretend to understand him.' My real quarrel with modern criticism is that very little of what it has said is relevant to such a reader's response, or can extend and intensify that enjoyment through the understanding of its continued allegory.

Surely no other poem impresses the reader so strongly with the sense of its poetic actuality. It everywhere insists upon itself as an artifact through rhetorical elaboration, verbal tricks, deliberate contrivance of the episodes, and the sheer invention displayed in the variety of the images presented. The poem is a product entirely of the poet's imagination. It is this quality which Coleridge praises in his note on 'the marvellous independence and true imaginative absence of all particular space or time in the "Faery Queene" '.[1] In reading Spenser we are not conscious of a framework of reference, or the intruding voice of the poet, as we are, say, in reading Milton. Even in Book I, where the religious framework is clearly implicit, the fiction triumphs over it. Similarly in Book II the fiction triumphs over the moral doctrine. We hear the voice not of one who records what has happened, nor the prophet with a message, nor the moralist, but only the poet singing. Or rather the poem being sung. Any stanza may be used to illustrate the kind of reality which the poet creates. To choose one purely descriptive:

> By this the Northerne wagoner had set
> His seuenfold teme behind the stedfast starre,
> That was in Ocean waues yet neuer wet,
> But firme is fixt, and sendeth light from farre
> To all, that in the wide deepe wandring arre:
> And chearefull Chaunticlere with his note shrill
> Had warned once, that *Phœbus* fiery carre
> In hast was climbing vp the Easterne hill,
> Full enuious that night so long his roome did fill. (1. ii. 1)

Here the stanza retains the Italian meaning of the word, 'a lodging, chamber, dwelling' (Florio), and its etymological derivation from *stare*, 'to stand'. It is a distinct unit and a detached block of meaning—as orthography and even the printed page suggest—integrated by tight internal rhyming. Coleridge comments perceptively

---

[1] *Lectures and Notes on Shakspere*, p. 514.

that it is 'a perfect whole . . . to which nothing can be added and from which nothing can be removed', and praises 'that wonder-work of metrical Skill and Genius! that nearest approach to a perfect Whole, as bringing the greatest possible variety into compleat Unity by the never interrupted interdependence of the parts!'[1] Such unity is gained in part by the three interlocking rhymes: these are held together by the middle rhyme which links the first three lines to the middle of the stanza where it repeats itself to form a centre for the whole, and then carried into the seventh line brings the third rhyme in its turn back to the centre. These rhymes never break. Even the danger of a break at the fourth and fifth lines is prevented by the invariable run-on of the couplet into the third rhyme. In this way the three rhymes converge towards the centre of the stanza, its whole movement being centripetal. Such a rhyme scheme, together with the alliteration through which the lines echo with puns and ambiguities, and with rhetorical devices more subtle than the scholastic division of turns can suggest, makes the stanza alive with internal movement and a radiating centre of meaning. Such internal movement and wholeness make the stanza *stand*, fixed for the moment as a globe for our contemplation, or as a painting to be read in spatial terms. It is not a point within a narrative line, begotten by the last stanza and begetting the next, not even Keats's magic casements opening 'in faery lands forlorn': it points to itself and it is that faery land. Moreover, its internal harmony suggests the kind of allegory which the poet writes, that is, an integration of multiple meanings into a perfect whole, into an image which makes us see. The separate stanzas form a mosaic whose pattern is organic rather than mechanical, and spatial rather than temporal. They form larger images which expand into that total image which is the poem. That total image is its own world, the faery land which is the poet's fiction. Though this image may be sustained by moral ideas, it insists too strongly upon its own reality ever to be dissolved into them.

[1] *Miscellanies, Æsthetic and Literary*, collected by T. Ashe (Bohn's Library, 1885), p. 333; *Inquiring Spirit*, ed. K. Coburn (New York, 1951), p. 158. Contemporary appreciation of Spenser's stanza is recorded by Gabriel Harvey who asks, 'is not the Verse of M. *Spencer* in his braue Faery Queene, the Virginall of the diuinest Muses, and gentlest Graces?' (*Works*, ed. Grosart, i. 266) and notes 'ye difference of ye last verse from ye rest in euerie Stanza, a grace in ye Faerie Queen' (*Marginalia*, ed. Moore Smith (Stratford, 1913), p. 168).

2

First I wish to establish a basis in Elizabethan criticism for reading Spenser's poem. For the poet himself, we may speculate, would seek some critical basis before projecting his continued allegory. We know that a happy alliance existed between criticism and literature in the Elizabethan age, and we know also how essential to writers was the support of critical theory. Critics taught poets how to write, and the age how to read. The English Parnassus became fruitful in the latter part of the sixteenth century partly because critics ploughed the land for the poets to plant. There was no division between them: 'either was the others mine'. While it is usual to find the critical basis for reading Spenser's allegory in the tradition of allegorical interpretation which seeks the truth beneath the fiction, I find it rather in Sidney's poetical theory with its emphasis upon the fiction itself.

The tradition of allegorical interpretation extends throughout the Middle Ages into the Renaissance, and any number of Elizabethan writers may be invoked to support a reading of poetry which describes the literal surface as a veil hiding the truth, or in various metaphors as husk enclosing the kernel, bark enfolding the pith, and sugar-coating to the pill. Harington is representative when he writes:

the ancient Poets haue indeed wrapped as it were in their writings diuers and sundry meanings, which they call the senses or mysteries thereof. First of all for the litterall sence (as it were the vtmost barke or ryne) they set downe in manner of an historie the acts and notable exploits of some persons worthy memorie: then in the same fiction, as a second rine and somewhat more fine, as it were nearer to the pith and marrow, they place the Morall sence profitable for the actiue life of man, approuing vertuous actions and condemning the contrarie. Manie times also vnder the selfesame words they comprehend some true vnderstanding of naturall Philosophie, or somtimes of politike gouerne- ment, and now and then of diuinitie: and these same sences that com- prehend so excellent knowledge we call the Allegorie.[1]

Here we would seem to have a critical basis for reading Spenser's allegory. But two points need to be noted. First, that the allegorical tradition is defensive: those who take no delight in poetry are urged to profit by its moral or doctrine.

Secondly, when the critics themselves comment upon poetry,

[1] 'A Briefe Apologie of Poetrie', in *Elizabethan Critical Essays*, ii. 201–2.

they display an intense imaginative exuberance which is not bound by a notion of allegorical levels of meaning. That most absolute allegorist, George Sandys, comments upon the fable of Narcissus in these terms:

Narcissus, a youth; that is, the soule of a rash and ignorant man; beholds not his owne face, nor considers of his proper essence or virtue, but pursues his shadow in the fountaine, and striues to imbrace it; that is, admireth bodily beauty, fraile and like the fluent water; which is no other then the shadow of the soule: for the mind doth not truly affect the body, but its owne similitude in a bodily forme. Such *Narcissus*, who ignorantly affecting one thing, pursues another; nor can euer satisfie his longings. Therefore he resolues into teares and perisheth: that is; the soule so alienated from it selfe, and doting on the body, is tortured with miserable perturbations; and dyes, as it were, infected with that poyson: so that now it rather appeareth a mortall body then an immortall soule. This fable likewise presents the condition of those, who adorned by the bounty of nature, or inriched by the industry of others, without merit, or honour of their owne acquisition, are transported with self-loue, and perish, as it were, with that madnesse. . . . But a fearfull example we haue of the danger of selfe-loue in the fall of the Angells; who intermitting the beatificall vision, by reflecting vpon themselues, and admiration of their owne excellency, forgot their dependance vpon their creator. Our *Narcissus*, now a flowre, instructs vs, that wee should not flourish too soone, or be wise too timely, nor ouer-loue, or admire our selues: which although hatefull in all ages, in youth is intollerable.[1]

Here he displays that eager curiosity with which the Elizabethan turned to fiction. He does not seek one meaning rather than another, but all meaning, there being literally no end to what he may find in the fiction. Neither does he limit the meanings to certain levels, nor reduce the myth to precept or example: in his hands it remains an image. The Elizabethan idea of correspondence leads him to interpret the myth through the various orders of existence upon the levels of nature and grace until it may be seen ultimately as an image of the Fall. Further, the Elizabethan faith in the concordance of all Scripture allows him to see the poet's fiction as an analogue to Holy Scripture. And in trying to see what both are analogues to, he gathers all meaning in the poet's fiction. All poetry becomes allegorical in the Elizabethan

---

[1] *Ovids Metamorphosis Englished, Mythologiz'd, and Represented in Figures* (London, 1632), p. 106.

age simply through the energy and exuberance, the intellectual vigour and imaginative intensity with which it was read. Necessarily it becomes an inexhaustible fountain of wisdom, as Chapman found in Homer 'not onely all learning, gouernment, and wisedome being deduc't as from a bottomlesse fountaine from him, but all wit, elegancie, disposition, and iudgement'.[1] In such terms Golding defines the appeal of Ovid:

in no one of all his bookes the which he wrate, doo lurke
Mo darke and secret misteries, mo counselles wyse and sage,
Mo good ensamples, mo reproofes of vyce in youth and age,
Mo fyne inuentions too delight, mo matters clerkly knit,
No nor more straunge varietie too shew a lerned wit.
The high, the lowe: the riche, the poore: the mayster, and the slaue:
The mayd, the wife: the man, the chyld: the simple and the braue:
The yoong, the old: the good, the bad: the warriour strong and stout:
The wyse, the foole: the countrie cloyne: the lerned and the lout:
And euery other liuing wyght shall in this mirrour see
His whole estate, thoughtes, woordes and deedes expresly shewd
    too bee.[2]

Such manifold appeal demands manifold meaning from poetry and reveals the intense delight which the Elizabethan reader took in the fiction. Metaphors such as tearing the veil, or breaking the husk, wrongly describe this way of reading which sees so many meanings held within the fiction, being present rather than hidden. Some other metaphor, that of seeing the meanings in fiction as the expanding petals of a multifoliate rose might do, or any other which describes the fiction as expanding from a clear centre, and our response as a living one which grows into greater understanding the more we read.

There was another tradition in Elizabethan criticism, represented by Sidney's *Apology for Poetry*, which is usually seen as opposed to the allegorical tradition; but it is one which, I believe, includes it. Though Sidney does not use the allegorical tradition, it is implicit in his central doctrine that the poet's fictions are 'things not affirmatiuely but allegorically and figuratiuelie written'.[3]

---

[1] Prefatory Epistle to *Achilles Shield*, in *Elizabethan Critical Essays*, ii. 299. Cf. Elyot who speaks of Homer as one 'from whom as from a fountaine proceded all eloquence and lernyng'. *The Boke Named the Gouernour*, ed. H. H. S. Croft (London, 1883), i. 58.

[2] Preface 'To the Reader', *The XV Bookes of . . . Metamorphosis* (London, 1575), Biii^{r-v}. Cf. Chapman on Homer, in *Elizabethan Critical Essays*, ii. 306.

[3] Ed. J. Churton Collins (Oxford, 1907), p. 39. This edition is cited throughout.

The difference between the two traditions may be seen in their defence of poetry. 'The first problem of Renaissance criticism', according to J. E. Spingarn, 'was the justification of imaginative literature.'[1] The most famous of the attacks upon literature was Agrippa's *De incertitudine et vanitate scientiarum et artium*, published first in 1530 and englished in 1569. Its argument is commonplace and orthodox enough: that all worldly arts and sciences are uncertain and vain for knowledge comes from Satan, and that certainty and truth are to be found only in the Word of God. On these grounds Gabriel Harvey praises the work:

> A thousand good leaues be for euer graunted *Agrippa*.
> For squibbing and declayming against many fruitlesse
> *Artes*, and Craftes, deuisde by the *Diuls* and *Sprites*, for a torment,
> And for a plague to the world: as both *Pandora*, *Prometheus*,
> And that cursed *good bad Tree*, can testifie at all times.[2]

It is distinguished, however, by its method; for Agrippa writes ambiguously with serious mockery and mock-seriousness, and his invective is devastating. His work may be read as a sceptical discourse which argues that *nihil scire felicissima vita* (placed as motto on the title-page of the 1532 Cologne edition); but equally it may be read as an elaborate joke whose whole point is that 'a demi-god in omnisufficiency of knowledge, a diuell in the practise of horrible Artes' (as Harvey calls him)[3] can use immense knowledge to denounce the use of knowledge. He concludes his treatise both with the serious exhortation that 'it is better therfore and more profitable to be Idiotes, and knowe nothing to beleue by Faithe and charitee, and to become next vnto God, then being lofty and prowde through the subtilties of sciences to fall into the possession of the Serpente' and with a *reductio ad absurdum* of his whole argument in a discourse upon the 'Mysteries of the Ass' where he affirms gravely: 'it is more manifest then ye sonne, that there is no beaste so able to receiue diuinitee as the Asse, into whome if yee shall not be tourned, yee shall not be able

---

[1] J. E. Spingarn, *A History of Literary Criticism in the Renaissance* (New York, 1899), p. 3. Cf. Gregory Smith: 'Elizabethan criticism arose in controversy. The early Essays are "Apologies" for Poets and Poetry against the attacks of a vigorous Puritanism.' *Elizabethan Critical Essays*, i, p. xiv.

[2] 'A Gallant familiar Letter', in *The Poetical Works of Edmund Spenser*, ed. J. C. Smith and E. de Selincourt (Oxford, 1912), p. 624.

[3] 'Pierce's Supererogation', in *Elizabethan Critical Essays*, ii. 246. 'How well he's read, to reason against reading!' as Shakespeare's King of Navarre says of Berowne.

to carrie the diuine misteries'.[1] The brilliance of his method made
the work a model in the literature of paradox, and Barnaby Riche
in his *Allarme to Englande* (1578) writes that it is diligently studied
by the young courtly gentlemen who desire 'to be curious in
cauilling, propounding captious questions, therby to shew a
singularitie of their wisedomes'.[2] Nashe inveighs against him as
the master of those who rail at the arts;[3] to Bacon he is 'that trivial
buffoon, who in reviewing the opinions of others distorts every
idea in order to give it over to ridicule'.[4] One defence of poetry
was made through the allegorical tradition. Harington condemns
Agrippa for 'a generall libeller' who does not see that the ancient
poets wrapped mysteries in their writings. Lodge berates Gosson
who was Agrippa's English counterpart, as a '*homo literatus*, a
man of the letter, little sauoring of learning . . . you remember
not that vnder the person of Æneas in Virgil the practice of
a dilligent captaine is discribed, vnder the shadow of byrds,
beastes, and trees the follies of the world were disiphered; you
know not that the creation is signified in the Image of Prometheus,
the fall of pryde in the person of Narcissus. . . .'[5] The terms of
this defence are everywhere the same: those who attack poetry
for its vanity see only the delightful surface, and not the truth
which lies hidden below.

Sidney's defence of poetry, besides being more subtle and

---

[1] *Of the Vanitie and Vncertaintie of Artes and Sciences*, Englished by Ja.(mes)
San.(ford) (London, 1569), p. 185ʳ. Since this translation was available to Sidney
I have used it throughout; but there were several Latin editions, and Sidney need
not have depended upon it. For the Latin text I have consulted the edition printed at
Cologne, 1568.

[2] *Allarme to England* (London, 1578), H₁ᵛ. Sanford, Agrippa's translator, writes in
his address to the reader: 'his intent is, not to deface the worthinesse of Artes and
Sciences, but to reproue and detecte theire euil vses, and declare the excellencie of
his wit in disprouinge them, for a shewe of Learning' (*Van.* iiiʳ). L. I. Bredvold
writes of the work: 'its importance lies chiefly in that it was regarded by its later
readers as an addition to the literature of *paradox*, a literary *genre* which frequently
became a vehicle for skeptical thought and added to the spicy flavour of the modern
skeptics, from Montaigne down.' *The Intellectual Milieu of John Dryden* (Ann Arbor,
1934), p. 29.

[3] 'Pierce Penilesse', in *Works*, ed. McKerrow, i. 191. Yet McKerrow notes that
Nashe is heavily indebted to the *Vanity*. 'It is hardly too much to say that the
greater part of Nashe's apparent learning is transferred wholesale from Agrippa's
work' (v. 134–5).

[4] *Temporis partus masculus*. For this reference I am indebted to F. H. Anderson,
The Philosophy of Francis Bacon (Chicago, 1948), p. 110.

[5] 'A Briefe Apologie of Poetrie', in *Elizabethan Critical Essays*, ii. 200, 201.
'Defence of Poetry', ibid. i. 65.

complex, differs. He begins by accepting Agrippa's argument on the
vanity of arts and sciences because their scope is limited by Nature.
'There is no Arte deliuered to mankinde that hath not the workes
of Nature for his principall obiect, without which they could not
consist, and on which they so depend, as they become Actors and
Players, as it were, of what Nature will haue set foorth.' Then he
lists the various sciences to show how they are 'tied to . . . such
subiection'.[1] Since Nature's world, being fallen, is brazen, all
these arts and sciences must err when they seek to affirm knowledge: 'the Astronomer, with his cosen the Geometrician, can
hardly escape [being a liar], when they take vpon them to measure
the height of the starres. . . . And no lesse of the rest, which take
vpon them to affirme.' He cites the historian who 'affirming many
things, can, in the cloudy knowledge of mankinde, hardly escape
from many lyes'; and it follows that those who look for truth in
history 'goe away full fraught with falshood'.[2] The same argument
is made by Agrippa who claims that truth cannot be apprehended
by the sciences, and he cites the approval of the academic philosophers who said 'that nothinge might be affirmed'. He too cites
the astronomer who must lie because 'there is no Astronomer
come downe from Heauen that hath benne able to teache the
true, and certaine mouing of the thinges that are thought not to
moue', and writes of the historian that 'it is impossible, but that
a number of them shoulde be verie Liers'.[3] Both agree in attacking
the uncertainty of the arts and sciences which offer only falsehood
while seeking to affirm fact. Further, they agree on the vanity of
knowledge which does not bring self-knowledge. Agrippa tells
the common story of the Astronomer who 'wente out of his
house to beholde ye starres, [and] . . . fell into a diche', and Sidney
tells how 'it was found that the Astronomer looking to the starres
might fall into a ditch'.[4] 'The Arithmetricians, and the Geo-
metricians number and measure al thinges', Agrippa writes, 'but
they make no accompte of the numbers and measures of soule
and life.' Sidney claims that 'the Mathematician might draw foorth
a straight line with a crooked hart'.[5] Of philosophers, Agrippa
says that they 'searche out the causes and the beginninges of
thinges, but God the Creatour of all thinges they neglect &

---

[1] *Apol.*, pp. 7, 8.   [2] *Apol.*, pp. 38, 39.
[3] *Van.*, pp. 43[r], 14[r].   [4] *Van.*, pp. 43[v]-44[r]; *Apol.*, p. 13.
[5] *Van.*, p. 179[v]; *Apol.*, p. 13.

know not'; Sidney says that 'the enquiring Philosopher might be blinde in himselfe'.[1] Both assume that the end of knowledge should be, in Sidney's words, 'the knowledge of a mans selfe'.[2] Agrippa describes his work as a Herculean attempt 'to chalenge into the fielde all theese moste hardie hunters of Artes and Sciences'; and the same may be said of Sidney's work where he shows himself to be, as he describes Agrippa, 'a playing wit' who can be 'merry in shewing the vanitie of Science'.[3]

Sidney's attack upon the arts and sciences is the basis upon which he defends the nature and end of poetry. He agrees with Agrippa that nothing can be affirmed, in order to defend the poet who offers fiction and therefore 'nothing affirmes'. Agrippa allows at one point that the writer may escape the tyranny of fact:

> there be moreouer many, whiche write Histories, not so mutche to tell the Truthe, as to delite that thei maie expresse, and depainte, the Image of a noble Prince, in whom they please. Whiche if any shal reproue for liynge, they saie, that they haue not so greate a regarde, to thinges done, as to the profite of the posteritee, and to the fame of witte, and therefore they haue not declared all thinges, as they haue benne donne, but how they ought to be declared, and that obstinately, they will not defende the truthe, but where the common vtilitee dothe require, either a faininge or vntruthe. . . . Such an example hath *Xenophon* sette out of *Cyrus*, not as it was, but as it ought to be, as a resemblance and paterne, of a singular good Prince.[4]

By exploiting such an argument, Sidney defends the poet who portrays 'so right a Prince as *Xenophons Cyrus*' to show us 'each thing to be followed; where the Historian, bound to tell things as things were, cannot be liberall (without hee will be poeticall) of a perfect patterne'. Accordingly, '*Xenophon*, who did imitate so excellently as to giue vs *effigiem iusti imperii*, the portraiture of a iust Empire vnder the name of *Cyrus* (as *Cicero* sayth of him),

---

[1] *Van.*, p. 179ᵛ; *Apol.*, p. 13. This distrust of learning shared by Agrippa and Sidney is, of course, traditional. Cf. de Mornay's *Discourse of Life and Death*, translated by Sidney's sister in 1590 (publ. 1592) in which he writes of knowledge: 'another by Geometry can measure fields, and townes, and countries: but can not measure himselfe. . . . The Astrologer lookes vp on high, and falles in the next ditch: fore-knowes the future, and forgoes the present: hath often his eie on the heauens, his heart long before buried in the earth. The Philosopher discourseth of the nature of all other things: and knowes not himselfe' (sig. C₄ʳ). It is interesting to note that de Mornay attacks learning in the course of arguing a paradox: 'what euill is there not in life? and what good is there not in death?' (sig. A₃ʳ).

[2] *Apol.*, p. 13. Cf. *Van.*, p. 186ʳ.

[3] *Van.*, sig. A₁ʳ; *Apol.*, p. 35.   [4] *Van.*, p. 16ʳ.

made therein an absolute heroicall Poem'.[1] While Agrippa argues
that the poet makes 'a clatteringe noise with the craftie coueringe
of fables, and disceitfullie to deuise all thinges vpon a matter of
nothinge', Sidney may argue that the poet's perfect pattern is
'not wholie imaginatiue, as we are wont to say by them that build
Castles in the ayre: but so farre substantially it worketh, not onely
to make a *Cyrus* . . . but to bestow a *Cyrus* vpon the worlde, to
make many *Cyrus's*'.[2] We have already seen how Agrippa's attack
is met by the allegorist's claim that beneath the 'clatteringe noise'
the poet has hidden truth. But clearly his attack is not countered
by their defence: Agrippa's point is that the clattering noise
covers a matter of nothing. The case of the allegorists rests upon
the truth which poetry yields, and they have no defence against
the charge that such truth is the fruit of the tree of the knowledge
of good and evil, and not the Word of God. Sidney, on the other
hand, defends the poet's fiction because it is fiction and does not
affirm. His case rests upon the fiction itself, and how its end
supplements the Word of God. If the difference between the two
defences may be summed up in a word, it is that between Lodge
finding '*vnder* the person of Æneas in Virgil the practice of a
dilligent captaine', and Sidney finding *in* Cyrus the perfect pattern
of a prince. The allegorists tried unwisely to counter Agrippa on
his own grounds: Sidney used Agrippa, and in his method of
paradox found a rhetorical means for defining the work of the
right poets. For this reason we may recognize a strong element
of paradox in the *Apology*: it opens with an attack upon all the
arts and sciences which affirm knowledge, and closes with the
praise of poetry because it can 'giue vs all knowledge'. He found
in the *Vanity* a framework to support his central argument, which
is not a negative defence of poetry but a positive statement of its

---

[1] *Apol.*, pp. 8, 21, 12.
[2] *Van.*, p. 12ᵛ; *Apol.*, p. 9. It is curious that the translator of the 1676 edition of
Agrippa's work echoes Sidney's words in this passage on the poets who are 'always
building Castles in the Air, as *Campanus* hath truly said of them' (p. 24). The Latin
reads: 'super fumo machinari omnia, sicuti alicubi cecinit Campanus' (1568 ed.).
Both agree in rejecting poets who write without knowledge: Agrippa speaks of
poets 'who never made it their study to speak or deliver in Writing any thing of
sound knowledge', Sidney of those who fail to use art, imitation, and exercise 'so
is oure braine deliuered of much matter which neuer was begotten by knowledge'
(p. 50). The one rejects poets who 'please the eares of foolishe men with wanton
Rithmes', the other objects that 'mans wit may make Poesie . . . to be *Phantastike*,
which doth . . . infect the fancie with vnworthy obiects' (*Van.*, p. 11; *Apol.*, p. 41).

nature and end. It is in this positive statement, specifically in his idea of the right poet, that I find the critical basis for reading Spenser's allegory.[1]

Sidney's argument arises from a division of poets into 'three seuerall kindes': the first who 'imitate the inconceiuable excellencies of GOD. Such were *Dauid* in his Psalmes, *Solomon* in his song of Songs . . . *Orpheus*, *Amphion*, *Homer* in his hymnes'; the second who deal with philosophical matters: 'eyther morrall, as *Tyrtæus*, *Phocylides*, and *Cato*; or naturall, as *Lucretius* and *Virgils Georgicks*; or Astronomicall, as *Manilius* and *Pontanus*; or historical, as *Lucan*'; and the third whom he calls 'indeed right Poets' (pp. 10, 11). Those of the first kind are not really poets: 'the first and most noble sorte may iustly bee termed *Vates*'; of the second kind, he remarks: 'whether they properly be Poets or no let Gramarians dispute'; and only the third kind are 'indeed right Poets' (p. 11). The first kind of poet is divinely inspired, and 'against these none will speake that hath the holie Ghost in due holy reuerence', while the second kind cannot be inspired because he is 'wrapped within the folde of the proposed subiect, and takes not the course of his owne inuention'. Only the right poet is properly inspired: not in the Platonic sense of inspiration as that suppression of intellect by which he is akin to the lunatic, but in the Christian sense of 'breathing into' by which he is 'lifted vp with the vigor of his owne inuention'.[2] Thus Sidney is led to reject Plato's view of poetry as 'a very inspiring of a diuine force, farre aboue mans wit', for he believes that the poet ranges 'within the Zodiack of his owne wit' (pp. 46, 8).

We may understand Sidney's threefold division of the poets, and sense its importance to the new poet Spenser, by relating the

[1] In 'Sidney's Idea of the "Right Poet" ', *Comparative Literature*, ix (1957), 51–59, I have maintained that the idea of the 'right Poet' which forms the argument of the *Apology* is original with Sidney, and not taken from the sixteenth-century Italian critics.

[2] *Apol.*, pp. 10, 11, 8. Chapman, in the 'Epistle Dedicatory' to *Homers Odysses* (London, 1616), similarly distinguishes the two kinds of poetic ecstasy: 'there being in *Poesie* a twofold rapture, (or alienation of soule, as the abouesaid Teacher [Ficino] terms it) one *Insania*, a disease of the mind, and a meere madnesse, by which the infected is thrust beneath all the degrees of humanitie: *& ex homine, Brutum quodammodo redditur*: (for which, poore *Poesie*, in this diseasd and impostorous age, is so barbarously vilified) the other is, *Diuinus furor*; by which the sound and diuinely healthfull, *supra hominis naturam erigitur, & in Deum transit*. One a perfection directly infused from God: the other an infection, obliquely and degenerately proceeding from man' (A$_4$^{v}).

Apology to the source of the critical tradition in Plato. For though
the *Apology* was occasioned by Gosson's *Abuse*, Sidney finds his
natural adversary in Plato. He uses the brilliant strategy of allow-
ing Plato's attack upon poetry to be directed against the first two
kinds of poets, and then formulates a third kind which Plato
could not recognize. In this way he may absorb Plato—of whom
he says 'the wiser a man is, the more iust cause he shall find to
haue in admiration' (p. 46)—while going beyond him. The first
kind, the divine poet, is denounced by Plato for telling false
things about the gods, though if he praises the gods he may be
admitted into the perfect commonwealth.[1] Sidney allows only
that the divine poet may cheer the merry and console the troubled;
and though he honours this 'most noble sorte' he does not defend
him. The second kind, the poet who takes his material from philosophical or historical matters, is attacked by Plato on the grounds
that such poetry is thrice removed from reality, being produced
at second-hand without knowledge of the subject. Sidney allows
Plato's argument when he says that such poets 'retaine themselues
within their subiect, and receiue, as it were, their beeing from it',
being simply 'takers of others'. As Plato compares poets to the
painter whose work is a copy of a copy, Sidney compares them
to 'the meaner sort of Painters, who counterfet onely such faces
as are sette before them'.[2] While Plato banishes these poets,
Sidney queries their right even to the name of poet.

But Sidney allows, as Plato does not, a third kind of poet who
'bringeth his owne stuffe, and . . . maketh matter for a conceite',
for 'all onely proceedeth from their wit, being indeede makers of
themselues' (pp. 34, 48). This kind is not like Plato's meaner sort
of painter, but like the more excellent who 'hauing no law but
wit, bestow[s] that in cullours vpon you which is fittest for the
eye to see' (p. 11). While the first two kinds take their matter at
second-hand from Nature, the right poet is set 'beyond and ouer
all the workes of that second nature' so that he 'bringeth things
forth far surpassing her dooings' (p. 9). Moreover, the work of
the right poet may not properly be regarded as an imitation 'of'
anything, but only as an imitation. Thus Sidney speaks of 'that
imitation, wherof Poetry is' (p. 26). The right poet imitates, then,
not by copying nature but by creating another nature, and as a
maker may be compared to the heavenly Maker. In Plato such

[1] *Republic*, ii. 378; x. 607.   [2] *Rep.* x. 599; *Apol.*, pp. 34, 48, 11.

a comparison explains the creative role only of the first two kinds of poets. As the Demiurge shapes the world out of pre-existing matter according to the Ideas independent of him, so the poet must struggle with intractable matter, and, lacking its Idea, must either yield himself in admiration (as the first kind of poet) or succumb to his material and render it sweetly (as the second kind). In Sidney the comparison illuminates the truly creative power of the right poet, for God creates *ex nihilo* and contains the Ideas within Himself. Hence Sidney may speak of the right poet who 'borrow[s] nothing of what is, hath been, or shall be', but 'maketh matter' and 'with the force of a diuine breath . . . bringeth things forth'.[1] While Plato must deny the poet any perception of Ideas, Sidney places these within the poet. 'That the Poet hath that *Idea* is manifest', he writes, 'by deliuering them forth in such excellencie as hee hath imagined them' (p. 9).

The background to Sidney's view of Nature is given by the neo-Platonic tradition which places reality in a super-sensuous world behind and above empirical fact. According to this tradition, the artist does not imitate external Nature but rather its reality which he perceives in his own mind. While the Aristotelian tradition, by placing reality within and through nature, required the artist to imitate the phenomenal world, neo-Platonism led artists to scorn fidelity to fact.[2] Sidney was heir to this tradition in its Christianized form. Since Nature is fallen, to imitate Nature only confines man in the fallen world. For this reason—and the reason is also Agrippa's—he rejects those arts and sciences which depend upon nature, such as the historian who brings 'images of true matters', or the moral philosopher who urges us to 'followe Nature'. By affirming the knowledge of good and evil, such arts

---

[1] *Apol.*, pp. 11, 34, 9. See M. C. Nahm, *The Artist as Creator* (Baltimore, 1956), pp. 63 ff.

[2] E. Panofsky, who has traced the influence of this tradition among Renaissance artists, writes: 'auf der einen Seite drückt sich das Ungenügen an der bloßen, "Wirklichkeit" nunmehr in einer der vergangenen Epoche fremden verächtlichen Geringschätzung derselben aus ("Ich lache über die, die jegliches Natürliche für gut achten" heißt es z. B. bei einem dieser Autoren); es wird von "Irrtümern" der Natur gesprochen, die "richtigzustellen" sind (wie bescheiden drückt sich dagegen noch der um 1550 — und in Venedig! — schreibende Dolce aus, bei dem es heißt: "Es muß der Maler bestrebt sein, nicht bloß die Natur nachzuahmen, sondern dieselbe auch teilweise zu übertreffen — ich sage teilweise, denn im übrigen ist es ja schon ein Wunder, wenn es gelingt, sie auch nur annäherungsweise nachzuahmen").' *Idea, Ein Beitrag zur Begriffsgeschichte der Älteren Kunsttheorie* (Leipzig, 1924), pp. 44–45.

only confirm man in his fallen state. The right poet alone is free from bondage to Nature: not 'beeing captiued to the trueth of a foolish world' (pp. 20, 7, 23), he may render that golden world whose 'reality' is contained within his own mind.

With this doctrine that the poet creates a golden world, Sidney was able to clarify and distinguish the poet's purpose and the end of his poetry, while the earlier critics, using Horace, always confuse the two. He sees that imitation alone constitutes poetry, and so applies Aristotle's theory of imitation to the work of the right poet. The poet's art of imitation is the art of feigning: 'it is that fayning notable images of vertues, vices, or what els, with that delightfull teaching, which must be the right describing note to know a Poet by' (p. 12). Aristotle defines the poet by virtue of the imitative element in his work, and what he means by plot or fable, Sidney comprehends in his term 'fiction'. The poet's entire purpose is to create his fiction: he does 'meerely [that is, entirely] make to imitate' (p. 11). The divine poet teaches delight, and the philosophical poet delightfully teaches; but neither end, nor both together, adequately describe the work of the right poet. Because Sidney believes that the poet's entire purpose is to feign his golden world of images, he goes beyond the Horatian account of the end of poetry and emphasizes wholly its rhetorical end of 'moving'. His defence of poetry rests upon its power to move men to virtuous action.

His view of the end of poetry is determined by the doctrine of the Fall. The firm Christian basis of his poetic is shown when he discusses the creative power of the poet who 'bringeth things forth far surpassing her [Nature's] dooings, with no small argument to the incredulous of that first accursed fall of *Adam*, 'sith our erected wit maketh vs know what perfection is, and yet our infected will keepeth vs from reaching vnto it'. Then he adds: 'but these arguments wil by fewe be vnderstood, and by fewer granted' (p. 9). If one may in all modesty suggest what may be understood by his argument, at least in part, it is that from our having eaten of the Tree, we know that we ought to do well; but our will is corrupt and by Nature we cannot be moved to do well. Accordingly, Sidney defines the work of the right poet in terms of the image which can move our infected will. Since poetry presents images of what should be, 'things not affirmatiuely but allegorically and figuratiuelie written', he urges readers that 'in

Poesie, looking for fiction, they shall vse the narration but as an imaginatiue groundplot of a profitable inuention' (p. 39). How he intends them to use the fiction only as an imaginative groundplot may be gathered from his own reading of heroical poetry:

The Poet nameth *Cyrus* or *Aeneas* no other way then to shewe what men of theyr fames, fortunes, and estates should doe.

Only let *Aeneas* be worne in the tablet of your memory . . . and I thinke . . . hee will be found in excellencie fruitefull.

Whom doe not the words of *Turnus* mooue, the tale of *Turnus* hauing planted his image in the imagination?

[The poet] bestow[s] a *Cyrus* vpon the worlde, to make many *Cyrus's*, if they wil learne aright why and how that Maker made him.[1]

From these remarks it is clear that Sidney believes that poetry may move the infected will because its images 'strike, pierce, [and] possesse the sight of the soule' (p. 17). When he writes that the poets 'deliuer' a golden world, and that their work may 'breed' fruitful knowledge and 'plant' goodness in the soul, it is clear that he sees poetry as a Garden of Adonis containing the forms to be planted as seeds in man's imagination. Its end is to guide man on the way to salvation: 'of all Sciences . . . is our Poet the Monarch. For he dooth not only show the way, but giueth so sweete a prospect into the way, as will intice any man to enter into it' (p. 25). Since poetry shows the way, Sidney constantly uses the metaphor of light to describe its power: poetry possesses 'the sight of the soule', by its images wisdom is 'illuminated or figured foorth', and its pictures give 'insight' into all the virtues in order to make us 'see the forme of goodnes'. The metaphor culminates in his claim that through poetry 'all vertues, vices, and passions [are] in their own naturall seates layd to the viewe, that wee seeme not to heare of them, but cleerely to see through them' (p. 18). What poetry presents is revelation, a vision of the golden world. Sidney gives poetry a power beyond moving which the earlier critics allowed: it moves *upwards*, and so supplements the working of grace. By re-creating its vision of the golden world, the reader may be moved to that virtuous action through which he may be redeemed. The only adequate analogue to Sidney's view of the end of poetry is Dante's statement that the end of the *Commedia*

[1] *Apol.*, pp. 40, 33, 26, 9.

is 'to remove those living in this life from a state of misery and to bring them to a state of happiness'.[1]

In this view of the end of poetry, we may understand why Sidney found in Agrippa 'another foundation then the superficiall part would promise', that is, something other than a scurrilous abuse of the arts. Agrippa wished to replace the knowledge of good and evil with the unfallen state of vision. Movingly he exhorts the reader: 'the knowledge of all things is compacte in you. . . . As he [God] than hath created trees ful of fruites, so also hath he created the soules as reasonable trees ful of formes & knowledges, but thorow the sinne of the first parent al things were reueled [concealed?] & obliuion the mother of ignoraunce stept in. Set you than now aside, which may, the veyle of your vnderstanding, which are wrapped in the darknes of ignoraunce. Cast out ye drincke of *Lethe* you whiche haue made yourselfes droncken with forgetfulnes, awaite for the true light you which haue suffered your selues to be taken with vnreasonable sleepe, and foorthwith when your face is discouered ye shall passe from the light to the light.'[2] This faith in regenerate man became the central faith of the Protestant humanist tradition, and it informs Sidney's view of the end of poetry.

In his *Apology* Sidney integrates the major tradition of literary criticism: his threefold division of the poets answers but also includes Plato's view of poetry, his poetic is firmly based upon Aristotle's theory of imitation, and he uses the sixteenth-century Italian critics in order to reach a fuller understanding of the poet's purpose and the end of poetry. The end of his treatise is through delightful teaching to defend poetry from the *Mysomousoi*, with the further end of virtuous action, to move the age to make the highest kind of poetry. Sidney's first editor, Olney, refers in the Preface to 'Excellent Poesie so created by this Apologie': it is this original argument of the Idea of the 'right Poet' which gives his

---

[1] 'Letter to Can Grande', in *The Letters of Dante*, trans. Paget Toynbee (Oxford, 1920), p. 202. Cf. Chapman's belief that poetry is the means 'to the absolute redresse, or much to be wished extenuation, of all the vnmanly degeneracies now tyranysing amongst vs: for if that which teacheth happinesse and hath vnpainefull corosiues in it, (being entertayned and obserued) to eate out the hart of that raging vlcer, which like a *Lernean Fen* of corruption furnaceth the vniuersall sighes and complaintes, of this transposed world; were seriously, and as with armed garrisons defended and hartned; that which engenders & disperseth, that wilfull pestilence, would bee purged and extirpate'. Ded. Ep. to *Achilles Shield* (London, 1598), A₄ᵛ.

[2] *Van.*, p. 186ʳ.

treatise its place as the *De Poetica* of our language. Its greatest creation is, I believe, *The Faerie Queene*.[1]

Sidney's idea of fiction became everywhere accepted in the Elizabethan age. Touchstone even informs Audrey that 'the truest poetrie is the most faining'. Sandys remarks that 'fiction, that spar of Gold, is the art; & truth well counterfeited, the honour of the Poet'. Jonson defines 'the very Fiction it selfe [as] the reason, or forme of the worke'. Again, Marston admonishes Hall:

> For tell me *Crittick*, is not *Fiction*
> The soule of Poesies inuention?
> Is't not the forme? the spirit? and the essence?
> The life? and the essentiall difference?
> Which *omni*, *semper*, *soli*, doth agree
> To heauenly discended Poesie?[2]

I believe that only this emphasis upon fiction could support allegory; for it is the primacy of the literal level which distinguishes allegory from merely allegorical poetry.

3

For the rest of this chapter I shall analyse an episode from Spenser's poem, the most obvious choice being the opening episode in

---

[1] One may only speculate upon any direct influence. See Carpenter, *Reference Guide*, pp. 95–96, and Atkinson, *Bibliographical Supplement*, pp. 39–42. But we do know that Spenser dedicated the *Calender* to Sidney, and that he was held 'in some vse of familiarity' (Letter from Leicester House, Oct. 1579, in *Elizabethan Critical Essays*, i. 89). One may surmise that he who 'all mens hearts with secret rauishment . . . stole away, and weetingly beguyld' (*Astrophel*, 21–22) would inspire England's new poet to attempt the heroic form. Much later in dedicating *The Ruines of Time* to Sidney's sister, Spenser writes of his 'entire loue and humble affection' for her brother 'which taking roote began in his life time somewhat to bud forth: and to shew themselues to him, as then in the weakenes of their first spring: And would in their riper strength (had it pleased high God till then to drawe out his daies) spired forth fruit of more perfection.' There is the testimony of W. L. that 'as *Vlysses* brought faire *Thetis* sonne / From his retyred life to menage armes: / So *Spencer* was by *Sidneys* speaches wonne, / To blaze her fame' (Commendatory verse to *The Faerie Queene*). Again, in the *Calender* Piers urges Cuddie who is the pattern of a poet to 'lyft vp thy selfe out of the lowly dust' (*Oct.* 38): in these terms Spenser later pays tribute to Sidney 'who first my Muse did lift out of the flore' (Dedicatory Sonnet to the Countess of Pembroke). But the influence may have been mutual. When Sidney composed his *Apology*, Spenser's critical treatise on *The English Poet* was presumably available to him. But Sidney's tradition was too central in Elizabethan criticism for there to be any need to argue direct influence.

[2] Sandys, *Ovids Metamorphosis*, p. 36; *Ben Jonson*, ed. Herford & Simpson, viii. 636; Marston, *The Metamorphosis of Pigmalions Image and Certain Satyres* (1598), E₆ʳ.

which the Red Cross Knight defeats Error. I shall compare it, since we have been considering the art of reading allegory, to the opening episode of Dante's *Commedia*. These are the only two major classics in modern literature which were conceived by their authors as allegories; yet, strangely enough, they have never been brought into any significant relationship.

Studies in the allegory of each work proceed independently, and what we understand by Dante's claim that his poem is polysemous has not been related to Spenser's similar claim that his poem is 'a continued Allegory, or darke conceit'. Our most distinguished Dante critic, C. S. Singleton, turns to the *Romance of the Rose* and Ariosto, he even puts Bunyan and Milton together in the vain effort to get Dante's kind of allegory and ignores Spenser.[1] Yet Dante's 'allegory of theologians', for which he argues so cogently, is uniquely paralleled by *The Faerie Queene* Book I. Spenser's critics, on the other hand, have considered only Dante's possible influence upon him, finding nothing sure. In the past there have been strong reasons for failing to connect the two poets, though they should not prevail now. Earlier critics made a barrier of age, the historical watershed dividing the medieval Catholic world from the Protestant Renaissance. Now we recognize that the watershed comes later, between us and the two poets. A stronger reason has been the differences between their traditions: Dante writes within a medieval theological tradition, Spenser within a Renaissance humanist tradition of the rediscovered classics. Though these differences are real, Spenser's tradition, as expressed in Sidney's *Apology*, regards Dante as the ideal poet. In defining the right poet as one who creates a golden world, Sidney cites Dante as one 'hauing all, from . . . his heauen to hys hell, vnder the authoritie of his penne'.[2] But more important, each poem makes an imaginative leap from anything that comes before. It was a leap which makes comparison of Dante with the *Romance of the Rose* ineffectual, and of Spenser with Ariosto mockery. Even with their own previous allegorical works, the *Convivio* and *The Shepheardes Calender*, there is a difference of kind. I believe that it is a leap which brings them together.

---

[1] *Dante Studies*, I (Harvard, 1954), p. 13. In commenting upon the Error episode, Upton notes: 'I must not forget that Dante opens his poem with this very same allegory' (*Spenser's Faerie Queene*, London, 1758, ii. 339).

[2] *Apol.*, p. 22.

Unless these poets write a common language of allegory, there is little we may ever understand about the genre; but if they do, comparison of the opening episodes of each poem should be mutually illuminating. At first the differences in matter and method may seem too striking. Dante's Wood is nasty, brutish, rough (to adapt Hobbes's relevant phrase), and fills his heart with fear; Spenser's is a pleasant Wood where the knight and his lady are beguiled with delight. Dante describes in concrete and very real terms a man of flesh and blood who is defeated by fear and doubt until Virgil aids him; Spenser uses allegorical devices of a chivalric combat between an armed knight and a monster which personifies Error. But such differences are not essential. Spenser's Wood is also dark, for the enshrouding trees 'heauens light did hide, / Not perceable with power of any starre' and leads to the monster's 'darksome hole'.[1] That Beatrice sends Virgil to aid Dante, and that Una accompanies her knight, reflect rather differences of religious faith than of poetical method. (The differences of method are more apparent than real, but I leave this point until later.) Moreover, these differences do not rule out striking similarities. In larger terms each episode presents an image of one lost in a Wood where he confronts certain monsters (Dante's three beasts, Spenser's threefold enemy in the woman-serpent with her brood) and is overcome by error and doubt. Dante is driven back into the dark pass where he struggles with death until Beatrice aids him: Spenser's knight wanders until he comes to the dark den where he is almost slain before Una aids him. (The *donna . . . beata e bella* and the 'louely Ladie' clearly suggest God's grace.) Then both begin their Exodus—the one treading that pass which had allowed none to go alive ('che non lasciò già mai persona viva') and the other taking by-ways 'where neuer foot of liuing wight did tread' (1. vii. 50)—until they are restored to the heavenly Jerusalem. Essentially, then, each episode is an initiation: the candidate wanders in a labyrinth or maze which prepares him for his salvation. It initiates the poet also by committing him to his kind of allegory. Further, it initiates the reader by offering a brief allegory of what is to come, and by teaching him the art of reading allegory.

---

[1] All references are to the opening episode of each poem, unless indicated otherwise. For Dante, I cite the edition of *La Divina Commedia*, ed. C. H. Grandgent (New York, rev. ed., 1933).

The literal level of an allegory seems the most difficult to read properly. Does the fiction exist in its own right, or is it a veil which must be torn aside to reach the allegorical levels beneath? The latter has been the usual fashion in which to read not only Spenser, as we have seen, but also Dante. Modern Dante criticism recognizes, however, that the *Commedia* does not respond to such allegorizing. On this subject Professor Hatzfeld writes:

> In passages where ... the allegorical sense *is* the literal one, the reader is even less entitled to ask extratextual and biographical questions, such as whether the dark wood means heresy, or fornication, or pursuit of worldly honors in Dante's life, or whether the leopard means Florence and the lion Charles of Valois. These questions refer only to potentialities, namely, Dante's life as raw material, and abandon the actually achieved world of Dante's poetical symbolism. In other words, the new Dante interpretation makes a strong point of the fact that Dante in his poetry (not in his prose) overcomes the usual mediaeval allegorism and fuses personal, theological, political, moral, even astronomical elements into symbols of a decidedly poetical and not didactic quality.[1]

But not modern Spenser criticism where, as we have seen, the poem's literal level is still translated into moral precept and historical example. We are told that in the episode of the Wandering Wood, the knight is Holiness, Una is Truth, Error is obvious error: *ergo*, the episode means that Holiness defeats Error with the aid of Truth. We are told this by the critics, not by Spenser who does not name the knight, nor the lady, and describes the monster in very real terms. Again without support from the text, we are told that the knight is England, Una is the true Church, Error is the Church of Rome: *ergo*, the episode means that England passed successfully through the dangers of Reformation.[2] Since both poems share a similar critical history—contemporary praise for their profound meaning, the neo-classical eclipse, the romantic age's rejection of the allegory for lyrical beauty (Livingston Lowes on Spenser, Croce on Dante), and yesterday's search for hidden meanings—probably Spenser criticism needs to catch up.

What seems so perverse about translating the literal level is that Spenser, like Dante, labours to render the fiction in its own

---

[1] Helmut Hatzfeld, 'Modern Dante Criticism', *Comparative Literature*, iii (1951), 297–8.

[2] See *Var. Sp.* i. 422 f., 449 f.

right. It is an image presented in realistic and visual detail. There is the precise physical detail of the monster's huge tail wound about the knight's body, his strangling her gorge, her filthy vomit, the serpents swarming about his legs, and the final gruesome beheading. There is the exact rendering of the monster 'vpon the durtie ground', her brood 'sucking vpon her poisonous dugs', her vomit 'full of great lumpes of flesh and gobbets raw'. The details are immediately repulsive to all the senses: to the *sight* with the monster half-serpent, half-woman, and her deformed brood sucking up her blood; to the *hearing* with the monster's loud braying and her brood 'groning full deadly'; to the *smell* with the 'deadly stinke' of her vomit; to the *taste* with the violent spewing of the flood of poison; and to the *touch* with the monster's tail strangling him. The realism of the episode is enforced by its dramatic action: the monster's brood creeping into her mouth 'and suddain all were gone', her rushing forth and retreating before the knight, the brilliant chiaroscuro effect of the knight's armour which casts 'a litle glooming light, much like a shade' into Error's dark hole, the brood with 'bowels gushing forth'. This monster has all the terrible reality of a nightmare, and even Fuseli who saw the nightmare could complain that 'when Spenser dragged into light the entrails of the serpent slain by the Red Knight, he dreamt a butcher's dream and not a poet's'.[1] Clearly the poet labours to make us see. His whole effort is to render a clearly-defined, exact, and visual image. No less than with Dante, Spenser's reader must respect the primacy and integrity of the poem's literal level.

Whatever the differences of their critical traditions, both poets clearly demand that the reader focus upon this literal level. For Dante it may be enough to point (as Mr. Singleton does) to Holy Scripture with its insistence upon the literal level. For the Renaissance poet there is the classically-derived doctrine that the poet gathers precept and example into a poetic image which he makes us see; and behind this doctrine is the neo-Platonic faith that if man once sees virtues and vices, he will embrace the one and shun the other. For the Protestant poet there is also the renewed emphasis upon the Bible's literal sense. But they may share a simpler basis for insisting upon the literal level of their poems. Ever since Plato, poets have recognized that they deliver fiction

[1] See E. C. Mason, *The Mind of Henry Fuseli* (London, 1951), p. 217.

rather than truth or morality. In the *Convivio* Dante claims that
'the literal sense ought always to come first, as being that sense
in the expression of which the others are all included, and without which it would be impossible and irrational to give attention
to the other meanings, and most of all to the allegorical'. Further,
the highest allegorical sense, the anagogic, sustains and illuminates
the literal by seeing in it the poem's total meaning: 'this occurs
when a writing is spiritually expounded, which even in the literal
sense by the things signified likewise gives intimation of higher
matters belonging to the eternal glory'.[1] The corresponding
Renaissance claim is Sidney's doctrine that 'in Poesie, looking but
for fiction [that is, *only* for fiction and not allegorical truth], they
[the readers] shal vse the narration but as an imaginatiue groundplot of a profitable inuention'.[2] Since the fiction is the groundplot
for readers of both Dante and Spenser, to strip it away leaves the
poem barren. As readers we must respect what they have given
us. To read their allegories we must accept as given that Dante's
matter is a history of what happened to him, and that Spenser's
'History' (he insists upon the term) is 'matter of iust memory'
(II. Pr. 1).

But how may we understand their opening episodes? Not
according to the usual medieval or Renaissance theories of
allegory: these, with their stress upon levels of allegorical meaning, only distract. If we seek more clear authority for the art of
reading than the *Letter to Can Grande* and the *Apology for Poetry*
provide, we must begin with the poems themselves, with the fact
that each within its tradition is a separate kind of allegory which
demands its own kind of reading. And this provides the clue we
need. The opening episode of each poem defines the art of reading
the allegory. The initiation which is described here both separates
and joins: it separates the candidate from us, from our way of
life, and enters him upon a pilgrimage which is treated in the
rest of the poem. It follows that there are two ways of understanding. The first is outward, that extrinsic meaning which
relates the episode (and the poem) to our world; the second is
intrinsic, that inner coherence which binds all parts of the poem.

---

[1] *Convivio*, trans. W. W. Jackson (Oxford, 1909), p. 74. See also his letter to Can
Grande in *The Letters of Dante*, trans. Paget Toynbee (Oxford, 1920).

[2] See the Ponsonby edition (ed. A. S. Cook (Boston, 1890), p. 36) whose version is here less elegant but more explicit.

Allegory's unique power is achieved through the contrapuntal relationship between the poem's world and our world, and by the centripetal relationship of its parts. More comprehensively and significantly than other genres, it points beyond itself and also to itself. The brazen world of fallen nature and the poem's golden world, reality and the ideal, fact and fiction become united in our reading.

In their opening episodes both poets exploit the metaphor of the labyrinth or maze, of one wandering lost in a Wood where he encounters beasts. Dante's source has been found in Horace's *Satires*,[1] Spenser's in medieval romance; but the more likely source is Holy Scripture. There we learn that Wisdom (with whom Beatrice and Una are identified) 'wil walke with him [her lover] by crooked waies, and bring him vnto feare, and dread, and torment him with her discipline vntill shee haue tried his soule, and haue proued him by her iudgementes. Then will she returne the streight way vnto him, and comfort him, and shew him her secrets.'[2] But the metaphor is universal, too centrally archetypal to be traced to any source. Or if any, it is that of Christ who, after His baptism, entered the Wilderness where He was with the wild beasts during his initiation into the role of Redeemer. (Dante's baptism is signified by the metaphor of the lake in which he struggles, the knight's baptism by the spiritual armour which he dons.) The Renaissance poet may mingle classical myth with Scripture: the labyrinthine wood with the monster in the middle invokes the myth of Theseus who enters the labyrinth to slay the Minotaur in the middle, and is guided out by Ariadne's thread. He may do so because Christ is the true Theseus who slew monsters, and the Word is 'the thread that will direct us through the winding and intricate labyrinths of this life'.[3]

Singleton has shown Dante's complex use of this metaphor,

---

[1] J. H. Whitfield, *Dante and Virgil* (Oxford, 1949), p. 74. Cf. Upton: 'what are these trees and labyrinths [of the Wandering Wood], but the various amusements and errors of human life? So Horace and Dante apply the similitude' (*Spenser's Faerie Queene*, ii. 339).

[2] Eccles. iv. 17–18. The Genevan version (London, 1580) which I cite throughout this study. The tropological significance of Spenser's episode, then, is that given by Fulke Greville to Sidney's *Arcadia*: 'his end in them was not vanishing pleasure alone, but morall Images, and Examples, (as directing threds) to guide every man through the confused *Labyrinth* of his own desires, and life' (*Life of Sir Philip Sidney*, ed. Nowell Smith (Oxford, 1907), p. 223).

[3] Alexander Ross, *Mystagogus Poeticus* (London, 1647), p. 254.

how it is designed to locate us by showing the way of our life.[1] It is *our* life, as Dante's opening line suggests, but his experience in the Wood is unique. He becomes lost only when he separates himself from the common herd, from our life, through love of Beatrice. As Christian alone in the City of Destruction knows that he bears upon his back the burden which plunges him deeper into hell, Dante in the Dark Wood is forced by the beasts back into the darkness.[2] In the beginning when he is with us, he is nameless; he may begin to find himself only by losing himself, that is, by finding himself lost; and finally Beatrice will restore him to himself, and name him Dante. As in Bunyan where the pilgrim in our city is anonymous—after he enters the way of salvation he is named Christian—and in Spenser where the knight is not named until after he endures the first test. We may say, then, that Dante's poem arises out of its opening episode: once he realizes the horror of our way of life, he is prepared to be initiated into a new way of life.

Spenser also exploits the metaphor in order to locate us within our world. When the knight has been chosen by Una and the Faery Queen, he goes out 'to winne him worship, and her grace to haue' until the tempest drives every one into hiding: 'euery wight to shrowd it did constrain, / And this faire couple eke to shroud themselues were fain.' All seek the shady grove where 'all within were pathes and alleies wide, / With footing worne, and leading inward farre.' The ominous phrase, 'so in they entred arre', announces the beginning of his initiation (literally, *inire*, to enter in). Within the Wood they no longer lead their way, but passively are led: 'led with delight' they 'wander too and fro in wayes vnknowne':

> That path they take, that beaten seemd most bare,
> And like to lead the labyrinth about;
> Which when by tract they hunted had throughout,
> At length it brought them to a hollow caue,
> Amid the thickest woods.

This is the path which 'euery wight' takes, but none returns. In

---

[1] *Dante Studies*, p. 7.

[2] Francis Fergusson acutely remarks of Dante's experience: 'once in the terror of the Dark Wood, he had to explore the full import of that experience before his spirit was free to take another direction'. *Dante's Drama of the Mind* (Princeton, 1953), p. 5.

the first stage of the initiation the candidates (both Dante and Spenser's knight) wander as we do in our life.

In the second stage they are proven worthy of being chosen. To pass this test separates them from us. In Canto II Dante's spirit is so overwhelmed by cowardice that he withdraws from what he has begun. Virgil abjures him:

> L'anima tua è da viltate offesa,
> La qual molte fïate l'omo ingombra,
> Sì che d'onrata impresa lo rivolve,
> Come falso veder bestia, quand' ombra.

Dante is freed from all doubts of his worthiness only after he is told by Virgil how Beatrice cares for him. Only through faith in her compassion may he enter upon his journey. (These doubts recur at the beginning of his final ascent, the 'dubbi' of *Paradiso* IV, but Beatrice herself is there to resolve them.) In Spenser the knight wanders lost (that is, he is overcome by Error) and in doubt—'the place vnknowne and wilde, / Breedes dreadfull doubts'—until he so persists that he sees Error herself. The battle with this monster is described in terms of her labyrinthine tail which 'her den all ouerspred, / Yet was in knots and many boughtes vpwound, / Pointed with mortall sting', for this is the labyrinth which he must overcome. In the encounter his courage is first overcome—l'anima tua è da viltate offesa—and he retreats. Only when the lady intercedes with the injunction: 'add faith vnto your force, and be not faint', does he slay the monster. Then the brood, the doubts bred by the earlier experience in the Wood, 'him encombred sore'—la qual molte fïate l'omo ingombra—but with the death of Error they cannot hurt him and only destroy themselves. Spenser's remark during the battle, 'God helpe the man so wrapt in *Errours* endlesse traine', points to our life here: this monster will devour us, as she devours all who take the beaten path to her den, unless God helps us. But when God intercedes through the Lady, the knight may go 'forward on his way (with God to frend)'. Then he is no longer led by the path, but keeps it:

> That path he kept, which beaten was most plaine,
> Ne euer would to any by-way bend,
> But still did follow one vnto the end.

(The straight march of the concluding line demonstrates his victory over the labyrinth.) In Una's address to him:

> Well worthy be you of that Armorie,
> Wherein ye haue great glory wonne this day,
> And proou'd your strength on a strong enimie,
> Your first aduenture,

the repetition of 'you' and 'your' emphasizes that the battle proves him worthy his armour.[1] (Yet worthy only within his armour: 'that Armorie, / *Wherein* ye haue great glory wonne': at first he uses 'all his force' to free himself from the monster, but defeats her only when he 'strooke at her with *more then manly force*'.) His worthiness which is sealed by his faith sets him apart from us, even as Dante is commended by the Virgin as 'il tuo fedele'. Through this victory over the world, that is, over our way of life, both Dante and Spenser's knight are initiated into their pilgrimage.

Dante's poetic method may seem to differ radically from Spenser's. Dante renders the experience directly as his own; he describes dramatically and concretely the fear and agony which he suffers in the Wood. In contrast, Spenser leaves the given for the less real: rather than describe a man in error and doubt, he shows a wandering knight battling with Error. These are the terms in which C. S. Lewis has taught us to regard allegory.[2] And such abstract personification, we say, is alien to the reality of Dante's poem. But what, in fact, does Spenser do? In similarly dramatic and concrete terms, he shows a man confronting a monster; and in the immediate visual terms which we have noted earlier, he describes the physical impact of the battle. His 'Allegoricall

---

[1] It is evident that the episode also proves Spenser worthy of his role as England's heroic poet. The catalogue of trees which he so carefully elaborates in stanzas 8 and 9 imitates Chaucer's *Parlement of Foules*, 169–82. It indicates that he now wears the mantle as England's poet. Behind both poets' use of the catalogue is Ovid's account of Orpheus, the archetype of the inspired poet, moving trees with his music. The power of Orpheus descends now to Spenser as he begins to create his faery land. Spenser's imitation of Chaucer is all the more apt since the poet in the *Parlement* enters a delightful Wandering Wood where he is overcome by error: 'no wit hadde I, for errour, for to chese, / To entre or flen, or me to save or lese' (146–7). Cf. Affrican's rebuke in 155–6. Since Chaucer is indebted to Dante's opening episode (see J. A. W. Bennett, *The Parlement of Foules* (Oxford, 1957), pp. 63–65), there is a nice historical connexion between Spenser and Dante.

[2] *The Allegory of Love* (Oxford, 1936), pp. 44 f.

deuices' serve to sharpen the sense of reality; they add to it; and render it more 'real'. Spenser's metaphor is overt: to yield to the world is to wander in an enchanting Wood; to seek the way out—how difficult it is to avoid metaphor!—is to battle a woman serpent. Dante's metaphor is half-submerged, but it is no less present. Beatrice sees Dante struggling with death: 'non vedi tu la morte che 'l combatte / Su la fiumana ove 'l mar non ha vanto.' This is the sea which Dante struggles to leave:

> E come quei che, con lena affannata,
> Uscito fuor del pelago a la riva,
> Si volge a l'acqua perigliosa e guata;

and Virgil, in the lines quoted previously, sees Dante's spirit *encumbered* with cowardice, *stricken* by doubts. Once Dante accepts Virgil as his guide, the beast no longer forces him back into the dolorous pass. In effect he has 'slain' the beast. Metaphorically? yes. But it is all metaphor: the Dark Wood, the beasts, even (though in a different way) Hell itself, the Wandering Wood, the monster with her brood, the dungeon of Orgoglio. Dante's three beasts are emblems of the three stages of his journey through Hell. Spenser's monster is an emblem of Error; but what does Error signify? Not vice, nor any simple psychological state such as we meet in the personifications of other poets. Error is all that which stands between the knight and his entering upon his salvation, that is, Hell itself and the death which he must suffer before he may be reborn. The dragon-figure suggests this all-encompassing significance, as it does again in the knight's final antagonist. More simply, Error is what Dante means by the Dark Wood and the three beasts.

Spenser's treatment is more sophisticated largely because his age allowed him to be.[1] For one thing, his knight is more obviously

---

[1] His elaborate personification follows Renaissance convention, and in this matter it is pertinent to refer to Harington's preference for Ariosto's personification over Dante's. 'This description of the monster of covetousnesse, is (in my fancy) very well handled by mine Author, far beyond the like in *Dant* who maketh her onely like a Wolfe, pined with famine; But *Ariosto* goeth farder, and more significantly, describing her first to be ugly, because of all vices it is the most hatefull; eares of an asse, being for the most part ignorant, or at the least carelesse of other mens good opinions; a Wolfe in head and breast, namely ravenous and never satisfied; a Lions grisly jaw, terrible and devouring; a Foxe in all the rest, wyly and craftie, and timerous of those that are stronger then himselfe; all which applications are so proper and so plaine, as it is needlesse to stand upon them.' *Orlando Furioso* (London, 1634), p. 213.

an ideal pattern of what man should be. His entrance into the enchanting wood where he slays the woman-serpent invokes the analogy to Adam who, at the beginning of his quest, entered the Garden of Eden where the enchantress Eve joined with the serpent conspired his fall. (Eden was traditionally linked with the labyrinth,[1] and in medieval-Renaissance iconography the woman-serpent is the common emblem for Satan.) As Adam was tempted by the fruit of the knowledge of good and evil, the knight is first overcome by the serpent's vomit 'full of bookes and papers'.[2] Through faith, however, the knight defeats the serpent-Eve and enters the path which leads to his salvation. But in one way Spenser's treatment is more primitive than Dante's. He uses the symbol of the cave which traditionally signifies rebirth. Yet surely Dante's metaphor of the struggle in the water suggests another primitive metaphor, such as that used in *Beowulf* where the hero grapples with the sea monster.

Besides this significant pointing to our world, the initiation described in the opening episode of each poem points inward to the poem's world. In Dante, as Mr. Singleton has shown, it serves as prologue.[3] The three beasts represent the three stages of descent into Hell, Beatrice reveals the role which the poem fulfils, and Dante's journey here corresponds to his journey through Hell. Thus it stands by itself as a brief epic, a 'dumb show' revealing the argument of the drama which will unfold. Virgil saves Dante from the beasts, as later he will guide him through Hell. It is Beatrice who persuades him to begin his journey, as later she

---

[1] Cf. Bartas' account of Adam in the Garden of Eden: 'musing, anon through crooked Walks he wanders, / Round-winding rings, and intricate Meanders, / False-guiding paths, doubtfull beguiling strays, / And right-wrong errors of an end-less Maze' (*Diuine Weekes and Workes*, trans. Sylvester (London, 1633), p. 86). Milton's Adam relates how he 'stray'd I knew not whither' at his creation until in vision God comes as his 'Guide / To the Garden of bliss'. Once in the garden he is so overcome by its delight that 'here had new begun / My wandring, had not hee who was my Guide / Up hither, from among the Trees appeer'd / Presence Divine' (*Paradise Lost*, viii. 283, 298–9, 311–14). This is the Red Cross Knight's state of innocence in which he conquers the labyrinth 'with God to frend'.

[2] That human knowledge comes from Satan is Agrippa's argument, and one passage from the *De Vanitate* serves as motto for the Error episode: 'Nothinge can chaunce vnto man more pestilente then knowledge: this is the very pestilence, that putteth all mankinde to ruine, the which chaseth awaie all Innocencie, and hath made vs subjecte to so many kindes of sinne, and to death also: whiche hath extinguished the light of Faith, castinge our Soules into blinde darkenesse: which condemninge the truethe, hath placed errours in the hiest throne' (p. 4ʳ).

[3] *Dante Studies*, pp. 5–6.

brings him to his final salvation. Spenser's opening episode points inward in the same significant way to the world of his poem. The woman-serpent is later revealed as Duessa, the 'goodly Lady' with 'her neather partes misshapen, monstruous', and by the composite symbol of Duessa upon the Dragon. The knight's victory over Error is an emblem, then, of his final victory over Duessa and the Dragon. Here Una reveals the role which the poem fulfils, as later she prepares the knight to battle the Dragon by leading him to the house of Holiness where he is confirmed in faith. As Dante leaves the labyrinth to enter the descending circles of Hell, the knight leaves the Wood only to lose faith in Una through Archimago's false vision, and to wander lost, 'all in amaze' upon that path which leads him into Orgoglio's dungeon. After his rescue by Arthur, as he girds himself for the second stage of his journey—it is also an ascent through Purgatory—he meets Despair. By using the same allegorical language, Spenser places the two scenes in close correspondence. As Error is 'a monster vile, whom God and man does hate', Despair is 'a man of hell', a 'Snake in hidden weedes'. The one lives in a 'darksome hole' in the thickest woods, the other in a 'darkesome caue' among 'old stockes and stubs of trees'.[1] Again the knight must enter the cave and fight the monster. But while the first struggle was outward and physical, this is inward and spiritual. It takes place within his conscience; therefore the labyrinth he treads is intellectual. Error's vomit of books and papers appears in Despair's learning. Earlier he wanders in a maze until Error's 'huge traine / All suddenly about his body wound', now he wonders in amazement until Despair's arguments charm him in 'his guilefull traine'.[2] Against Error Una urges him to 'shew what ye bee': now she reminds him what he is, one chosen by God. As before, she offers faith, that is, faith in God's mercy. Each encounter tests the knight: the earlier proves him worthy his armour, the later to be worthy as one chosen by God.

More than this, we may say, in Singleton's phrase, that Spenser's opening scene also 'figured and forecast, as well as any single scene might do, the whole configuration of the journey beyond'. The knight's token entrance into the cave—he only looks in—is fulfilled later when he descends into the dark depths of Orgoglio's

---

[1] Cf. 1. i. 13 and 1. ix. 28; 1. i. 14 and 1. ix. 34, 35. After the knight defeats Error, 'then mounted he vpon his Steede againe': after he defeats Despair, 'vp he rose, and thence amounted streight' (1. i. 28; 1. ix. 54).   [2] 1. i. 18 and 1. ix. 31.

dungeon. Through Una's intercession again, he is redeemed when
Arthur makes his deep descent to restore him to light. Later he
pays tribute to her 'whose wondrous faith, exceeding earthly
race, / Was firmest fixt in mine extremest case.' Then in his last
battle he 'descends' into the cave: his sword plunges into the
Dragon's mouth which 'wide gaped, like the griesly mouth of
hell'. As he slays Error by adding faith to his force, here his
'baptized hands' wielding 'his godly armes' defeat the Dragon.
The first battle against the Dragon initiates his fall: this last battle
initiates him to that restored state signified by his marriage to
Una. In the cycle of fall and ascent he progresses from light to
darkness to light. But with this difference: that 'his glistring
armor made / A litle glooming light, much like a shade' as he
peers into Error's cave, while at the end 'those glistring armes
. . . heauen with light did fill' (1. xi. 4). The opening episode which
shows his primal state of innocence becomes a measure of his
later descent into sin, and a promise of his final ascent.

The two kinds of reading which we have applied to Dante and
Spenser, the one pointing outward to our world, and the other
turning inward to the poem's world focus in our single vision
of the poem as fiction. That fiction is 'an ideal space', as Curtius
terms Dante's poem,[1] or a 'golden world' in Sidney's phrase.
Though allegory usually suggests a way of writing in which one
thing is said but another is meant, our poets tell 'of Forests, and
inchantments drear, / Where *more* is meant then meets the ear.'[2]
We read the fiction not by translating, but by retaining the fiction
as metaphor. Earlier poets had written fiction, but for Dante and
Spenser both the matter and form of their poetry were transformed
by Holy Scripture. Mr. Singleton has convinced us that Dante
imitates Scripture: 'the literal sense is given as an historical sense
standing in its own right, like Milton's, say—Not devised in order
to convey a hidden truth, but given in the focus of single vision'.[3]
Here Spenser's kind of allegory may seem antithetical to Dante's.
Dante moves towards greater reality as his poem proceeds: Spenser moves in an unreal world of giants and dragons where Dr.
Johnson would never stub his toe. But what does this difference
amount to? Dante's fiction is that his matter is fact; Spenser's
fiction is that his matter is romance. The one establishes the illusion

[1] *European Literature and the Latin Middle Ages*, trans. Trask (New York, 1953),
p. 18.   [2] *Il Penseroso*, 119–20.   [3] *Dante Studies*, p. 15.

of historical reality, the other of faery land. For both poets, their fiction is a metaphor of Holy Scripture. Dante's position is clear; but what of Spenser? To consider briefly the knight's final battle against the Dragon. We say that here Spenser exploits the allegorical devices of the armed knight facing a fire-breathing Dragon while his lady retires to a hill. But where is the truth of this fiction? It is not the moral truth that Holiness defeats Sin or Death, or the historical fact that England defeats the powers of Antichrist. Its truth is given by Holy Scripture. The knight's three-day battle in Eden against the Dragon in order to release Una's parents, Adam and Eve, imitates Christ's harrowing hell, His three-day descent through which mankind is restored to the Tree and Well of Life. The fiction of both poets, then, whether it is given as an historical sense or as romance, is a metaphor of Holy Scripture. Once we see that each poet writes metaphor, then one poem becomes a metaphor of the other. And it is this fact which allows them to be compared.

Once we allow that in reading Spenser's poem we should focus upon the image, rather than upon some idea behind the image, our understanding gathers around our response to the poem's literal level because it arises from it. Our sense of that other reality to which the poem points, by first pointing to itself, grows from our sense of the poem's reality. We may be said to understand—literally to under-stand—the poem because we bear the whole poem in our response. That response is integrated because the intense delight given by the poem determines, at the same time, our understanding of its meaning. Our delight and understanding being integrated, our awareness of the literal and allegorical levels is continuous and simultaneous, and our vision of the poem whole. This simple, yet radical, alteration of focus may be achieved by reading the poem not for its hidden truth but rather for its fiction. Instead of treating the narration as a veil to be torn aside for the hidden meaning, we should allow Sidney's art of reading poetry by using the narration 'but as an imaginatiue groundplot of a profitable inuention'. Once we allow this art of reading, then Spenser's allegory need not be read as a complicated puzzle concealing riddles which confuse the reader in labyrinths of error, but as an unfolding drama revealing more and greater significance as it brings the reader full understanding of its complex vision.

II

'The Wel-head of the History'

> Master EDMUND SPENSER was the very first among us,
> who transferred the use of the word, LEGEND, from Prose
> to Verse: nor that unfortunately; the Argument of his
> Bookes being of a kind of sacred Nature, as comprehend-
> ing in them things as well Divine as Humane. And surely,
> that excellent Master, knowing the weight and use of
> Words, did competently answere the *Decorum* of a LEGEND,
> in the qualitie of his Matter, and meant to give it a kind
> of Consecration in the Title.   DRAYTON

IN this chapter I shall consider the '*Idea* or fore-conceite' of *The Faerie Queene*. First, we must approach the poem as Spenser did, by way of *The Shepheardes Calender*. Writing this pastoral poem prepared him, as reading it prepares us, for his later allegory. Some understanding of the kind of interpretation it requires should help us understand the more complex heroic poem. Lacking Spenser's treatise on *The English Poet*, we have found in Sidney's *Apology* a critical basis for understanding Spenser's allegory. But there is also the letter to Ralegh which he annexed to the 1590 edition of his poem 'for that it giueth great light to the Reader, for the better vnderstanding'. This letter should offer us some further insight into the idea or argument of the allegory, what Spenser calls 'the wel-head of the History'. Finally in this chapter I shall consider Book I as an image which answers to that '*Idea* or fore-conceite'.

I

The critical attention given Spenser's *Shepheardes Calender*, apart from praise of the work as a brilliant poetical exercise, has mainly been to identify certain historical allusions. While the poem is deliberately designed, so it would seem, to provoke from the reader E. K.'s delighted response to 'a prety Epanorthosis in these two verses' or 'a very Poeticall παθος', its brilliant rhetorical

surface deliberately conceals reference, as E. K. hints many times
in his glosses, to certain persons and events. Accordingly, the
poem provokes the critic to turn from the display of sheer poetic
skill in order to uncover some historical allegory. Yet even a
probable identification of Rosalind or Dido or Cuddie does not
take one very far into the poem which is read then only as a cipher
or intellectual puzzle. The poem was not so read in Spenser's own
age. In his *Skialetheia* Guilpin praised 'deep *Spencer*' for 'his pro-
found-prickt layes'; to Whetstone it was 'a work of deepe learning, iudgment & witte'.[1] Unless we dismiss this praise as jingoism,
we must allow that the poem has depths of meaning which cannot
be probed by removing an allegorical veil. This is to say the
obvious, perhaps; yet criticism of the *Shepheardes Calender* has not
been much more than footnotes to E. K.'s glosses.

What is so perverse about this effort to identify historical
allusions is that Spenser has laboured so carefully to conceal them.
Why, then, should the critic turn from what the poet says to what
he has left unsaid? Certainly parts of the poem 'reflect'—though
in no simple one-to-one correspondence—the contemporary historical situation, awareness of which would then provide an added
social impact for the contemporary reader; but the poem's substance, its meaning, is not there. Again to say the obvious, Rosalind
or Dido or Cuddie is clearly in the poem, while whoever in the
age may be doubtfully identified with one of these poetic facts is
not, unless we confuse art and life. Spenser conceals private
meaning in his poem, it is true; but he does so in order to turn
the reader from the particular to the universal. A general moral
meaning is dominant throughout the poem: E. K. writes that
'the keeping of sheepe . . . is the argument of *all* Æglogues', and
Spenser affirms that his purpose is 'to teach the ruder shepheard
how to feede his sheepe'. Moreover, Spenser insists in the Epilogue
that his *Calender* be not confined to any particular historical setting:

> Loe I haue made a Calender for *euery* yeare,
> That steele in strength, and time in durance shall outweare:
> And if I marked well the starres reuolution,
> It shall continewe till the worlds dissolution.

As E. K. paraphrases these lines: 'all thinges perish and come to
theyr last end, but workes of learned wits and monuments of

---

[1] *Skialetheia, or, A Shadowe of Truth* (London, 1598), E₁ʳ; *Sir Phillip Sidney, his
honorable life . . . by George Whetstone* (London, 1586), B₂ᵛ margin.

Poetry abide for euer'.[1] Spenser is not writing a history of his time, but prophecy; or rather, as a poet he ranges 'into the diuine consideration of what may be, and should be'.[2] That Milton read the *Calender* in this way is evident from his comment upon 'that false Shepheard *Palinode* in the Eclogue of *May*, under whom the Poet lively personates our Prelates, whose whole life is a recantation of their pastorall vow, and whose profession to forsake the World, as they use the matter, boggs them deeper into the world: Those our admired *Spencer* inveighs against, not without some presage of these reforming times.'[3] Spenser's intent in choosing 'rather to vnfold great matter of argument couertly, then professing it', is not to set up an historical maze, but to seek the universal level of significance. By his time, the pastoral form had become the vehicle for such higher meaning. Drayton believed that 'the most High, and most Noble Matters of the World may bee shaddowed in them', and he held Spenser to be 'the prime *Pastoralist* of *England*'.[4]

The argument of the *Shepheardes Calender* is the rejection of the pastoral life for the truly dedicated life in the world.[5] For Spenser, this means the life of the heroic poet whose high religious calling is to serve the Queen by inspiring her people to all virtuous action. Upon the level of merely private allusion, the poem may refer covertly to Spenser's circle of friends, to local gossip and other topical matters; but such allusion is carefully submerged, being occasional, digressive, and extrinsic to the poem's unity. Upon another level, the personal, the poem records Spenser's progress from his apprenticeship to pastoral poetry towards the heroic poem. Like the Red Cross Knight, he is a 'clownishe younge man' described in the letter to Ralegh who 'rested him on the floore, vnfitte through his rusticity for a better place' until the Faery Queen appoints him his task. (A year after the *Calender* appeared, Spenser started to write *The Faerie Queene*.) This level of meaning is transmuted through the pastoral conventions into an allegory of human life within the order of Nature. Through the device of the calender, human life is seen in the perspective of the

---

[1] Gloss on December emblem. All quotations of the poem are from *Spenser's Minor Poems*, ed. E. de Selincourt (Oxford, 1910).   [2] *Apol.*, p. 11.

[3] *Animadversions, Works* (Columbia edition), iii. 165–6.

[4] 'To the Reader of his Pastorals', in *Works*, ed. Hebel, ii. 517–18.

[5] In this paragraph I use some of the conclusions which I reached in 'The Argument of Spenser's *Shepheardes Calender*', *E.L.H.* xxiii (1956), 171–82.

fall and the Nativity: the one bringing the state of death out of which man must escape through rejecting the pastoral Paradise, the other promising rebirth which he may gain through seeking the truly dedicated life in the world.

The most obvious parallel between the *Calender* and the later poem is that each is radically allegorical. That designation, however, is ambiguous. There would be less critical confusion if one could refer to the earlier work as an 'allegorical poem', and to the later work as an 'allegory'. There is that distinction between them as between the *Convivio* and the *Commedia*: the one being an allegory of poets, the other an allegory of theologians.[1] Yet despite the confusion in terminology, the reader responding to each work distinguishes clearly a difference in the kind of reality which each projects.

The difference may be illustrated by comparing parts where the allegorical reference is 'parallel'. In the *Calender* the five moral eclogues form its allegorical core: in their songs of innocence we hear the songs of experience. In the arguments and glosses E. K. reveals that the debates and fables in the pastoral world refer to the political and religious events of the age. In the *May* eclogue, 'vnder the persons of two shepheards Piers and Palinodie, be represented two formes of pastoures or Ministers, or the protestant and the Catholique'; the debate refers to 'the Pope, and his Antichristian prelates', and the tale of the Fox and the Kid to 'the false and faithlesse Papistes', who deceive 'the simple sorte of the faythfull and true Christians'. The *July* eclogue is made 'to the shame and disprayse of proude and ambitious Pastours', and the debate concerning Pan refers to the Pope. In the *September* eclogue the attack upon Rome and the popish prelates is understood to be an attack upon England and the Puritans: Diggon is deceived by the 'loose liuing of Popish prelates'. In glossing Thomalin's emblem in the *July* eclogue, E. K. writes 'that vertue dwelleth in the middest, being enuironed with two contrary vices', and his statement suggests a parallel to Book II of *The Faerie Queene* where Spenser again treats moral virtue as the mean between two extremes. If E. K. were to gloss its ecclesiastical allegory, he would identify Guyon as the patron of the Church of England, that *via media* environed with two contrary foes, the zealous Puritans together with the Anabaptists or Family of Love who

[1] See C. S. Singleton, *Dante Studies*, I, pp. 84–98.

seek to despoil true religion, and that natural religion in league with man's fallen nature, the Church Militant seen as the Church of Rome. This state is described in the house of Medina where Guyon is linked with Medina who dwells between the rash and melancholy Huddibras (whom Samuel Butler rightly identified with the Puritans) linked with the discontented Elissa, and the lusty Sansloy linked with the sensual Perissa (the lawlessness and sensuality of the Roman faith). Consequently, the descriptions in the two poems correspond. In the *September* eclogue Diggon denounces the false shepherds who

> bene fraight with fraud and spight,
> Ne in good nor goodnes taken delight:
> But kindle coales of conteck and yre,
> Wherewith they sette all the world on fire (84–87),

where plainly he refers to the Puritans. In *May* Palinode links himself with such shepherds in confessing that 'when choler is inflamed with rage, / Wanting reuenge, is hard to asswage' (136–7). In Book II such characteristics describe Guyon's foes: Pyrochles 'inflam'd with rage' and Cymochles 'inflam'd with fell despight' are aroused by Atin who in their minds 'coles of contention and whot vengeance tynd' to despoil his prostrate body.[1] His other set of antagonists represents the intemperate indulgence in sensual pleasures: Phaedria who tempts him to wanton idleness, Mammon who offers worldly bliss, and Acrasia who uses 'vaine delightes, / And idle pleasures' to bind her victims 'in chaines of lust and lewd desires'.[2] These characteristics also define the antagonists in the moral eclogues. Palinode wants to join the May revels and spend his life 'at ease and leasure'; but such shepherds who 'mis-liue in leudnes and lust . . . heaping vp waues of welth and woe' (66, 87, 93) are condemned by the virtuous Piers. The proud and ambitious Morrell who sits in idleness upon his hill of delight is clearly a servant of Philotime, as was Diggon when he was 'bewitcht / With vayne desyre, and hope to be enricht' (*Sept.* 74–75) by the popish prelates. Palinode's argument on idleness, 'ah *Piers*, bene not thy teeth on edge, to thinke, / How great sport they gaynen with little swinck' is echoed in Phaedria's song, 'behold, O man, that toilesome paines doest take'; and his question 'what shoulden shepheards other things tend' is echoed in the song in

---

[1] II. viii. 12; v. 37; viii. 11.   [2] II. v. 27; i. 54.

Acrasia's Bower, 'ah see, who so faire thing doest faine to see'.[1]
Morrell inhabits a place of delight which he compares to Eden,
even as does Acrasia: his motto could be used for the Bower of
Bliss, *in summo fælicitas*; but Thomalin's emblem is Guyon's: *in
medio virtus*.

Yet how differently we read each poem! The reader of *The
Shepheardes Calender* may turn to the allegorical level to which the
literal meaning insistently points, and read the poem as an allegory
of the Reformation. If the reader of *The Faerie Queene* does so, he
will identify Acrasia as the Church of Rome, which in one sense
she is, but in so doing he will have short-circuited a matrix of
meanings. While the reader may seek some reality behind Morrell,
he must allow that Acrasia exists only in a poetic world. She may
be related to the Church of Rome only when both are interpreted
allegorically as analogues. That feminine enchantress who enshrouds her victims may then be compared to the Church Militant,
'that sensuall vnsatiable vaste wombe / Of thy seene Church' in
Fulke Greville's phrase,[2] that Dragon-figure of the Antichrist
which Reformation writers found in the harlotry of the Church
of Rome. Yet even in the earlier poem the allegorical reference
remains general rather than particular—Morrell is equated to
proud Pastors who live in every year, Palinode with the 'form'
of Catholic ministers—and overt rather than hidden, so that when
Diggon is exhorted to be 'not so dirke' he is ready 'playnely to
speake'. Such universal reference prevents our translating events
in the poem into direct historical terms. We may translate only
the other way: at most we can associate certain historical figures
with the characters in the poem. The earlier poem gains part of
its effect by focusing the outer world upon the poem; but the
later poem creates its own world, and first points insistently to
its own reality. For this reason I believe that the romantic critics
were right, though only partly right, in appreciating the beauty
and pleasure of the Bower. They were wrong only in limiting
their response to Grill's anger at Guyon's act of destroying it and
in refusing to accept that higher state which Guyon offers.

Yet what of Medina and her sisters? Since they represent the
Aristotelian concept of temperance as the mean between the two
extremes of excess and defect, is not their 'reality' to be found in

---

[1] *May*, 35–36, and *F.Q.* II. vi. 15; *May*, 63, and *F.Q.* II. xii. 74.
[2] *Caelica*, cix. *Poems and Dramas*, ed. G. Bullough (Edinburgh, 1938), i. 153.

moral doctrine? Certainly such doctrine lies behind the description of the golden-haired Medina between the froward Elissa and
the forward Perissa. But Spenser relates them to the suitors and
Guyon, and in their confused battle represents the Platonic concept of temperance as the struggle between the rational part of
the soul (Guyon) and the irrational, the latter being divided into
the irascible (Huddibras) and the concupiscent (Sansloy). When
he shows Medina and Guyon dominating the sisters and their
suitors, he achieves a synthesis of Plato and Aristotle which no
philosopher could achieve. When he shows them sitting down at
a feast, he brings this 'moral doctrine' to a symbolic point which
may be linked with the Christian understanding of virtue, but had
best be kept in its own poetic reality.

2

We may expect to find in *The Faerie Queene* an Idea or argument
which unifies the whole poem, and in terms of which, as Sidney
claims, the poet's skill is to be judged: 'any vnderstanding knoweth
the skil of the Artificer standeth in that *Idea* or fore-conceite of the
work, and not in the work it selfe'.[1] That a poet should plan his
poem before writing was common practice sanctioned at least as
far back as Geoffrie de Vinsauf:

> The hand that seeks a proper house to raise
> Turns to the task with care; the measured line
> Of th'inmost heart lays out the work to do,
> The order is prescribed by the inner man,
> The mind sees all before a stone is laid,
> Prepares an archetype . . .
> So in the poet's secret mind the plan
> Unwitting grows, and only when 'tis grown
> Comes poetry to deck the frame with words.[2]

Spenser would know that Virgil had expressed the Idea of his
poem in prose before writing it. Evidence that he did the same is
found in his letter to Ralegh.

All discussion of Spenser's allegory must begin with his letter
to Ralegh. It is his only critical treatise which has survived, one
written expressly to direct the reader's understanding 'to the

[1] *Apol.*, p. 9.
[2] For this reference and translation I am indebted to J. A. W. Bennett, *The Parlement of Foules* (Oxford, 1957), p. 5.

wel-head of the History, that from thence gathering the whole intention of the conceit, ye may as in a handfull gripe al the discourse, which otherwise may happily seeme tedious and confused'. Early editors quite rightly placed it as preface to the poem. Recently, however, it has become an obstacle to our understanding. It is generally agreed that it diverges from the poem, especially in what is given as the occasion of the Knights' quests.[1]

If the letter is so at variance with the poem, one must infer that Spenser deliberately misrepresents what he wrote. Since such an inference is so unreasonable, one must assume that it describes an earlier plan which was modified during the actual writing. Yet its date, 23 January 1589 [90], shows that it was written just before the poem was published; and its presence in the 1590 edition would still involve deliberate misrepresentation. Does it attempt to rationalize what was being published? but how odd to rationalize a poem by misrepresenting it. Does it offer, as a recent critic suggests, a new plan proposed by Ralegh but not carried beyond Book I? But how much more odd that Spenser, having spent ten years planning and writing, should attempt such drastic revision while the poem was being printed. Or is the letter simply irrelevant to our reading?[2] Such ways out are tempting, but none is satisfactory.

What Spenser chooses to tell us in the letter—and also not to tell us—is puzzling until we understand its relation to the poem. The first part in which he defines and defends the method of the

---

[1] Though the letter stands as preface in most editions of Spenser since the seventeenth century, the divergencies went unnoticed, even by Upton and Todd, until 1932 when Lawrence Blair pointed them out ('The Plot of the *Faerie Queene*', *P.M.L.A.* xlvii. 81–88). He concluded simply that 'Spenser did not tell the truth about his plot when he wrote to Raleigh'. In reply, R. H. Perkinson accused him of making an 'astonishing error' through not reading the letter more carefully ('The Plot of the *Faerie Queene*, *P.M.L.A.* xlviii (1933), p. 295). Then Blair retracted his error (ibid., p. 298); but the heresy had been sown.

[2] These speculations are made by Mrs. Bennett and W. J. B. Owen in *M.L.R.* xliii (1948), 239–41, and xlv (1950), 511–12. Owen grants that 'the presence of the letter in the 1590 edition is all the more remarkable since Spenser had an opportunity to revise or remove it when he prepared the cancel signed Qq in the second issue of the book'. ' "In These XII Books Seuerally Handled and Discoursed" ', in *That Soueraine Light*, Essays in Honor of Edmund Spenser, 1552–1952, ed. W. R. Mueller & D. C. Allen (Baltimore, 1952), p. 85, n. 1. However, since he believes that 'we are observing the difficulties of a literary theorist who, for the moment and for whatever reason, is sadly muddled', he concludes: 'to devise schemes to help the poet out of his difficulty is to assume that he himself knew what he meant' (ibid., p. 88). It is not Spenser who is sadly muddled.

poet who offers fiction rather than affirms discipline suggests that he is addressing a middle-class audience. For such readers he must underline his purpose and the didactic end of his poem, and justify his choice of the history of Arthur. Then he describes his method, and outlines the disposition of his History according to the method of the 'Poet historical'. (One indication of his careful writing here is the almost equal space he gives to the definition, defence, description, and disposition of his method.) His account of the poem's structure is deliberately formalized: the twelve knights as patrons of the twelve virtues set out on the twelve days of the Faery Queen's feast 'vppon which xii. seuerall dayes, the occasions of the xii. seuerall aduentures hapned, which being vndertaken by xii. seuerall knights, are in these xii books seuerally handled and discoursed'. From the last phrase it is clear that the poem's structure is not repetitive: the adventures are 'seuerally [that is, differently] handled and discoursed'. But in a preface which serves to introduce the poem, he need not describe, what can only be given in the poem itself, how they are differently handled. Thus the letter suggests the parallel structure of Books I and II while, as we shall see later, the poem works out that parallel in terms of significant contrast. Again, he may speak of the various knights as patrons of the twelve virtues 'as Aristotle hath deuised', without adding what is well known: that while Temperance is specifically Aristotelian virtue, Holiness is purely Christian. He tells only enough to arouse, but not to satisfy, curiosity; and he need not, were such possible, tell all. It is sufficient that he declare his purpose in order to avoid 'gealous opinions and misconstructions', and that he outline the pattern of his history which will not then seem 'tedious and confused'.[1] To use his own phrase, he directs our understanding 'to the *wel-head* of the History', rather than to that History itself. For Spenser that 'wel-head' is a formalized pattern or argument, rather than a narrative summary or digest of his poem. It follows that the reader should not expect the letter to provide more than a pattern or schematic form which the poet will embody in the poem.

[1] The absence of the letter from the 1596 edition has provoked speculation that Spenser's plans had changed (see Owen, in *M.L.R.* xlv (1950), p. 512, and Bennett, *Evolution*, p. 37). But it is a sufficient explanation that by 1596 Spenser had no reason to fear 'gealous opinions and misconstructions'. Since the letter is intended only to give light to the reader, it is not needed with the publication of the six books—they offer sufficient light in themselves.

Yet what of the account which Spenser offers of the occasion of Book II? Is there a 'discrepancy' here with the poem? There is—but only if we insist that the letter paraphrase the content of the poem. Instead, he presents the occasion of Book II in deliberately schematic terms which are adequate for the first three books. A witness who suffers directly from some wrong complains to the Faery Queen: Una complains that her parents are besieged by a Dragon, the bloody-handed Babe is presented by the Palmer who complains in his stead that its parents have been slain by Acrasia, and the Groom complains that his Lady is held captive by Busirane. This account is presented as an allegorical pageant which provides the pattern for the knights' quests which follow. Only later in the poem do we see how this pattern is achieved: that Truth laments man's spiritual bondage signified by the imprisonment of Una's parents, Adam and Eve, within the brazen Castle which is the brazen body of the Dragon, and how the Red Cross Knight slays the Dragon to release mankind who then may enter the unfallen Eden. And that Reason (the presence of Truth in man's nature) laments man's fleshly bondage signified by the Babe's bloody hands, and how Guyon destroys Acrasia's Bower to release Verdant, who is mankind, from bondage to the fallen Eden. But all this is rightly withheld from the letter. The schematic nature of Spenser's statement is also seen in the 'time' sequence: the knights are said to leave on twelve successive days, while in the poem a knight begins his quest only when his predecessor has completed the quest assigned him. Finally, this schematic account illustrates, as the context shows, the difference in method between the historiographer and the poet. The former 'discourseth of affayres orderly as they were donne, *accounting as well the times as the actions*' (my italics), while the latter 'thrusteth into the middest, euen where it most concerneth him, and there recoursing to the thinges forepaste, and diuining of thinges to come, maketh a pleasing Analysis of all'. While the historiographer must present the occasion of Guyon's adventure as given in the letter, the poet is free to re-create the time and the action as his allegory demands. He omits the occasion of Book I—it merely supplements the matter of the poem—in order to reveal the knight at the beginning of his quest already transformed by his borrowed armour, one appointed to the service of the Faery Queen, 'to winne him worship, and her grace to haue'. The account of 'a tall clownishe younge man, who ... rested him on the floore, vnfitte through his rusticity for a better place' balances the final vision which the poem projects of Saint George dwelling in the New Jerusalem. After describing the occasion of Guyon's quest, Spenser adds: 'which is the beginning of the second booke', the beginning, that is, for the historiographer. The allegory of Book II requires that the action begin *in medias res*. The book opens with Archimago in power, and the parents already slain by Acrasia. Into this fallen world Guyon enters to take the quest upon himself, as a self-appointed act of vengeance on behalf of mankind. Unlike the Red Cross Knight, he is (so Archimago addresses him) the 'faire sonne of *Mars*, that seeke with warlike spoile, / And great atchieu'ments great your selfe to make' (II. i. 8). The simple allegorical pageant given in the *Letter* is quite properly displaced by the poem's pleasing analysis.

If the letter is properly read, I would claim that there are no divergencies with the poem. Instead of remaining an obstacle, it should give 'great light to the Reader, for the better vnderstanding', as Spenser intended.

In the letter Spenser declares that the general end of his poem is 'to fashion a gentleman or noble person in vertuous and gentle discipline'. When we allow that 'fashion' means to 'form' or 'create', and that 'discipline' in the Christian humanist tradition as expressed by Milton 'is not only the removall of disorder, but if any visible shape can be given to divine things, the very visible shape and image of vertue',[1] we see that he means something more than that his work has a didactic bent. Its end is such as Jonson ascribes to Virgil:

> that, which he hath writ,
> Is with such iudgement, labour'd, and distill'd
> Through all the needfull vses of our liues,
> That could a man remember but his lines,
> He should not touch at any serious point,
> But he might breathe his spirit out of him.[2]

Or as Fulke Greville describes Sidney's end in the *Arcadia*: 'to limn out such exact pictures, of every posture in the minde, that any man being forced, in the straines of this life, to pass through any straights, or latitudes of good, or ill fortune, might (as in

---

[1] *Reason of Church Government*, in *Columbia Milton*, iii. 185.
[2] *Poetaster*, v. i. *Works*, ed. Herford and Simpson, iv. 29.

a glasse) see how to set a good countenance upon all the dis-countenances of adversitie, and a stay upon the exorbitant smilings of chance.'[1] This is the tropological level of significance in which the work turns to the reader to re-create him in the image of a perfect man. It is behind Milton's claim that the poet 'ought him selfe to bee a true Poem'.[2]

But this end is carefully distinguished from the poet's own pur-pose which Spenser outlines as the method of the 'antique Poets historicall':

In which I haue followed all the antique Poets historicall, first Homere, who in the Persons of Agamemnon and Vlysses hath en-sampled a good gouernour and a vertuous man, the one in his Ilias, the other in his Odysseis: then Virgil, whose like intention was to doe in the person of Aeneas: after him Ariosto comprised them both in his Orlando: and lately Tasso disseuered them againe, and formed both parts in two persons, namely that part which they in Philosophy call Ethice, or vertues of a priuate man, coloured in his Rinaldo: The other named Politice in his Godfredo. By ensample of which excellente Poets, I labour to pourtraict in Arthure, before he was king, the image of a braue knight, perfected in the twelue priuate morall vertues, as Aristotle hath deuised, the which is the purpose of these first twelue bookes: which if I finde to be well accepted, I may be perhaps en-coraged, to frame the other part of polliticke vertues in his person, after that hee came to be king.

What is surprising is the scope of his poem. Homer's heroes are contained in Aeneas: presumably the Odyssean wanderings in the first six books being Virgil's image of a virtuous man, and the effort to found a city in the second six books being his image of a good governor. As Virgil includes Homer's heroes in his Prince Aeneas, and Tasso follows Homer in dividing the heroes, and Ariosto follows Virgil in combining them in one person, Spenser plans to follow them all by displaying the image of a virtuous man in Prince Arthur and the image of a good governor in Arthur as king. While the end of his poem may be ethical, his purpose is to fashion the image of a brave knight perfected in the moral virtues. Like Sidney, he distinguishes the second kind of poet who treats moral doctrine from the right poet who delivers an image. For while this second kind may seek to fashion a gentleman in virtuous

---

[1] *Life of Sidney*, ed. Nowell Smith, p. 16.
[2] *Apology for Smectymnuus*, in *Columbia Milton*, iii. 303.

discipline, the right poets (to recall Sidney's phrase) 'doo meerely make to imitate' (and 'meerely' means both *wholly* and *purely*).

When Spenser elaborates Arthur's particular meaning in the separate books, he may seem to have a moral purpose, namely, to display the virtues: 'In the person of Prince Arthure I sette forth magnificence in particular, which vertue for that (according to Aristotle and the rest) it is the perfection of all the rest, and conteineth in it them all, therefore in the whole course I mention the deedes of Arthure applyable to that vertue, which I write of in that booke. But of the xii. other vertues, I make xii. other knights the patrones, for the more variety of the history.' It is not the virtues which he displays, however, but the knights as patrons of the virtues. Thus the Red Cross Knight is not Holiness but the patron of holiness, that virtue being his *persona*. Each knight has a moral *persona* because the virtues and vices are seen so clearly that they take on human form. Jonson expresses this point exactly: 'wee doe not require in him [the poet] meere *Elocution*; or an excellent faculty in verse; but the exact knowledge of all vertues, and their Contraries; with ability to render the one lov'd, the other hated, by his proper embattaling them.'[1] Since Arthur contains the perfection of all the virtues, he is the sum of all the knights, the circumference or zodiac which includes them all. Or we may say that since the separate knights are made the patrons of the virtues only for variety, each is an aspect of Arthur in his particular meaning as magnificence. In Spenser's general purpose he is the image of a brave knight. This is the ideal expressed by Sidney, that in the work of the right poet 'all vertues, vices, and passions [are] so in their own naturall seates layd to the viewe, that wee seeme not to heare of them, but cleerely to see through them'.[2] It is in this way that moral ideas may inform and sustain the poet's fiction, but the fiction triumphs over them.

The image of a brave knight in Arthur is an image of what should be. Though Spenser recognizes that his method will not be pleasing to those who 'had rather haue good discipline deliuered plainly in way of precepts, or sermoned at large, as they vse', he follows Plato in offering 'doctrine by ensample':

But such, me seeme, should be satisfide with the vse of these dayes, seeing all things accounted by their showes, and nothing esteemed of, that is not delightfull and pleasing to commune sence. For this cause

[1] *Discoveries*, in Herford and Simpson, viii. 595.   [2] *Apol.*, p. 18.

is Xenophon preferred before Plato, for that the one in the exquisite depth of his iudgement, formed a Commune welth such as it should be, but the other in the person of Cyrus and the Persians fashioned a gouernement such as might best be: So much more profitable and gratious is doctrine by ensample, then by rule. So haue I laboured to doe in the person of Arthure.

He follows Sidney in scorning 'playne setting downe' and in choosing to present 'pictures what should be, and not stories what haue beene'; only while Sidney grants that the *Cyropaedia* is 'an absolute heroicall Poem', Spenser rejects that work on Sidney's own ground that the poet ranges only 'into the diuine consideration of what may be, and should be'. There is almost haughty defiance in thus ranging himself with the ancient poets against the modern age which takes pleasure only in the superficial shows of things. Though the allegorists also defended the ancient poets against those who took pleasure only (or none at all) in the superficial shows, they sought rather doctrine by rule upon the allegorical level. The difference between doctrine by 'ensample' and by rule is that between what should be and what might be, between the poet who offers an image and the one who offers doctrine (whether directly or upon the allegorical level). Yet Spenser's method does not deny, but rather includes, the allegorical. Against those who see only pleasure offered by the literal level of poetry, the allegorists point to the profit of the doctrine hidden beneath. Spenser finds 'doctrine by ensample' more profitable than doctrine by rule, and also more 'gratious' (a term denied to the allegorists in their defence of poetry). His method, like that of the ancient poets, is to 'ensample' a virtuous man, that is, to deliver an image of the virtuous man rather than to hide doctrine under the historical fiction of the adventures of a hero. It is that difference we noted before between finding doctrine *in* Aeneas or *under* him, or that between looking through the image or outside it. Spenser absorbs rather than contradicts the literal level both by asserting the primacy of the poet's purpose over the poem's end, and by asserting its primacy over doctrine.

From the letter it is clear that Spenser regards the works of the ancient poets as allegories which form a single and integrated tradition. Each poet seeks to fashion an image of the virtuous man and the good governor, and each follows the same method in presenting what should be. Each poem is deliberately articulated within the tradition. When Spenser says that he has followed '*all* the antique Poets historicall', he implies that the entire tradition is gathered into his poem, being recreated in the image which he delivers. He does not move beyond his originals but rather returns to gather them into a fresh statement, according to his time's need. The metaphor of ripples upon water when a stone is dropped suggests this kind of developing tradition in which each work begins from a common centre—the poet's purpose to deliver an image of the virtuous man—and moves outward to envelop its originals. There is no dead hand of the ancients to burden the later poets. That '*Idea* or fore-conceite' by which the skill of the poet is judged belongs to all poems in the tradition, and we judge each by the idea, not by the work itself. Tradition, for this reason, became so vital and liberating during the Elizabethan period.

3

For the rest of this chapter I shall consider how this Idea is realized as an image in Book I. In the 'doctrine by ensample' which Spenser offers, the *ensample* is my immediate concern; the *doctrine* will be considered later. To see Book I as an image means to see its shape or structure; and while that structure has been seen as an exposition of moral virtue, spiritual biography, and also that of Renaissance theological treatises,[1] it must be seen primarily in its own terms as a poetic structure. Failure to see the structure of the book as an image accounts, in part, for the difficulties in interpreting the allegory.

One need hardly insist upon what is apparent to every reader, that Book I tells a story. We see the knight as a man suffering and enduring all things: after the first moment of triumph over Error, his agony of jealousy and rage believing Una disloyal, the foolish passion with which he entertains Duessa, the terror of his meeting with Fradubio, his scorn of the flattering courtiers in the house of Pride and the wrathful fight with Sansjoy, then staggering before Orgoglio as a 'man forlorne, / And left to losse.' After Arthur's entrance we hear his piteous voice in the dungeon wailing for

---

[1] See *Var. Sp. Book I*, pp. 422 f.; and V. K. Whitaker, 'The Theological Structure of the *Faerie Queene*, Book I', in *That Soueraine Light*, pp. 71–84. In *S.P.* lv (1958), 533–48, I argue that Book I and *Piers Plowman* are analogues, revealing the same Christian vision drawn from Scripture and presented in a common language of allegory.

death, and see his flesh 'shronk vp like withered flowres'. When
he is rescued we see how he yields in terror to Despair, and how
he suffers for his sins in the house of Penance until the vision of
hell opening below him is replaced by the vision of the New
Jerusalem waiting above; we see his bravery and endurance in
fighting the Dragon; and finally we see him enjoying the bliss of
his marriage to Una. Everywhere the story points to its own
reality, rather than to any underlying allegory of moral virtue.
It is significant that the term 'holiness' is never used with reference
to the knight, and the term 'holy' only once.[1]

The defining structure of Book I is taken from Scripture. The
myth of man's fall and restoration which is developed throughout
the Old and New Testaments gathers in the Book of Revelation
into a final image: the Woman fleeing into the wilderness, being
vexed by the Dragon which is linked with Rahab, the Whore of
Babylon. Through this image of the true Church of Christ opposed
by the Church of Antichrist,[2] Spenser shows Una opposed by
Duessa: each claims the Red Cross Knight for her own, the one
conspiring his fall into Orgoglio's dungeon and the other leading
him towards his ultimate restoration in the Heavenly City, until
Duessa's claim is denied and he marries Una. Since it was generally
held that the final Book includes all Holy Scripture,[3] Spenser's
imitation is correspondingly inclusive.

The Red Cross Knight's story is bisected by the coming of
Arthur: the first part is a tragedy which ends with his fall into
Orgoglio's dungeon, the second part is a comedy which ends with
his marriage to Una. At the mid-point of the story, the Dwarf
declares to Una the 'whole discourse' of her knight's 'wofull
Tragedie' in these terms:

> The subtill traines of *Archimago* old;
> The wanton loues of false *Fidessa* faire,
> Bought with the bloud of vanquisht Paynim bold:
> The wretched payre transform'd to treen mould;

[1] I. x. 45. That Spenser carefully distinguishes holiness from virtue is suggested
in his dedication of the poem to the 'magnificent Empresse renowmed for pietie,
vertue, and all gratious gouernment'. Here piety or holiness is distinct from virtue,
and both from the political virtues. All are contained in her magnificence, the term
which he uses in the letter to Ralegh to name Arthur's perfection.

[2] See John Bale, *The Image of Both Churches*, in *Select Works* (Parker Society, 1849).
Cf. Bennett, *Evolution*, pp. 108–14.

[3] Cf. Bale: 'the very complete sum and whole knitting up is this heavenly book
(*Revelation*) of the universal verities of the bible'. *The Image of Both Churches*, p. 252.

The house of Pride, and perils round about;
The combat, which he with *Sansioy* did hould;
The lucklesse conflict with the Gyant stout,
Wherein captiu'd, of life or death he stood in doubt.

(1. vii. 26)

These five movements, separated by semi-colons, outline the first half of the story as the five acts of a tragedy. They tell the story 'of hym that stood in greet prosperitee, / And is yfallen out of heigh degree / Into myserie, and endeth wrecchedly.'[1] Each act ends with a choric lament: after the knight flees from her, Una 'gan . . . waile and weepe, to see that woefull stowre' (1. ii. 7); after he has bought Duessa's love, she laments before the lion, 'redounding teares did choke th'end of her plaint' (1. iii. 8); after he enters the house of Pride, Duessa, who has taken Una's place, laments to Sansjoy; after his combat with Sansjoy, '*Duessa* wept full bitterly' (1. v. 17); and the fifth act concludes with Una's threnody bewailing the downfall of the hero:

Tell on (quoth she) the wofull Tragedie,
The which these reliques sad present vnto mine eie.

Tempestuous fortune hath spent all her spight,
 And thrilling sorrow throwne his vtmost dart;
Thy sad tongue cannot tell more heauy plight,
 Then that I feele, and harbour in mine hart:
 Who hath endur'd the whole, can beare each part.
 If death it be, it is not the first wound,
 That launched hath my brest with bleeding smart.
 Begin, and end the bitter balefull stound;
If lesse, then that I feare, more fauour I haue found.

(1. vii. 24–25)

At the end Arthur comes as the *deus ex machina* to slay Orgoglio and release her knight. The curtain falls on the first part of the knight's story when Arthur advises him 'that blisse may not abide in state of mortall men' (1. viii. 44), and despoils Duessa to reveal her ugliness. Then the story fulfils Sidney's definition of 'the high and excellent Tragedy, that openeth the greatest wounds, and sheweth forth the Vlcers that are couered with Tissue; that . . . teacheth the vncertainety of this world, and vpon how weake

---

[1] Chaucer, Prologue of *The Monk's Tale*.

foundations guilden roofes are builded'.[1] The genre would be suggested to Spenser by his model in Book I, the *Book of Revelation*, which was generally regarded as the archetype of tragedy.[2] I shall use this five-act division in order to comment upon Spenser's method of presenting Book I as an image.

Act I. The Red Cross Knight's meeting with Error is, as we have seen, a prelude or argument to his story. Balanced against this event in the second part of Canto 1 is the story of his deception by the guileful Archimago. After he meets the enchanter and asks of strange adventures, he is told 'of daunger which hereby doth dwell, / And homebred euill' yet is to be found 'far hence . . . in wastfull wildernesse . . . by which no liuing wight / May euer passe, but thorough great distresse' (1. i. 31, 32). We understand by this equivocation of the fiend that Orgoglio is the cursed creature whom he means, and in journeying to him, the knight will suffer great distress; yet that evil is home-bred, for the knight will meet there his fallen self. Una advises him to rest:

> with the Sunne take Sir, your timely rest,
> And with new day new worke at once begin:
> Vntroubled night they say giues counsell best.

Unwittingly, her words are strongly ironic: like the sun, this son of Day[3] takes his rest, but the night will bring the troublesome dreams which counsel him to leave her, until the new work he begins at once with the new day is his flight which ends only with his 'rest' in Orgoglio's dungeon. Accordingly, Archimago mocks her answer:

[1] *Apol.*, p. 31. It is interesting to observe that the plot of Book I reproduces the ritual forms preserved in Greek tragedy: an *Agon* or contest (the Knight battles Sansfoy and Sansjoy); a *Pathos* of the Year-Daimon, generally a sacrificial death (the knight's death in Orgoglio's dungeon); a Messenger who announces the *Pathos* (the Dwarf who tells of the knight's fall); a *Threnos*, or Lamentation (by Una); and an *Anagnorisis*—discovery or recognition—of the slain and mutilated Diamon, followed by his Resurrection or Apotheosis, or, in some sense, his Epiphany in glory (the theme of the second part, with the knight's discovery in the dungeon, his appearance before Una, and his restoration to Una through slaying the Dragon). See Gilbert Murray, 'Excursus on the Ritual Forms preserved in Greek Tragedy' in Jane Harrison, *Themis* (Cambridge, 1912), pp. 341–63.

[2] Milton writes that 'the Apocalyps of Saint *John* is the majestick image of a high and stately Tragedy, shutting up and intermingling her solemn Scenes and Acts with a sevenfold *Chorus* of halleluja's and harping symphonies', and cites the authority of Pareus. *Reason of Church-Government*, in *Columbia Milton*, iii. 238. He makes the same point in the Introduction to *Samson Agonistes*. See A. S. Cook, 'Milton's View of the Apocalypse as a Tragedy', *Archiv*, cxxix (1912), 74–80.

[3] Night calls him one of 'the sonnes of Day' (1. v. 25).

> Right well Sir knight ye haue aduised bin,
> (Quoth then that aged man;) the way to win
> Is wisely to aduise: now day is spent;
> Therefore with me ye may take vp your In
> For this same night. The knight was well content. (1. i. 33)

Una has advised the way for her to lose. Now day *is* spent; and
the son of day will be gathered up by Night. The clash of 'night'
and 'knight' in the final line is deliberate: when night falls, the
knight falls; and this night endures until darkness is slain in the
form of the Dragon. The 'In' which he enters brings another
initiation, now into the role of Duessa's lover, in which state he
wanders in a labyrinth of doubt and error which brings him into
the darkness of Orgoglio's dungeon. The pleasure of the enchanting wood is rendered in the 'wanton blis and wicked ioy' of the
dream conjured by 'that great Enchaunter', that infernal Prospero
who uses magic books, as Error had done, to defeat the knight.
That earlier opposition between Error's 'darksome hole' and the
knight's glistering armour which made 'a litle glooming light'
is revealed to be a conflict between the powers of darkness and
light, as Archimago summons the 'Prince of darknesse and dead
night' and curses 'highest God, the Lord of life and light' (1. i. 37).
Only now the knight, drowned in sleep, lies in the power of
darkness. Archimago's wicked sprights—like Error's brood they
are compared to flies for both signify doubtful thoughts—seek to
make the sleeping knight doubt Una's loyalty, and so forget that
faith by which he had triumphed over Error. They bring the
dream through which he seems to see his lady lying by him:

> And she her selfe of beautie soueraigne Queene,
> Faire *Venus* seemde vnto his bed to bring
> Her, whom he waking euermore did weene
> To be the chastest flowre, that ay did spring
> On earthly braunch, the daughter of a king,
> Now a loose Leman to vile seruice bound:
> And eke the *Graces* seemed all to sing,
> *Hymen iō Hymen*, dauncing all around,
> Whilst freshest *Flora* her with Yuie girlond crownd. (1. i. 48)

When he awakes he sees this wicked spright as his 'Lady trew'
and she deceives him by telling the truth falsely. As Una seeks
a knight who her 'captiue langour should redeeme' (1. vii. 49),
this false Una is captive to love as she pleads, 'let me not dye in

languor and long teares' (I. i. 52). She tempts him to become her
lover rather than her knight. 'Your owne deare sake forst me at
first to leaue / My Fathers kingdome' is her great lie. It is Una's
'wondrous faith' (I. ix. 17) which always sustains the knight, but
this false Una seeks faith in him: 'my weaker yeares . . . fly to
your faith', in order to arouse his selfhood. Only later do we
understand how this false vision parodies Arthur's vision of the
Faery Queen, in which

> Me seemed, by my side a royall Mayd
> Her daintie limbes full softly down did lay:
> So faire a creature yet saw neuer sunny day.

> Most goodly glee and louely blandishment
> She to me made, and bad me loue her deare,
> For dearely sure her loue was to me bent,
> As when iust time expired should appeare. (I. ix. 13–14)

The vision is the same, only the false Una offers love now and
not when just time has expired. For the knight that time expires
only after he slays the Dragon. Then Una will appear, as she
seems to appear now, crowned with 'a girland greene' (I. xii. 8)
with the graces singing around her as she is brought to his bed.
Then the first state of being 'bathed in wanton blis and wicked
ioy' will be fulfilled—as the development of the metaphor suggests—when he is seen 'swimming in that sea of blisfull ioy'
(I. xii. 41). He is tempted to seize for himself what ultimately will
be given him by God's will, even as Adam was tempted to seize
godhead before just time expired. Neither Una's arms nor the
faith she offers defends him now against this false vision whose
serpentine nature is revealed when she leaves 'so slyding softly
forth, she turnd as to her ease' (I. i. 54). For once he tries 'to
proue his sense, and tempt her faigned truth' he forgoes the faith
which had defeated the female serpent. Such Milton's Adam came
to understand:

> Let none henceforth seek needless cause to approve
> The Faith they owe; when earnestly they seek
> Such proof, conclude, they then begin to faile.
>
> (P.L. ix. 1140–2)

Once he yields faith, he enters an intellectual maze: 'long after
lay he musing at her mood' (I. i. 55) so that when Archimago tells
him that Una and the squire 'haue knit themselues in *Venus*

shamefull chaine' he awakens 'all in amaze' (1. ii. 4, 5).[1] At the
sight of the false couple 'in wanton lust and lewd embracement'
(an infernal parody of Paul's exhortation to gird one's loins with
truth!)

> he burnt with gealous fire,
> The eye of reason was with rage yblent,
> And would haue slaine them in his furious ire.   (1. ii. 5)

By morning he has 'wandred far away, / Still flying from his
thoughts and gealous feare; / Will was his guide, and griefe led
him astray' (1. ii. 12). Since God's image in man, the eye of reason,
is blinded, his own will leads to his fall. As he seemed to see before
in his dream, he saw in the false vision; and since he sees Una as
a harlot with her lover, he himself will become that lover of
feigned truth in the harlot Duessa.

   Act II. In the Red Cross Knight's battle against Sansfoy, they
fight with 'equall puissaunce'—they are aptly compared to two
rams butting with equal force—but the Cross saves him:

> Curse on that Crosse (quoth then the *Sarazin*)
> That keepes thy body from the bitter fit;
> Dead long ygoe I wote thou haddest bin,
> Had not that charme from thee forwarned it.   (1. ii. 18)

Though Sansfoy's blow hews a large share from his helmet—his
eye of reason being blinded—his shield saves him from further
harm, and his return blow splits his enemy's head. His armour
defends him, but now it is not his source of strength. Earlier he
defeats Error by adding faith to his force: he defeats Sansfoy by
becoming 'wondrous wroth' (1. ii. 19). Since his own will is his
guide, Duessa need only appeal to his 'mighty will' to have his
wrath change into lust. Now he accepts the harlot that before 'he
thought haue slaine . . . in his fierce despight'. Duessa's 'seeming
glorious show, / Did much emmoue his stout heroicke heart'

---

[1] It is illuminating to compare Milton's treatment of the labyrinth. We have
already noticed how Adam overcomes his wandering in the Garden by having
'God to frend' (to use Spenser's phrase). In the temptation of Eve by the serpent,
she is at first 'not unamaz'd' (*P.L.* ix. 552), then 'yet more amaz'd' (614) until she
treads his serpentine path—'hee leading swiftly rowld / In tangles, and made intricate
seem strait' (631–2)—and is lost, like 'th'amaz'd Night-wanderer' to whom she is
compared. Upon learning her trespass, Adam 'amaz'd / Astonied stood and Blank'
(889–90) and is prepared to reject life 'in these wilde Woods forlorn' (910). After his
fall, he seeks to live 'in some glade / Obscur'd, where highest Woods impenetrable /
To Starr or Sun-light, spread thir umbrage broad' (1085–7).

(I. ii. 21). After he defeats Error, he goes forward in the company of Una 'with God to frend'; now he finds a 'new friend' (I. ii. 27) in Duessa. His own force that before proves him worthy his armour, now corrupts him further: he defeats Sansfoy only to be defeated by the wanton Duessa. In the beginning Una chooses him because he was 'a fresh vnproued knight, / Whose manly hands imbrued in guiltie blood / Had neuer bene' (I. vii. 47); the irony of his present Pyrrhic victory over Sansfoy is that he buys Duessa 'with the bloud of vanquisht Paynim bold'. Now his hands are imbrued in guilty blood, and he brings retribution against not only himself but Una. Sansjoy seeks him out in the house of Pride; Sansloy defeats Una's false champion and so gains her as his prize; and Night prophesies that 'he the man that made *Sansfoy* to fall, / Shall with his owne bloud price that he hath spilt' (I. v. 26) as we see in his death before Orgoglio. This unfolding drama of the knight's temptation and fall reverses that pattern of his victory over Error. His original state of innocence is succeeded by the fallen state.

We have noticed that Book I draws upon Scripture, but at this point of his story Spenser significantly turns aside to draw upon classical mythology. When the knight plucks a bough to weave a garland for Duessa, he hears Fradubio tell the pitiful story of his metamorphosis into a tree. The theme of the bleeding bough derives ultimately from Virgil, while the metamorphosis is Ovidian. Fradubio's story stands here as a brief allegory of the knight's fall and restoration which is later rendered in Christian terms. Each has doubted his own lady, and left her for the witch Duessa by whom he is defiled. But much more pitiful than Fradubio's wretched state of being exposed to the weather and 'banisht from liuing wights, our wearie dayes we waste', the knight goes 'where neuer foot of liuing wight did tread, / That brought not backe the balefull body dead', until 'in balefull darkenesse bound . . . his better dayes hath wasted all'.[1] Moreover, he will be transformed into that terrifying image of fallen man seen in Orgoglio, that 'monstrous masse of earthly slime, / Puft vp with emptie wind, and fild with sinfull crime' (I. vii. 9). When Fradubio reveals that he may be restored by being 'bathed in a liuing well', the knight is ignorant of what this means. With a pun he replies: 'O how, said he, mote I that well out find, / That

---

[1] I. ii. 42; vii. 50; viii. 28, 38.

may restore you to your wonted well?' (I. ii. 43). Later he will be
restored by the Well of Life, but only after he is rescued by Arthur,
passes through the house of Penance, and fights the Dragon. Now
he hears Fradubio's 'piteous yelling voyce' pleading not to be
injured; later his more poignant voice will be heard by Arthur
pleading rather for death. Now he sees 'the wretched payre transform'd to treen mould'; later he will appear as 'a ruefull spectacle
of death and ghastly drere' (I. viii. 40). Thus the classical version
of the fall rendered in Fradubio's story prepares us through
parallel with contrast for our understanding the Red Cross
Knight's fall and restoration in Christian terms. Then the melancholy of exile from the company of men will be replaced by the
full Christian horror of man's exile from God, that more terrifying
metamorphosis of man's fallen state seen in Orgoglio and the
knight's appearance as a corpse, and the means of restoration only
hinted at in Fradubio's phrase will be fully realized in the knight's
journey under Una.

Fradubio's voice at first overcomes him with horror, and his
story leaves him full of fear. Though he thrusts the plucked bough
into the ground 'that from the bloud he might be innocent', it is
too late. He turns to comfort Duessa:

> Her eylids blew
> And dimmed sight with pale and deadly hew
> At last she vp gan lift: with trembling cheare
> Her vp he tooke, too simple and too trew,
> And oft her kist.

His kiss—like the kiss which Shakespeare's Adonis offers fainting
Venus until 'her two blew windowes faintly she vpheaueth'—
seals his doom.

Act III. The progress of the knight's tragedy is held up by one
of the most famous 'set-pieces' of the poem, the description of
the house of Pride with its medieval pageant of the seven deadly
sins. It seems to be the most blatantly allegorical episode in
Book I, one to be interpreted in moral terms as a house of *Pride*.
The moral meaning is everywhere present, to be sure: here is
pride in all its manifestations. Yet this moral meaning *is* present,
rather than disguised, and it is the literal description which is
insisted upon throughout. Later when the knight enters the corresponding house of Holiness, not one line will be spared to describe
the place. If we approach the present episode within its context,

we shall find neither mere description nor simple moral meaning
but an image pregnant with many meanings.

The description of the 'goodly building, brauely garnished' is
richly iconographical:

> A stately Pallace built of squared bricke,
>   Which cunningly was without morter laid,
>   Whose wals were high, but nothing strong, nor thick,
>   And golden foile all ouer them displaid,
>   That purest skye with brightnesse they dismaid:
>   High lifted vp were many loftie towres,
>   And goodly galleries farre ouer laid,
>   Full of faire windowes, and delightfull bowres;
> And on the top a Diall told the timely howres.   (I. iv. 4)

The squared brick links the palace with Egypt, the fallen world;
it is laid without mortar being the fallen city whose walls are
daubed with untempered mortar (Ezek. xiii. 10); that its brightness
dismays the sky shows that it reflects light; the golden foil declares
its deception; the lofty towers link it with the tower of Babel; the
delightful bowers display its worldliness; and the dial shows that
it belongs to the fallen world of time. Its foundation 'on a sandie
hill' reveals its fate in Christ's warning: 'it fell, and the fall thereof
was great'. In its infinite throngs of people about Lucifera's throne
where Duessa and the knight 'to the *Presence* mount', in one word
we see how Lucifera's palace parodies Him whose Presence is
salvation. Here, we may say, is Saint Augustine's earthly city, the
reflection of the City of God, that city founded upon 'self-love in
contempt of God unto the earthly', which seeks 'the glory of
men', and 'exalts itself in self-glory'.[1] We may say so, but Spenser
does not; so far he has not named the palace but only described it.
Later the dwarf sees the throngs taken captive in the dungeon:

> How mortgaging their liues to *Couetise*,
> Through wastfull Pride, and wanton Riotise,
> They were by law of that proud Tyrannesse
> Prouokt with *Wrath*, and *Enuies* false surmise,
> Condemned to that Dongeon mercilesse,
> Where they should liue in woe, and die in wretchednesse.
>
> (I. v. 46)

and when the knight flees from the palace:

[1] *De Civitate Dei*, xiv. 28 (Everyman ed., ii. 58–59).

> Scarse could he footing find in that fowle way,
>   For many corses, like a great Lay-stall
> Of murdred men which therein strowed lay,
> Without remorse, or decent funerall:
> Which all through that great Princesse pride did fall
> And came to shamefull end. And them beside
> Forth ryding vnderneath the castell wall,
> A donghill of dead carkases he spide,
> The dreadfull spectacle of that sad house of *Pride*.   (I. v. 53)

With great care Spenser refrains from naming the Palace until the final phrase of the concluding stanza: at the end the whole episode focuses in the name: 'that sad house of *Pride*'. If it were offered at the beginning, the reader would be invited to reduce its meaning to a moral one; but as it is given at the end, he must shape and hold the entire episode in his mind as an image. And only in this final stanza is the opening description fulfilled: the hinder parts which were called 'ruinous and old' (I. iv. 5) are now realized in terrifying literal terms in 'that fowle way'. Lucifera upon her throne above with the lay-stall of corpses below is that image of the woman-serpent Error, and it anticipates the despoiling of Duessa whose borrowed light is laid away to reveal her nether parts in all their foulness. If the image is held in its wholeness upon the literal level, and seen in its context of the book and even the whole poem, its meanings are complex. It is the fallen world anatomized according to the deadly sins, Dante's *Inferno*, which leads ultimately to the figure of Orgoglio-Satan at the centre. It is that world in which 'the motions of sinnes, which were by the Lawe, had force in our members, to bring forth fruit vnto death' (Rom. vii. 5). As an image within the poem it may be seen as Duessa upon the Dragon whose tail destroys all things. Its lofty towers are an earthly counterpart to the lofty towers of the Heavenly City. The 'mayden Queene, that shone as *Titans* ray' is Elizabeth in her *self* rather than in her 'true glorious type' (I, Pr. 4). The image means many things, and to pursue those meanings yields an increasingly clear vision of the whole book as an image.

Act IV. That the Red Cross Knight should now meet Sansjoy is inevitable. When he first appears 'full iolly knight he seemd', but with this difference, that he was 'too solemne sad'. Once he doubts Una's loyalty, wrath and grief lead him astray; and though he tries to feign 'seemely merth' (I. ii. 27) with Duessa, Fradubio's

story leaves him 'full of sad feare and ghastly dreriment' (I. ii. 44).
These emotions of wrath and grief are manifest in Sansjoy: he
enters 'enflam'd with fury and fiers hardy-hed', and when he sees
the knight's dwarf carrying Sansfoy's shield, he seizes the 'enuious
gage' (I. iv. 38, 39). He is the patron saint of the *'sad* house of
Pride', being fallen human nature subject to wrath and grief like
those in the dungeon 'prouokt with *Wrath,* and *Enuies* false surmise' (I. v. 46). The Red Cross Knight is the victim of these same
emotions, and in fighting Sansjoy he fights himself, that is, the
fallen human nature which seeks to overcome him. Earlier he had
fought against Sansfoy; now he fights for Sansfoy's shield and for
Duessa. The outcome is even more ironic than before: he becomes
what he fights against when victory brings his defeat. At the
beginning of the battle Sansjoy seeks blood and vengeance while
the knight fights for praise and honour; at the end it is the knight
who seeks to 'quench the flame of furious despight, / And bloudie
vengeance' (I. v. 14) by bathing his sword in the blood of his
enemy. After he is persuaded to forgo his vengeance,

> he goeth to that soueraine Queene,
> And falling her before on lowly knee,
> To her makes present of his seruice seene:
> Which she accepts, with thankes, and goodly gree,
> Greatly aduauncing his gay cheualree. (I. v. 16)

That last phrase is bitterly ironic. He is no longer the servant of
the Red Cross who seeks the grace of Gloriana, but the servant of
Lucifera. His adventure is not to slay the Dragon for which his
name is to be enrolled in the heavens, but gay chivalry, matter to
be chronicled in the house of Pride by those who record 'warres
for Ladies doen by many a Lord' (I. v. 3). He was chosen to slay
the Dragon after which he will be acclaimed

> With shaumes, and trompets, and with Clarions sweet;
> And all the way the ioyous people sings,
> And with their garments strowes the paued street, (I. xii. 13)

and with Una brought to their marriage bed. But now he chooses
worldly fame with Lucifera:

> So marcheth home, and by her takes the knight,
> Whom all the people follow with great glee,
> Shouting, and clapping all their hands on hight,
> That all the aire it fils, and flyes to heauen bright. (I. v. 16)

and being brought 'home', he is laid in bed where music seeks 'him to beguile of griefe and agony'. Being so overcome by Sansjoy, he will only plead for death in Orgoglio's dungeon, and emerge as 'the chearelesse man, whom sorrow did dismay' (1. viii. 43), the victim of that *tristicia* which makes him the victim of despair.[1] Only when he passes through the house of Penance may he learn 'himselfe to chearish' (1. x. 29) and gain the strength to engage the Dragon.

To describe Duessa's descent into hell with Night to restore the wounded Sansjoy through the art of Aesculapius, Spenser turns again to classical mythology. As Upton and Todd first observed, he closely imitates Virgil's account of Aeneas's descent into the underworld. Numerous details set up the episode as a deliberate imitation; but to what end in this imitation of Holy Scripture? In Virgil Aeneas's descent climaxes the first half of his adventures. He hears the prophecy of his woes to be fulfilled in the second half of his journey, and he learns his full destiny. In Spenser Duessa's descent climaxes the Red Cross Knight's wanderings— he leaves the house of Pride only to fall before Orgoglio. Night prophesies his fall, and reveals that his adversaries are Night's children. Duessa, like Aeneas, invokes the powers of Night; and Night's account of the macrocosmic conflict between the children of Night and the sons of Day expands Anchises' account of the fiery life-seeds shut up in the dark dungeon of the body. Clearly Spenser means to parody Virgil. In his poem the adversary, not the aged priestess of Phoebus, makes the prophecy of woe; and the great mother of the hero's adversaries, not the hero's sire, reveals the hero's destiny. And when we remember that in the Renaissance, Aeneas's descent was understood as his renewal, the purpose of Spenser's treatment of Virgil becomes clear. The classical statement of man's restoration is seen in Aesculapius endeavouring to cure Sansjoy's wounded body through his 'famous might / In medicine' (1. v. 43), again a borrowing from Virgil. But this is counterpointed by the story of Arthur redeeming the Red Cross Knight when he slays Orgoglio and descends

---

[1] After the seven deadly sins comes *Tristicia*, that sin which Chaucer's parson defines as 'the synne of worldly sorwe . . . that sleeth man, as seith Seint Paul. For certes, swich sorwe werketh to the deeth of the soule and of the body also; for therof comth that a man is anoyd of his owene life.' *The Parson's Tale*, lines 724–5 ff. Miss Spens suggests that an original draft of Book I treated the sin of *accidie* (*Spenser's Faerie Queene*, p. 30).

into the dungeon 'as darke as hell'. Then he restores the knight to Una through whose efforts 'that soule-diseased knight' (I. x. 24) will be fully cured. As before, the classical version—here of man's redemption—prepares us through parallel with contrast for understanding the Red Cross Knight's redemption in Christian terms. Duessa who brings Night to aid Sansjoy contrasts with Una who brings Arthur to slay the enemies of her knight through his bright blazing shield. The uncertain might of the reluctant Aesculapius parallels and contrasts the 'greedie great desire' with which Arthur enters the dungeon and the 'constant zeale, and courage bold' with which he restores the Red Cross Knight to light. Spenser chose Aesculapius because he is the false Christ, the 'Scolapius falsator' in Alcuin's phrase,[1] himself an emblem of fallen man, one thrust from heaven into hell where 'endlesse penance for one fault I pay', unable even to heal himself, 'and slake the heauenly fire, that raged euermore'.[2] Like the fallen knight who is held in the dungeon 'remedilesse, for aie', he is 'emprisond . . . in chaines remedilesse'.[3] In contrast Arthur is patterned after Christ who is 'the true *Aesculapius*, the Son of God, and the God of Physick . . . he only who was struck with the thunderbolt of his Fathers wrath, and sent to Hell, to deliver us from Death and Hell'.[4] As the classical descent into hell signifies man's renewal, Arthur's descent to aid the fallen knight shows how 'heauenly grace doth him vphold, / And stedfast truth acquite him out of all' (I. viii. 1). Spenser parodies the classical account precisely because it is itself a parody of the Christian statement. Such episodic treatment of classical mythology in Book I helps us to understand what Spenser means when he renders Virgil's *arma virumque cano* as 'I this man of God his godly armes may blaze' (I. xi. 7).

Act V. In his three-day descent into the dungeon of Orgoglio, the knight faces three foes. On the first day he defeats Sansfoy and proves his armour. On the second day, which begins with his coming forth at dawn and ends with the coming of Night, he proves himself wanting: though he defeats Sansjoy through faith awakened by Duessa's call, at the end he lies wounded. He has yielded to the irascible emotions on leaving Una, and to the

---

[1] See E. J. and Ludwig Edelstein, *Asclepius* (Baltimore, 1945), ii. 134.
[2] I. v. 42, 40.
[3] I. vii. 51; v. 36.
[4] Alexander Ross, *Mystagogus Poeticus*, p. 18.

concupiscent on joining Duessa. Once he lays his armour aside, he will fall victim to the threefold Orgoglio.

When Spenser comes to the climax of the knight's fall before Orgoglio, his language is highly charged with meaning. Not with moral meaning primarily, but with poetic meaning which the poem itself creates and accumulates. This quality of Spenser's verse may be illustrated in the three stanzas which describe Duessa's meeting with the knight after his flight from the house of Pride.

> Who when returning from the drery *Night*,
>   She fownd not in that perilous house of *Pryde*,
>   Where she had left, the noble *Redcrosse* knight,
>   Her hoped pray, she would no lenger bide,
>   But forth she went, to seeke him far and wide.
>   Ere long she fownd, whereas he wearie sate,
>   To rest him selfe, foreby a fountaine side,
>   Disarmed all of yron-coted Plate,
> And by his side his steed the grassy forage ate.
>
> He feedes vpon the cooling shade, and bayes
>   His sweatie forehead in the breathing wind,
>   Which through the trembling leaues full gently playes
>   Wherein the cherefull birds of sundry kind
>   Do chaunt sweet musick, to delight his mind:
>   The Witch approching gan him fairely greet,
>   And with reproch of carelesnesse vnkind
>   Vpbrayd, for leauing her in place vnmeet,
> With fowle words tempring faire, soure gall with hony sweet.
>
> Vnkindnesse past, they gan of solace treat,
>   And bathe in pleasaunce of the ioyous shade,
>   Which shielded them against the boyling heat,
>   And with greene boughes decking a gloomy glade,
>   About the fountaine like a girlond made;
>   Whose bubbling waue did euer freshly well,
>   Ne euer would through feruent sommer fade:
>   The sacred Nymph, which therein wont to dwell,
> Was out of *Dianes* fauour, as it then befell. (1. vii. 2–4)

It is the movement of the stanzas which, I suppose, discourages many readers from finding little more than decoration. The first stanza tells of Duessa's search for the knight and finding him at rest; the second simply inverts the first; and the third describes their meeting by the fountain. Upon the narrative level they tell us that Duessa meets the knight who rests by a fountain, and prose might use just so many words. But the movement of Spenser's stanzas denies any narrative flow, for the stanzas evolve through stages of expansion. The movement is circular rather than linear: each gathers significant meaning rather than leaving one fact to tell another. Instead of moving in a straight line, they rise outwards from a centre which here is the theme of the knight's fall. In expressing that theme, each phrase is deeply significant. The 'green boughes decking a gloomy glade' and 'the cherefull birds of sundry kind [that] / Do chaunt sweet musick, to delight his mind' repeat the setting of the knight's entrance into the Wandering Wood with its 'shadie groue . . . that heauens light did hide' where he joys to 'heare the birdes sweete harmony'. As that setting before prepared for the entrance of the female serpent, here it prepares for Duessa's. The 'boyling heat', 'the trembling leaues', and 'the cooling shade' repeat the setting of the Fradubio episode where the knight and Duessa sought to escape the sun 'so scorching cruell hot' in the 'coole shade' with the 'greene leaues trembling' (I. ii. 28, 29). As this earlier setting was background to Fradubio's story of his fall and metamorphosis by the Witch, here it becomes the setting for the knight's fall and metamorphosis by the same Witch. The green boughs which 'about the fountaine like a girlond made' also recall that episode where the knight seeks to frame a garland for Duessa—a garland to crown the witch who betrays him, as here it surrounds the water of the evil fountain which consumes his strength. Beyond these facts there is the gathering significance of the actions: the contrast between Duessa's search for the knight whom 'ere long she fownd', and Una's endless search; Duessa's reproach and Una's 'faire fearefull humblesse' (I. iii. 26) before the disguised Archimago whom she takes for her knight. That the knight appears 'disarmed all of yron-coted Plate' in this 'gloomy glade' is foreboding: in the darkness of Error's den, his armour is the light that guides him to see the monster. Even that 'his steed the grassy forage ate' portends his fall. In the beginning 'his angry steede did chide his foming bitt' even as he 'did earne / To proue his puissance': now, like his horse, he 'feedes vpon the cooling shade'. As the horse follows his appetite, he yields to conspiring nature. (There is, further, the implicit connexion between the horse and the passions.) The 'boyling heat' shows the enmity of the sun as Phaeton who 'inflames the skyen, / With fire not made to burne, but fairely for to shyne' (I. iv. 9). This destructive power of the sun together with the 'ioyous shade' (a contradictory term in Spenser's language) express the conflict between the false light and the true, and between light and darkness. The music of the birds suggests the enchantment of fallen nature, their music being the antithesis of the music of the spheres which the knight hears at his marriage. Each fact that we are given is significant and inevitable within the unfolding drama of the knight's fall.

More than this, there is usually in Spenser's episodes a central revealing action which renders its entire significance, what Joyce terms an epiphany. We have met such an act earlier in his 'falling' before Lucifera after his battle against Sansjoy. Here it is that moment when he drinks from the stream whose water is cursed by Phoebe so that 'all that drunke thereof, did faint and feeble grow':

> Hereof this gentle knight vnweeting was,
>   And lying downe vpon the sandie graile,
>   Drunke of the streame, as cleare as cristall glas;
>   Eftsoones his manly forces gan to faile,
>   And mightie strong was turnd to feeble fraile.
>   His chaunged powres at first them selues not felt,
>   Till crudled cold his corage gan assaile,
>   And chearefull bloud in faintnesse chill did melt,
> Which like a feuer fit through all his body swelt.   (I. vii. 6)

He has been sitting where he feeds upon the shade, now he lies upon the sandy 'graile'—the term is coined by Spenser to force a pun on grail—and through these infernal sacraments of communion and baptism he is metamorphosed into the fallen state. The moment marks his total defeat and fall into the dungeon of Orgoglio. Now Eden where 'Phison and Euphrates floweth by, / And Gehons golden waues doe wash continually' (I. vii. 43) is without a Champion. Duessa upon her Dragon rules the West, carrying her golden cup

> Which still she bore, replete with magick artes;
> Death and despeyre did many thereof sup,
> And secret poyson through their inner parts,
> Th'eternall bale of heauie wounded harts.   (I. viii. 14)

His drinking from the fountain is the first stage of his descent. Like the nymph in its water who 'sat downe to rest in middest of the race', he 'wearie sate, / To rest him selfe' in the midst of his quest; and as she became 'such as she her selfe was then in place', his 'well of life' waxes dull and slow. As he lies upon the ground, not being god-like erect, drinking from the stream 'as cleare as cristall glas' there is the hint of Narcissus whose transformation was understood to be a version of man's fall. His drinking the water signifies more immediately his yielding to the senses. In one magnificent phrase Spenser expresses all his present state when he describes the knight as he makes goodly court to his Dame 'pourd out in loosnesse on the grassy grownd' (I. vii. 7).

Now when he is without his armour, his powers transformed by the fountain, possessed by his Dame upon the ground, 'at the last' comes the apocalyptic thunder of Orgoglio's tread.

> The greatest Earth his vncouth mother was,
>   And blustring Æolus his boasted sire,
> Who with his breath, which through the world doth pas,
>   Her hollow womb did secretly inspire,
>   And fild her hidden caues with stormie yre,
> That she conceiu'd; and trebling the dew time,
>   In which the wombes of women do expire,
> Brought forth this monstrous masse of earthly slime,
> Puft vp with emptie wind, and fild with sinfull crime.   (I. vii. 9)

This threefold Giant is the Satanic image of the 'trinall triplicities on hye' (I. xii. 39). His creation out of earth inspired by the wind parodies God's creation of man. Being made in the image of earth, in size after its likeness, 'this monstrous masse of earthly slime' (I. vii. 9) is earthly man. Since man's body is a mixture of earth and water, it is commonly described by Spenser as 'fleshly slime', 'sinfull mire', or 'like to that Ægyptian slime'.[1] Being made from earth, even as the knight himself who is Georgos, this 'hideous Geant' is the knight's fallen state. There is no battle between them: the knight is already 'disarmd, disgrast, and inwardly dismayde'; and the pun on that last word points to his transformation. He has lost the whole armour of God which alone protects him; he has forgone all grace, both human and divine; and by his fall he is literally dis-made. Later Una calls him 'disarmed,

---

[1] II. x. 50; III. vi. 3, 32; II. ix. 21.

dissolute, dismaid', where the added term carries its etymological sense of *dissolved*.

What we witness in his descent is a passage through the elements of fire, air, water, and earth. When he escapes the sun's 'boyling heat' (fire) and bathes his forehead 'in the breathing wind' (air), he drinks from the stream (water) as he lies poured out on the ground (earth). Then he is defeated by Orgoglio who is a mass of earthly slime (earth and water) 'puft up with emptie wind'. The wind from the Giant's blow fells him to the earth, that 'all his sences stound': the wind that parodies the breath of the Holy Ghost, through which man is dis-made into a 'slombred sencelesse corse'. Where Scripture records that Nebuchadnezzar 'did eate grasse as the oxen', Spenser writes that 'into an Oxe he was transform'd',[1] that is, he becomes the state in which he exists. Of the knight we may say, then, that as he feeds upon the shade, drinks from the stream, and lies poured out upon the ground, he becomes earth and water, that earthly slime which is Orgoglio. God's image being erased in him, though not totally, he is re-created in Satan's image. Like Una's previous champions against the Dragon who 'all still shronke, and still he greater grew' (I. vii. 45), the knight's unfallen self shrinks to a 'pined corse' deep in the dungeon while Orgoglio reigns triumphant above with Duessa upon her Dragon.

The 'death' of the hero, this climax to the five acts of his temptation and fall, is rendered as an image. In Orgoglio we *see* the image of fallen man in all its terrible reality. Behind this image there is the Calvinist doctrine of man's total depravity; yet Spenser 'nothing affirmes', and all that he offers the reader is 'allegorically and figuratiuelie written'. Where theological doctrine exerts its strongest pressure upon our reading, as it does in this episode, the folk-lore elements are the strongest. The Giant with his great club who knocks the hero to the ground even with the wind of his blow, and then throws him into a deep dungeon, appeals to the reader's memories of folk-lore rather than his religious faith.

In imitating Holy Scripture in Book I, Spenser's whole effort is to write in accord with the Word while preserving his word, his fiction. By submitting, he finds perfect freedom. As Scripture

---

[1] Dan. iv. 30; *F.Q.* i. v. 47. According to the Genevan version we are to understand 'not that his shape or forme was changed into a beast, but yet he was either striken mad, and so auoided mans company, or was cast out for his tyrannie, and so wandred among the beasts, and ate herbes and grasse' (marginal gloss).

accommodates God's Truth to man, Spenser's fiction accommodates the same truth through his allegorical devices. The vision of glory must be covered by a veil:

> O pardon me thus to enfold
> In couert vele, and wrap in shadowes light,
> That feeble eyes your glory may behold,
> Which else could not endure those beames bright,
> But would be dazled with exceeding light.   (II, Proem v)

Fortunately he wrote in an age which allowed the concordance of all Scripture.

Spenser's skill in realizing the truth of Holy Scripture within his fiction is evident in Arthur who intercedes at the mid-point of Book I to rescue the fallen knight. After slaying Orgoglio and rending the iron door of the dungeon which encloses the knight, in the fortieth stanza—the inevitable number when we consider the theme of redemption—he descends to rescue him:

> Where entred in, his foot could find no flore,
> But all a deepe descent, as darke as hell,
> That breathed euer forth a filthie banefull smell.

> But neither darkenesse fowle, nor filthy bands,
> Nor noyous smell his purpose could withhold,
> (Entire affection hateth nicer hands)
> But that with constant zeale, and courage bold,
> After long paines and labours manifold,
> He found the meanes that Prisoner vp to reare;
> Whose feeble thighes, vnhable to vphold
> His pined corse, him scarse to light could beare,
> A ruefull spectacle of death and ghastly drere.   (I. viii. 39–40)

No reader can fail to see the figure of Christ in this image. The 'long paines and labours manifold' through which 'this good Prince redeemd the *Redcrosse* knight from bands' (I. ix. 1) reveal Him who, when mankind 'in bands were layd . . . harrowd hell with heauie stowre, / The faultie soules from thence brought to his heauenly bowre' (I. x. 40). Arthur saves 'this man forlorne, / And left to losse', even as Christ 'is come to seeke, and to saue that which was lost'.[1] Spenser could trust his readers to be curious enough to see in Arthur's actions the stages of Christ's manifestations upon earth. When he first disarms Orgoglio, 'large streames

---

[1] I. vii. 10; Luke xix. 10.

of bloud out of the truncked stocke / Forth gushed, like *fresh* water streame from riuen rocke',[1] an act which suggests the miracle of Moses as a prototype of Christ smiting the rock out of which water came that his people could drink. The Giant's club is compared to Jove's thunderbolt (i. viii. 9): the sight of Arthur's shield is like 'th'Almighties lightning brond' (i. viii. 21). While the former can batter to dust (i. vii. 14), the latter may transmute 'dust to nought at all' (i. vii. 35). Orgoglio is earthly; but the light from Arthur's shield is more than earthly: 'that heauens light did pas' (i. viii. 19). Again, Arthur's fall when 'his shield, that couered was, / Did loose his vele by chaunce, and open flew' suggests Christ's death which rends the veil of the Church. The rending of the veil of Arthur's shield marks the violent irruption of divine grace into the natural world through which man may be freed from the bondage of the Law to live under the covenant of Mercy. The harrowing of hell follows when Arthur enters Orgoglio's castle 'with greedie great desire' to save the knight who is held 'remedilesse, for aie' (i. viii. 28; vii. 51). One who has taken by-ways 'where neuer foot of liuing wight did tread,/ That brought not backe the balefull body dead' (i. vii. 50)—like Everyman, he was surprised by Death—and bound in that darkness where 'he his better dayes hath wasted *all*' (i. viii. 28), is brought to life and light. Spenser begins the episode by commenting upon the perils which make man fall 'were not, that heauenly grace doth him vphold, / And stedfast truth acquite him out of all', and then shows Una or Truth bringing Arthur to the castle where 'he found the meanes that Prisoner vp to reare'. Here we *see* how 'heauenly grace doth him vphold'. Later Spenser may have made a slip of the pen when he describes how the knights exchange gifts: 'the *Redcrosse* knight him gaue / A booke, wherein *this* Saueours testament / Was writ', but the slip was quite properly corrected to 'his' in the next edition. Throughout the episode the archetype is pressing almost too closely.

Yet the fiction is maintained. Arthur is not displayed as an allegory of Christ but rather as the image of a brave knight in whom we see the perfection of all the virtues. Where we see most clearly that larger image surrounding him, the poet stresses (and necessarily for the integrity of his art) the 'romantic' description— his magnificent glistering armour, the blazing baldric shining

[1] i. viii. 10 (my italics).

like Aaron's breastplate, the haughty helmet with its golden dragon and the 'bunch of haires discolourd diuersly' which so seized Marlowe's imagination. There is the native courage which he displays against Orgoglio: 'and at him fiercely flew, with courage fild, / And eger greedinesse through euery member thrild' (i. viii. 6); the temperance he displays when provoked by Ignaro yet 'calmd his wrath with goodly temperance' (i. viii. 34) (the only use of the word in Book I); his chastity shown in the story of his chaste desire towards the Faery Queen; the 'fast friendship' (i. ix. 18) which he offers to the Red Cross Knight (again the only use of the word in Book I); the Justice he exercises against Duessa; and his Courtesy in aiding Una, so that she speaks of him as 'faire braunch of noblesse, flowre of cheualrie' (i. viii. 26). Spenser may project such an image of a brave knight because of John's vision of the Dragon-slayer, one who in Langland's phrase is lord of 'al manere vertues; *dominus virtutum*',[1] but he contains his image within his poem. Further, Arthur's actions do not refer us outward to Christ's ministry, but inward to the story of the Red Cross Knight. For Orgoglio is surprised in just that state in which he had surprised the Red Cross Knight. At the sound of Arthur's horn, Orgoglio is 'dismaied', and rushes forth from making goodly court to Duessa 'as one astownd' (i. viii. 5). We remember when the knight with Duessa heard the 'dreadfull sownd' of the giant's tread and rose as one 'astownd'. Orgoglio, too, is 'disarmd' when Arthur 'smote off his left arme', and quite literally 'dismayde' when Arthur smites off his head, whereupon his body 'vanisht quite'.

The plot of the second half of Book I also has five acts: (i) the knight, overcome by the arguments of Despair, is saved by Una; (ii) he is led to the house of Penance where (iii) he combats Sin; (iv) he slays the Dragon, and finally (v) marries Una. These five acts complete the entire narration as a comedy, showing the change of fortune from a sad beginning to a happy ending. Each act ends with Una's intercession, and the entire action concludes with a *komos*:

> Great ioy was made that day of young and old,
> And solemne feast proclaimd throughout the land,
> That their exceeding merth may not be told:

[1] *Piers the Plowman*, ed. Skeat (Early English Text Society, 1869), B text, Passus xviii. 316.

Suffice it heare by signes to vnderstand
The vsuall ioyes at knitting of loues band.   (i. xii. 40)

Moreover, the acts within each half correspond, with the result that the entire movement is articulated within a pattern.

As the knight's meeting with Error is prelude to his quest, his meeting with Despair is prelude to his spiritual pilgrimage. Their correspondence has already been treated. It extends even to the mechanical detail of length: each is twenty-two stanzas (i. 7–28; ix. 33–54). There is the same deliberate care to form a distinct image, even to the extent of rounding out the episode by repeating a stanza (ix. 20 and x. 2). Since the labyrinth he treads is an intellectual one, the meeting with Despair corresponds also to his earlier meeting with Archimago which is itself, as we have seen, a counterpart to the meeting with Error. Despair's arguments charm the knight in 'his guilefull traine' even as he was caught in 'the subtill traines of *Archimago* old';[1] only, of course, Una intercedes to restore his faith that he is her chosen knight. The difference now is that the knight has been defiled by Duessa: from her cup he has drunk 'death and despeyre . . . th'eternall bale of heauie wounded harts'. In the dungeon he lives in that final state of despair, pleading for death which will not come; and when he emerges with his 'sad dull eyes deepe sunck . . . bare thin cheekes . . . rawbone armes', and 'his visage pale and wan', he is seen as Despair with his 'hollow eyne [and] raw-bone cheekes' (i. viii. 41, 42; ix. 35). Since the law of retribution invoked by Night demands that he 'shall with his owne bloud price that he hath spilt' (i. v. 26), it is the greatest irony that he should call upon law and justice against Despair for causing the death of Terwin:

Thou damned wight,
The author of this fact, we here behold,
What iustice can but iudge against thee right,
With thine owne bloud to price his bloud, here shed in sight?

(i. ix. 37)

For he himself is a damned wight who, according to law and justice, deserves only damnation.

The monster Error was aided by books and papers, and Archimago by his magic books; but Despair with his treacherous art of charmed speeches draws upon the Word of God. Or rather, upon

[1] i. ix. 31; vii. 26.

one half of God's Word, for he blots out the other half. He shows
God's Justice but not His Mercy; the Law but not the Gospel.[1]
Such is the common trick of Satan. 'The manner of Satan, which
is the common adversary of all men, is, when any man is grievously
sick and like to die, straightways to come upon him at the beginning very fiercely, and to shew himself terrible unto him, and to
cast before his eyes such a mist, that except he taketh heed, he
shall see nothing but the fierce wrath and terrible judgment of
God against sinners.'[2] Despair poses the riddle of God's justice:

> Is he not iust, that all this doth behold
> From highest heauen, and beares an equall eye?
> Shall he thy sins vp in his knowledge fold,
> And guiltie be of thine impietie?
> Is not his law, Let euery sinner die:
> Die shall all flesh?   (I. ix. 47)

So powerful are his arguments that he can say that 'death is the
end of woes', and show the horror of damnation. Here he asks a
rhetorical question which shouts the answer, 'yes, Christ will fold

---

[1] See E. Sirluck, 'A Note on the Rhetoric of Spenser's "Despair"', *M.P.*, xlvii
(1949), 8–11.
[2] Thomas Becon, *The Sick Man's Salve*, 1561 (Parker Society, 1844), iv. 156. When
the sick man in his despair fears his transgression of the law, he is reminded that
scripture consists of the law and the gospel. 'For the law was given by Moses; but
the gospel, that is, grace, favour, remission of sins, truth, faithfulness, and ever-
lasting life came by Jesus Christ. The law maketh afraid; but the gospel comforteth.
The law troubleth; but the gospel quieteth. The law uttereth sin; but the gospel
pardoneth and forgiveth sin. The law declareth the fierce wrath of God against
sinners; but the gospel preacheth the great and exceeding mercies of God toward
penitent sinners. . . . The law driveth to desperation; but the gospel ministereth
consolation and comfort' (p. 162). In Calvin's terms the Red Cross Knight's present
despair is 'Repentaunce of the Law, by which the sinner wounded with the searing
iron of sinne, & worne away with feare of the wrath of God, sticketh fast in that
trouble & can not wind him selfe out of it' (*The Institution of Christian Religion*, trans.
by Th. Norton (London, 1582), p. 193ʳ). Later in the house of Penance, the knight
undergoes 'the other Repentance they call of ye Gospell, by which the sinner is in
deede greeuously vexed with him selfe, but he riseth vp higher and taketh holde of
Christ, the salue of his sore, the comforte of his feare, the hauen of his miserie' (ibid.).
Calvin explains further: 'of the repentaunce of the lawe they put those examples:
Cain, Saul, and Iudas. Whose repentance when the scripture rehearseth vnto vs,
it meaneth that they acknowledging the greeuousnesse of their sinne, were afraide
of the wrath of God, but in thinking vpon God onely as a reuenger and iudge, they
fainted in that feeling. Therefore their repentance was nothing else but a certaine
entrie of hell, whereinto they being entred into this present life beganne alreadie to
suffer punishment, from the face of the wrath of Gods Maiestie. The repentaunce of
the Gospell, wee see in all them, that . . . refreshed with confidence of the mercie of
God are turned vnto the Lord' (ibid.).

up our sins in his knowledge and be guilty of our impiety', yet
the knight is reduced to silence. But Una solves the riddle:

> In heauenly mercies hast thou not a part?
> Why shouldst thou then despeire, that chosen art?
> Where iustice growes, there grows eke greater grace,
> The which doth quench the brond of hellish smart,
> And that accurst hand-writing doth deface.   (I. ix. 53)

Christ is the straight way by which the mind escapes from the
circular maze of pagan thought, as Saint Augustine found. Such
spiritual armour now arms the Red Cross Knight.

Other episodes in the two parts of Book I correspond. Briefly,
'that sad house of *Pride*' to which Duessa makes the knight bend
his pace corresponds to 'that sad house of *Penaunce*' to which Una
brings him. One is the fallen world anatomized as the *Inferno*
which culminates in the vision of hell in its dungeon; the other is
the world anatomized as *Purgatorio* which culminates in the vision
of the Heavenly City. The house of Penance relieves 'the needes /
Of wretched soules, and helpe[s] the helpelesse pore', that is, those
few who escape from the house of Pride 'with balefull beggerie,
or foule disgrace'.[1] The battle with Sansjoy in the house of Pride
corresponds to the knight's battle with Sin in the house of
Penance. In effect, he casts out Sansjoy by undergoing true repentance and learns 'himselfe to chearish'. The pageant of the
seven beadmen replaces the pageant of the seven deadly sins.
After Arthur slays Orgoglio, Duessa casts her golden cup to the
ground: when the Red Cross Knight is led to the house of Penance,
he is instructed by Faith who

> in her right hand bore a cup of gold,
> With wine and water fild vp to the hight,
> In which a Serpent did himselfe enfold,
> That horrour made to all, that did behold.   (I. x. 13)

Her cup is the means by which he may be restored to the true
sacraments, the Well and the Tree of Life which renew him in his
fight against the Dragon. Before when he drank from the waters
which 'waxed dull and slow', all his powers grew feeble; but once
he drinks the silver flood which 'fast trickled' being 'full of great
vertues', he gains more than human power.[2] After drinking from
the fountain, he could scarcely wield his blade; but he rises from

---

[1] I. x. 3; I. iv. 3.   [2] I. vii. 5; I. xi. 29.

the Well of Life 'high brandishing his bright deaw-burning blade'
(I. xi. 35). Before he had fed upon the shade only to sink deeper
into sin; now he is nourished all night by the true healing balm
of the Tree of Life which restores his strength. His three-day
battle against the Dragon in order to release Adam and Eve from
their bondage in the brazen tower imitates Christ's harrowing
hell. But Spenser again turns this image inward to the poem:
the knight imitates Arthur who had descended into hell to redeem
man, and he slays the Dragon which Arthur had wounded.

The image whose shape or structure we have been describing
is only part of a larger image which Spenser renders in Book I.
After reading Book I, what larger outlines hold the separate
episodes together, to give unity to what we have read? The
reader may remember certain images: Error with her inky brood
lurking in her dark hole, Archimago's wicked spright descending
into hell, Una wandering, the glittering house of Pride with its
dungeon below, Duessa's meeting with Night and their descent
into hell, the hideous giant Orgoglio, Despair brooding in his
cave, the vision of the damned in hell, the house of Penance with
the holy hospital, the vision of the New Jerusalem, the fiery
Dragon, and the final marriage rites. Or he may remember certain
actions: Error retreating, Lucifera's pageant into the fields, Sansloy
snatching Una's veil to reveal her shining face, Orgoglio's blow,
the uncovering of Arthur's shield, Orgoglio's fall, Arthur's
descent, Una's sudden intercession to save her knight, the belching
flames from the Dragon's mouth, and the final vision of Una
unveiled in all her glory. Or of memorable speeches: Fradubio's
story, Una's lament, Arthur's dream vision, and Despair's counsel.
What is so remarkable about this larger outline is the role of the
Red Cross Knight. After his initial defeat of Error, he remains
curiously passive, almost like the prostrate figure of Everyman
over whom greater forces battle to possess his soul. In Spenser's
story of arms and the man, the arms rather than the man is his
theme: 'that I this man of God his godly armes may blaze' (I. xi. 7).
Moreover, these are Una's arms, and he is the most recent of her
many champions, all of whom have been slain by the Dragon.
She relates to Arthur how her knight was abused by false Duessa,

> Mine onely foe, mine onely deadly dread,
> Who with her witchcraft and misseeming sweete,
> Inueigled him to follow her desires vnmeete.   (I. vii. 50)

Her contest with Duessa provides the action of the whole book. Their opposition is seen first in the opening iconographical description of Una veiled upon 'a lowly Asse more white then snow', while Duessa 'clad in scarlot red' rides upon a 'wanton palfrey all . . . ouerspred / With tinsell trappings.'[1] In their genealogies Una is the only daughter

> Of ancient Kings and Queenes, that had of yore
> Their scepters stretcht from East to Westerne shore,
> And all the world in their subiection held;
> Till that infernall feend with foule vprore
> Forwasted all their land, and them expeld.   (1. i. 5)

while Duessa declares that she

> Was, (O what now auaileth that I was!)
> Borne the sole daughter of an Emperour,
> He that the wide West vnder his rule has,
> And high hath set his throne, where *Tiberis* doth pas.
>
> (1. ii. 22)

Una's parents *once* held the world in their subiection, that is, they ruled the East, the unfallen Eden; Duessa's father *now* rules the West, the fallen world.

The Red Cross Knight is Una's chosen knight, but when he leaves her, Duessa becomes his Dame. The climax to the first half of the book comes when Duessa is disrobed, and the knight sees her in all her foulness; and the climax to the second half when Duessa, in seeking to claim the knight, is denounced by Una before all as 'that false sorceresse' (1. xii. 33). The contest between them is expressed in the imagery as the contest between day and night, light and darkness, or more exactly, between the true light and the false.

The first book is an expanded metaphor of the conflict between light and darkness. Una is light. When she first lays aside her veil

> her angels face
> As the great eye of heauen shyned bright,
> And made a sunshine in the shadie place.   (1. iii. 4)

When Sansloy snatches the veil from her face, 'then gan her beautie shine, as brightest skye' (1. vi. 4). In contrast, Duessa is descended from Night, and appears in 'borrowed light' (1. viii. 49). The three Sans brothers are 'great *Nightes* children', while the

[1] 1. i. 4; 1. ii. 13.

Red Cross Knight is called one of 'the sonnes of Day' (I. v. 23, 25,.
Therefore, when the knight battles Sansjoy he appears as Phoebus:

> At last the golden Orientall gate
> Of greatest heauen gan to open faire,
> And *Phœbus* fresh, as bridegrome to his mate,
> Came dauncing forth, shaking his deawie haire:
> And hurld his glistring beames through gloomy aire.
> Which when the wakeful Elfe perceiu'd, streight way
> He started vp, and did him selfe prepaire,
> In sun-bright armes, and battailous array:
> For with that Pagan proud he combat will that day. (I. v. 2)

Since the children of Night are disguised in light—even Night
herself is deceived by Duessa's brightness—the real conflict is
between luminous light and reflected light. Spenser distinguishes
carefully between 'glistring' and 'glittering': one emits light, as
the Red Cross Knight's 'glistring armor', the other reflects light,
as the walls of the house of Pride which are covered with golden
foil. He distinguishes also between light which shines and light
which burns. Lucifera shone 'like *Phœbus* fairest childe . . . With
fire not made to burne, but fairely for to shyne' (I. iv. 9). It is the
burning heat of the sun which forces the Red Cross Knight to
seek the shade with Duessa, and at the mid-point of the book,
Una's 'light, and shining lampe of blis' must 'liue perforce in
balefull darkenesse bound'.[1] At this nadir of the action, Una in
her despair rejects 'loathed light' and seeks 'eternall night' (I. vii.
22). At this moment Arthur comes; and he is all light. 'His
glitterand armour shined farre away, / Like glauncing light of
Phœbus brightest ray'; his baldric 'shynd, like twinkling stars';
its stone within 'exceeding shone, / Like *Hesperus* emongst the
lesser lights'; his helmet bred 'glorious brightnesse', and his
diamond shield

> so exceeding shone his glistring ray,
> That *Phœbus* golden face it did attaint,
> As when a cloud his beames doth ouer-lay;
> And siluer *Cynthia* wexed pale and faint,
> As when her face is staynd with magicke arts constraint.[2]

(There is the further conflict given here between created light and
the source of light, between the light of the sun and He Whom
Milton addresses as 'bright effluence of bright essence increate'.[3])

---

[1] I. iii. 27; viii. 38.   [2] I. vii. 29, 30, 31, 34.   [3] *Paradise Lost*, iii. 6.

Through the heavenly light of the shield, Arthur brings the Red Cross Knight to light; and when Duessa is shorn of her 'borrowed light', light is divided from darkness, and a new creation begins.

Una's victory over darkness is achieved through the knight's defeat of the Dragon. In the first day the knight wields his sword with 'three mens strength' (I. xi. 20), that is, with the greatest human power; but the Dragon's fire (the light that burns) his 'fyrie steele now burnt, that earst him arm'd' (I. xi. 27). At the end of the first day he falls where he is baptized by the Well of Life. In the second day his 'bright deaw-burning blade' (I. xi. 35) pierces the Dragon's armour, that is, he fights with Arthur's strength. When the sun of day falls the son of Day also falls. Now the Dragon's burning fire and Night's burning torch (reflected light) rule, and Una is left to 'watch the noyous night, and wait for ioyous day' (I. xi. 50). When day conquers darkness, at the moment when dawn 'gan her selfe to reare', the anointed knight 'freshly reare[s]' to slay the dragon.[1] As Arthur tells later, 'dayes dearest children be the blessed seed, / Which darknesse shall subdew, and heauen win' (III. iv. 59). Now Una may put aside her black veil, and appear as light itself:

> As bright as doth the morning starre appeare
> Out of the East, with flaming lockes bedight,
> To tell that dawning day is drawing neare,
> And to the world does bring long wished light.

(I. xii. 21)

The action of the book is resolved when she is restored to 'sure peace for euermore'.

Una, in her contest with Duessa, forms that larger image through which we may understand the continued allegory of Book I. Spenser 'contains' her within the poem by counterpointing her adventures with the Red Cross Knight's. Her fall begins when she seeks the secret shadow where she lies on the grass and removes the veil which is her armour. Like the knight she accepts one masquerading as the truth in the disguised Archimago. She serves royal power in the lion as the knight serves Lucifera, and sojourns among the Satyrs as does her knight in the house of Pride. She falls again into the hands of Sansloy who defiles her as Duessa again finds the knight to defile him. Her wandering too ends in despair until heavenly grace, in the form of Arthur, assists her.

---

[1] I. xi. 51, 52.

There is a progressive revelation of her significance as the story unfolds. When her knight confronts Error, she appears as Wisdom who warns him of the perils of the place: 'yet wisedome warnes, whilest foot is in the gate, / To stay the steppe' (I. i. 13). (This explains the proverbial language which she uses: 'oft fire is without smoke', 'vntroubled night they say giues counsell best', &c.) She is the faith which sustains the knight:

'

> O fairest virgin, full of heauenly light,
> Whose wondrous faith, exceeding earthly race,
> Was firmest fixt in mine extremest case.   (I. ix. 17)

More broadly, she is Truth, a term which Spenser uses to describe her role. As such, she is veiled, for 'truth may seeme, but cannot be'.[1] (It is tempting to see in Shakespeare's line a commentary upon Spenser's first book.) Only when the Dragon is slain may she seem to be as she is: 'who in her selfe-resemblance well beseene, / Did seeme such, as she was, a goodly maiden Queene' (I. xii. 8). When she brings her knight promise of election to defeat the arguments of Despair, she is the Church. Her opposition to Duessa is that between the Protestant Church and the Church of Rome: in de Mornay's terms the pure Church who is that Woman put to flight by the dragon described in Revelation, and the Church of Rome 'nothing else but falshood and lyes' to whose followers he writes:

Thou contemnest this poore and ragged Church, though not so full of wrinkles, and proudly disdainest her natural colour, though it be white, louing rather (delicious and delicat as thou art) a Church proud and glorious, in her vestments of scarlet, painted with colours more glittering, though borrowed, wantonly lusting after nouelties. It is therefore no maruell if thou haue embraced that Babylonian whore, beautified with false and counterfeit colours.[2]

When she guides the knight to the house of Penance, she appears as the Church Militant, as Spenser suggests in a pun when Coelia addresses her:

---

[1] *The Phoenix and the Turtle*, 62.

[2] *The Mysterie of Iniquitie*: that is to say, The Historie of the Papacie, Englished by Samson Lennard (London, 1612), sig. A$_{iii}$^{v}. The theme of his history is how Antichrist obtained 'a Soueraigne Empire in spirituall things throughout the West' (p. 652).

O happie earth,
Whereon thy innocent feet doe euer tread,
Most vertuous virgin borne of heauenly berth,
That to redeeme thy woefull parents head,
From tyrans rage, and euer-dying dread,
Hast wandred through the world now long a day;
Yet ceasest not thy wearie soles to lead.   (1. x. 9)

In the knight's battle against the Dragon, her rising marks the coming of Dawn (1. xi. 33, 51).

In her final revelation she appears as light itself in 'the blazing brightnesse of her beauties beame, / And glorious light of her sunshyny face' (1. xii. 23). She is the woman clothed with the sun, one who is beyond the lunar realm.

However extended her significance, she appears finally as the bride whose marriage to the Red Cross Knight is described in the immediate sensuous terms of the Epithalamion. Or rather one may say, that through realizing her significance, as in John's apocalyptic vision, the woman clothed with the sun is also the bride. The only comparable treatment of the beloved in profane scripture is Dante's Beatrice, yet at the end she remains in the spirit while Spenser shows his pilgrim 'possessed of his Ladies hart and hand, / And euer, when his eye did her behold, / His heart did seeme to melt in pleasures manifold' (1. xii. 40). In her we see the woman fleeing from the Dragon, wandering in anguish, lamenting in despair, but also light itself, to be given to the knight according to God's promise. 'He that ouercommeth, and kepeth my workes vnto the end, to him will I giue . . . the morning starre.'[1] Una is, with Beatrice, one of the most complex figures in poetry. Wisdom, Truth, Faith, the Protestant Church, the Church Triumphant, the body of the Redeemed, the morning star of Revelation; yet she remains upon the literal level 'a goodly maiden Queene', a woman whom her lover possesses.

[1] Rev. ii. 26, 28.

III

The Architectonike *of the Poem*

> The highest end of the mistres Knowledge, by the Greekes
> called *Architectonike* . . . stands, (as I thinke) in the know-
> ledge of a mans selfe, in the Ethicke and politick con-
> sideration, with the end of well dooing and not of well
> knowing onely . . . so that, the ending end of all earthly
> learning [is] vertuous action.   SIDNEY

PREVIOUSLY I have treated the '*Idea* or fore-conceite' of *The
Faerie Queene*, and the method by which Spenser realizes that Idea
as an image in Book I. I wish to consider now his intention which
is realized in the end or working of his poem. As the Idea is
embodied in an image, the intention is realized in an argument.
Though Spenser rightly distinguishes in the letter to Ralegh
between his purpose and the poem's end, we may see that they
closely correspond: as he labours to deliver the image of a brave
knight perfected in the virtues, the poem itself fashions a gentleman or noble person in virtuous and gentle discipline. The image
which the poet creates is thus re-created in the reader. Strictly
speaking, its Idea is not fulfilled in the writing of the poem—
perhaps this is why Sidney, 'in which Architectonical art he was
such a Master',[1] judges a work by its idea—but in the act of reading. Sidney tells us further that the end of the heroical poet who
fashions the image of a brave man is accomplished when the
reader understands 'why and how that Maker made him'.[2] How
Spenser fashioned his image was the subject of our last chapter,
and we must turn now to the problem of why he made him. In
considering the 'doctrine by ensample' which the right poet delivers, we turn, then, from the ensample to the doctrine itself.

The term 'architectonike' suggests both the chief end and also
structure. I shall proceed upon the hypothesis which I hope the
following pages will support, that Book I is central and unifying

[1] Fulke Greville, *Life of Sidney*, ed. Nowell Smith, p. 18.
[2] *Apol.*, p. 9.

within the poem's structure. In the first book the image is rendered for its own sake while the allegorical and tropological levels of significance remain implicit: in the second book that image may be understood in its tropological significance through the parallel structure of the first two books. From this point of advantage we may consider the doctrine more precisely, and I shall consider the theological allegory of Book II.

I

We may understand the doctrine of Book I by relating the allegory inward to the poem itself, specifically to the parallel structure of the first two books. In paralleling the structure of the first two books, Spenser deliberately points to the *doctrine* of his *ensample*, that is, its tropological significance. And the more precisely we are aware of the nature of that paralleling, the more precisely we may understand the allegory of the whole poem.

It has been commonly observed, of course, that these books are parallel in structure. In each the knight who represents a particular virtue (Holiness, Temperance) leaves the court of the Faery Queen with a guide (Una, the Palmer) and later defeats two chief antagonists (Sansfoy and Sansjoy, Pyrochles and Cymochles); upon being separated from his guide, he enters a place of temptation (the house of Pride, the cave of Mammon), and later falls. Then being rescued by Arthur and united with his guide, he enters a place of instruction (the house of Holiness, the castle of Alma) and finally fulfils his adventure (killing the Dragon, destroying the Bower of Bliss).[1] Such paralleling has been considered part of Spenser's design expressed in the letter to Ralegh, to write twelve books in which twelve knights, as patrons of the twelve virtues, undertake parallel adventures assigned by the Faery Queen. That the later books do not follow this repetitive structure has been variously explained as the need to avoid monotony, to modify the design according to the virtue being treated, or simply

---

[1] See E. A. Strathmann in *Var.Sp.* ii. 467; H. S. V. Jones, *A Spenser Handbook* (New York, 1930), pp. 172–4; Bennett, *Evolution*, pp. 124–37; and especially A. S. P. Woodhouse, 'Nature and Grace in *The Faerie Queene*', *E.L.H.* xvi (1949), 204–8. Greenlaw observes that Book II 'is exactly parallel, in structure, to the first book, and without question the two books were designed by the author to complement each other and to present his fundamental thought'. This remark is made without further expansion in his *Studies in Spenser's Historical Allegory* (Baltimore, 1932), p. 89.

—all too simply—as a change of plan. It was left to A. S. P. Woodhouse to explain for the first time the basis of the parallel structure of the first two books. He suggests that the two orders of nature and grace which were universally accepted as a frame of reference in the Renaissance are here carefully differentiated: 'what touches the Redcross Knight bears primarily upon revealed religion, or belongs to the order of grace, whatever touches Guyon bears upon natural ethics, or belongs to the order of nature'.[1] It follows that the parallel structure is designed to bring into relief differences which depend upon these two orders. He finds that this difference leaves its mark chiefly upon the education received by the two knights: the Red Cross Knight shows the bankruptcy of natural man who must utterly depend upon heavenly grace whereas Guyon shows how natural man realizes the potentialities of his nature by ruling his passions through reason. At times he insists more strongly than does Spenser upon an absolute separation of the two orders: Guyon's reference to 'the sacred badge of my Redeemers death' confuses the separation, as does the Palmer's benediction: 'God guide thee, *Guyon*, well to end thy warke.'[2] Even more confusing is Guyon's invocation to Christ for His Mercy at the moment when, like Longinus, he levels his spear against the Cross: 'Mercie Sir knight, and mercie Lord, / For mine offence and heedlesse hardiment, / That had almost committed crime abhord.' However, thanks to Professor Woodhouse, there seems no doubt now that the distinction between the two orders of nature and grace provides a necessary frame of reference for understanding the parallel structure of the first two books.

It does not follow, of course, that Spenser seeks to *illustrate* this distinction. The two orders of nature and grace provide no more than a basis upon which Spenser erects his pattern of meaning. Strictly speaking, they provide an intellectual framework by which the poem may be referred outwardly to a background of related ideas; as such, they cannot be identified with that 'antique Image' in its inner syntactic meaning. And it is the pattern of inner meaning realized by the parallel structure of the first two books,

[1] 'Nature and Grace', p. 204.
[2] See Woodhouse, p. 205, n. 17, and the subsequent discussion: R. Hoopes, ' "God guide thee: *Guyon*": Nature and Grace Reconciled in *The Faerie Queene*, Book II', *R.E.S.* N.S. v (1954), 14–24; and Woodhouse, 'Nature and Grace in Spenser: a Rejoinder', *R.E.S.* N.S. vi (1955), 284–8.

rather than reducible historical background, which is a key to the allegory. By my reading, this parallel is more exact than has been previously observed, and also more significant to our understanding the poem's doctrine. Further, to read the two books together offers perspective from which to see the whole poem's unity. Their parallel structure reveals that such unity would not be found in the projected Book XII, as is commonly surmised, but is already provided by Book I.

When Spenser writes in the letter to Ralegh that the adventures of his twelve knights are 'seuerally [that is, differently] handled and discoursed', he prepares the reader for a structure which provides parallel with contrast. Such structure may be seen in the opening episodes of the first two books. Each begins with a prelude designed to manifest the knight's nature. Guided by Una, the Red Cross Knight enters the pleasing Wandering Wood where he confronts Error, the female serpent who is an emblem of his twofold enemy later seen as Duessa riding the Dragon; and he triumphs, as he does later, by adding faith (the power of grace) to his force, so proving himself worthy of his armour. At the end, Una blesses her chosen knight as he leaves upon his adventure 'with God to frend'. The opening episode of Book II shows Guyon aroused to wrath by Archimago who seeks through Duessa 'to deceiue good knights, / And draw them from pursuit of praise and fame, / To slug in slouth and sensuall delights, / And end their daies with irrenowmed shame' (II. i. 23). The wrathful Guyon so deceived by the enchantress is an emblem of his later foes: his inner foe being the irascible and concupiscent affections embodied in Pyrochles and Cymochles, and his outer foe being Acrasia in her Bower of Bliss. He, too, is led into a Wandering Wood, 'a pleasant dale, that lowly lay / Betwixt two hils, whose high heads ouerplast, / The valley did with coole shade ouercast' (II. i. 24), where he attacks the Red Cross Knight. But when he recognizes him and confesses his offence, the Red Cross Knight 'streight way . . . knew / His error' (II. i. 28); and Guyon is saved through mercy and the return of reason (the Palmer). At the end he leaves upon his adventure with the Red Cross Knight's blessing and the Palmer's injunction, 'God guide thee'. Being thus parallel, these opening episodes significantly contrast the knights and their adventures. The Red Cross Knight's victory over Error shows his unfallen state: with Una, he enjoys that state of grace within which he may triumph over his enemies. When Una persuades him to 'shew what ye bee', he shows himself to be under her guidance what Sidney calls the poet's image of what 'should be'. Guyon, on the other hand, is an image of what the knight of temperance should not be, when he leaves his guide to be led by Archimago and in intemperate wrath attacks the patron of Holiness. The contrast between them is sharpened by the Red Cross Knight's presence in Book II where they are set apart by the phrases 'that godly knight' and 'a goodly knight' before the opening episode, and the address of 'Saint' and 'Sir' at the end. In Book I the armour is stressed, while the knight himself remains anonymous, the conventional 'full iolly knight'. In Book II the knight himself is described, demure, temperate, stern, and terrible in sight, and he is named while the arms are conventional: the 'many-folded shield' which is mentioned later is the familiar classical shield in Homer. 'I know your goodly gouernaunce', the Red Cross Knight says to Guyon, but of himself he knows that he is governed by God 'who made my hand the organ of his might'. In the opening episode of Book I the knight is seen in a higher state of righteousness to which he originally and finally belongs. Guyon, on the other hand, is circumscribed by the fallen world of good and evil. The opening line of the book, 'that cunning Architect of cancred guile', and the opening stanzas which describe Archimago's Satanic perversion, 'for to all good he enimy was still', plunge the entire action into the fallen world.

Since Guyon does not belong to any higher state, the opening episode of Book II is patterned upon the Red Cross Knight's next adventure when he falls into the power of Archimago and reverses his former state. Guyon is similarly abused by Archimago disguised as an aged sire, and that enchanter's deception proceeds as before in two stages. First, there is the false tale of the Lady overcome by lust which is told by the wicked spright in Book I, and by Archimago in Book II. Here the Red Cross Knight shows temperance, 'hasty heat tempring with sufferance wise, / He stayde his hand' (i. i. 50), while Guyon overcome with 'zealous hast away is quickly gone' (ii. i. 13). Then in each book follows the false vision of the dishonoured lady shown in the spright who seems to be Una embraced by the lusty Squire, and in Duessa disguised as the virgin who has been raped. Now both knights are overcome by wrath: the one 'pricked with wrath and fiery fierce disdaine' (I. ii. 8), the other 'inflam'd with wrathfulnesse' (II. i. 25). Wrath leads the Red Cross Knight into lust: after defeating Sansfoy, the sight of the wanton lady now 'did much emmoue his stout heroicke heart' and at her story 'he in great passion all this while did dwell' (I. ii. 21, 26). Being thus overcome by intemperate affections, his eye of reason blinded, and guided by his will, he falls helplessly into sin. Nothing within himself can restore him to his former state. Guyon, on the other hand, seeks to resist his fall by asserting the power of temperance over his affections. Though at first overcome by intemperance, he begs for Mercy at the sight of the Red Cross. Mercy being freely granted, reason returns as his guide, and he becomes 'knit in one consent' with Holiness. This parallel with contrast set up between the Red Cross Knight's deception by Archimago and Guyon's overcoming that deception relates the arguments of the two books. While Book I traces the cycle of events occasioned by man's fall from grace into sin, Book II shows how temperance may prevent that fall.

This relation between the arguments of the two books is illustrated by the succeeding episodes, the story of Fradubio in Book I and the story of Amavia in Book II. These episodes are parallel, each being an allegory of the knight's adventures. After each knight begins his pageant, he travels for a long time with his companion (Duessa, the Palmer) until he seeks shade under a tree from the scorching sun. At the sound of a lamenting voice, he is rapt in astonishment. Then he hears a tragic story of excessive love which brings death: Fradubio's lament, 'my deare loue, / O too deare loue, loue bought with death too deare' (I. ii. 31) betrays that same intemperate love expressed in Amavia's lament for Mortdant, 'my Lord my loue; my deare Lord, my deare loue' (II. i. 50). Fradubio and Amavia tell a similar story of the witch who so transforms man's weak nature that, when he seeks to escape her power, her charms bring death. Through the witch's enchantment, Fradubio cannot be released until he is bathed in a living well, while the Babe's hands may not be cleansed in the well. We have seen how Fradubio's story contains the Red Cross Knight's adventure: how, like him, he has left his lady for the witch Duessa by whom he is defiled, and may not be restored until he is bathed in the Well of Life. Guyon's purpose, to which he now dedicates himself, is to destroy the witch's enchantment through his own power which, however, must be supplemented by grace. Amavia dressed as the Palmer may cure Mortdant through 'wise handling and faire gouernance', but he is later slain through Acrasia's charms. By this we understand that Guyon needs more than the Palmer's guidance before he may not only cure intemperance but destroy its power. But the present condition of the two knights is contrasted. Guyon, not being involved in the witch's power, may heed Amavia's warning: 'if euer there ye trauell, shonne / The cursed land where many wend amis' (II. i. 51). But with powerful tragic irony, the Red Cross Knight is already within the witch's power. Though Fradubio warns him, 'fly, ah fly far hence away, for feare / Least to you hap, that happened to me heare' (I. ii. 31), he cannot escape. Guyon is moved by pity to revenge Amavia 'till guiltie bloud her guerdon doe obtaine'; and though the vow recoils upon him, for he shares that guilty blood, he goes forward to display all heroic virtue. But the Red Cross Knight is far from being the self-reliant hero, such as Guyon, who moves steadily towards final victory. For he is not the hunter, but the hunted; not victor, but the victim; and not hero, but the antagonist of a divine drama which brings him 'in darkesome dungeon, wretched thrall, / Remedilesse, for aie' (I. vii. 51). Later Una complains to Arthur that all her knights have failed through 'guilt of sin'. The Red Cross Knight, too, becomes infected with 'guilt of sin' for his hands are imbrued in the guilty blood of Sansfoy. Only at the end of his last adventure may he 'wash [his] hands from guilt of bloudy field' (I. x. 60). His guilt is expressed emblematically in Book II by the blood upon the Babe's hands which is interpreted by the Palmer as a token of man's 'bloudguiltinesse'. When Guyon dedicates himself to the task of avenging the bloody-handed Babe, he seeks to avenge the 'guilt of sin' through which man's nature is defiled. The difference between their adventures may be summed up in a word: the Red Cross Knight seeks 'to *redeeme* [Una's] woefull parents head', Guyon '*t'auenge* his Parents death': the aim of the one is redemptive, and he must submit and suffer in order to free mankind from a wicked moral order; the aim of the other is retributive, to assert a just moral order.

Since Guyon seeks to resist man's fall into sin through the power of Temperance, the occasion of his adventure is given by that moment of the fall represented by the Red Cross Knight's imprisonment in Orgoglio's dungeon. Being left, then, to lament, Una rejects life and light, and in despair wishes for death. But at this nadir of the action, help comes to her. She is aided first by the Dwarf who lifts her up: 'thrise did she sinke adowne in deadly swownd, / And thrise he her reviu'd with busie paine', and then by Arthur who persuades her 'to vnfold the anguish of your hart . . . [for] found neuer helpe, who neuer would his hurts impart' (I. vii. 24, 40). After she tells her story, he vows to redeem her knight. This moment appears in Book II where Amavia also laments her knight's fall and lovingly (as is her nature) embraces death: 'come then, come soone, come sweetest death to mee, / And take away this long lent loathed light.' As Una laments that Duessa 'with her witchcraft . . . Inueigled [the knight] to follow her desires vnmeete' (I. vii. 50), Amavia laments that 'with words and weedes of wondrous might', the witch Acrasia 'my lifest Lord she thus beguiled' (II. i. 52). (Amavia yields to despair, of course, unlike Una who later rises to seek her knight.) And in the same manner as help comes to Una, Guyon lifts Amavia up, 'thrise he her reard, and thrise she sunke againe', and persuades her 'your griefe vnfold. . . . He oft finds present helpe, who does his griefe impart' (II. i. 46). After she tells her story, he vows vengeance. In relation to the pattern set up in Book I, Book II begins *in medias res*. The fall is accomplished; the witch has triumphed; and human nature seen in the Babe is already defiled. At this point Guyon enters, and he seeks, as does Arthur in Book I, to reverse man's fall.

Throughout his adventure Guyon manifests the power of temperance over those affections through which the Red Cross Knight falls into the bondage of sin. In Book I we see the knight yield to grief and wrath when he believes Una disloyal, and then to lust when he meets Duessa. In Book II we learn how temperance may subdue these affections.

After the opening exemplum of intemperance given by Mortdant and Amavia, the Palmer declares that through temperance man may avoid both lust and the fury that drives man to grief:

> temperance (said he) with golden squire
> Betwixt them both can measure out a meane,
> Neither to melt in pleasures whot desire,
> Nor fry in hartlesse griefe and dolefull teene.   (II. i. 58)

The succeeding episode, the story of Phedon, presents in romantic terms the occasion of the Red Cross Knight's leaving Una: each knight believes he sees his lady in wanton lust with a base squire, and through his love, each is overcome by wrath, jealousy, and grief. The Palmer sermonizes upon such intemperate affections which war against 'fort of Reason, it to ouerthrow', and Guyon counsels Phedon that his hurts 'may soone through temperance be easd' (II. iv. 33, 34). Later Wrath is embodied in Pyrochles in whom wars 'outrageous anger, and woe-working iarre, / Direfull impatience, and hart murdring loue' (II. v. 16), and Wrath merging into Lust in his brother Cymochles who 'by kind, / Was giuen all to lust and loose liuing' (II. v. 28). Both are subdued by the knight of Temperance. Pyrochles' wrath finally immerses him in the Idle Lake where he seeks vainly to quench his inner flames, while Cymochles' lust confines him to Phaedria's Isle; but Guyon leaves both and proceeds upon his voyage.

The further power of Temperance to resist temptation is displayed by Guyon's descent into Mammon's Cave. This descent clearly parallels the Red Cross Knight's passage through the house of Pride. The house of Richesse corresponds to the house of Pride, both being places of glittering wealth to which the knights are led by a broad beaten highway. Philotime sitting in her 'glistring glory' with the suitors around her throne is an infernal Lucifera: her 'broad beauties beam great brightnes threw' (II. vii. 45), even as Lucifera's 'bright blazing beautie . . . shone as *Titans* ray' (I. iv. 8). Guyon descends to see the damned chained in hell where Tantalus, Pilate, and 'infinite moe [are] tormented in like paine' (II. vii. 63), even as the Dwarf sees 'the endlesse routs of wretched thralles' (I. v. 51) in the dungeon below the house of Pride. Such parallels only point up the difference between the two knights. The Red Cross Knight chooses at first to remain aloof from the worldlings of the house of Pride, but after his fight with Sansjoy he yields to Lucifera. Guyon, who is explicitly tempted to serve Mammon, must choose by asserting the virtue by which he stands; and this he does throughout triumphantly. (Though the virtue is his own, it is sustained by God: against the lust within the heart which is seen in the fiend who follows Guyon, Spenser prays: 'Eternall God thee saue from such decay.') He resists vigorously the temptations to which the Red Cross Knight finally yields. Though the Red Cross Knight flees the house of Pride in fear, he is readily found by Duessa where he sits resting by a fountain and feeding upon the cool shade. This climactic stage of his fall into Orgoglio's power is reproduced in the culminating episode of Guyon's temptation in the Garden where Mammon seeks 'to doe him deadly fall / In frayle intemperance through sinfull bayt':

> Thou fearefull foole,
> Why takest not of that same fruit of gold,
> Ne sittest downe on that same siluer stoole,
> To rest thy wearie person, in the shadow coole.
>
> (II. vii. 63)

But Guyon neither feeds nor rests, and through the power of temperance does not yield.

The relation of Books I and II to the theme of man's fall becomes more explicit when each knight falls into the power of his enemies. Guyon's fall which heralds the coming of Arthur parallels the same mid-point of the narrative in Book I where the Red Cross Knight whose powers are similarly weakened also falls to the ground and is imprisoned until he is rescued by Arthur. As Una is the means by which Arthur intercedes for the Red Cross Knight, the Palmer is the means by which Arthur pledges to aid Guyon. Afterwards the knight praises Una as one 'whose wondrous faith, exceeding earthly race, / Was firmest fixt in mine extremest case', even as Guyon joys to see the Palmer: 'firme is thy faith, whom daunger neuer fro me drew' (I. ix. 17; II. viii. 53). More important, however, is the significant contrast which the parallel provides. After his fall to the ground, the Red Cross Knight, being 'disarmd, disgrast, and inwardly dismayde' (I. vii. 11), suffers a second fall into Orgoglio's dungeon where 'all his vitall powres / Decayd, and all his flesh shronk vp like withered flowres' (I. viii. 41). Since he undergoes spiritual death, Arthur faces a double task: first, to slay Orgoglio, and then to descend into the dungeon. Guyon, however, is only 'dead seeming': his death-like trance renders allegorically an event that happens literally in Book I, as far as the conventions of romance allow. Being so dominated by the affections, he too needs grace: 'for every man with his affects is born, / Not by might master'd, but by special grace.'[1] His foes are prevented by Arthur from disarming and disgracing his fallen body; accordingly, when they are slain, he 'from his traunce awakt, / Life hauing maistered her sencelesse foe.'

[1] *Love's Labour's Lost*, I. i.

Arthur's roles in Book I as the instrument of divine grace, and in Book II as the symbol of magnanimity, appear so different that he has been considered two distinct persons. Yet the parallel between his two roles shows them to be compatible in one person. We have seen how his rescue of the knight in Book I imitates Christ's harrowing of hell. In Book II Spenser uses the same analogue though in terms appropriate to the argument. We see Arthur claim Guyon's fallen body from the Satanic forces represented by Pyrochles and Cymochles. Against the enemies who seek in their wrath to inflict punishment for sin, he sues for pardon. In the debate which follows he is called Guyon's 'dayes-man' (II. viii. 28): such was sought by Job to mediate between him and God's wrath. He suffers the symbolic wound in the right side, 'wyde was the wound, and a large lukewarme flood, / Red as the Rose, thence gushed grieuously' (II. viii. 39). Finally he slays his foes, and like Christ, claims man's body in the name of Mercy.

Spenser contrasts the scope of each book at certain key points. In Canto X of the first book where the opening stanza sums its argument, the final lines provide a formula for the whole book : 'if any strength we haue, it is to ill, / But all the good is Gods, both power and eke will.' The first line summarizes the knight's moral history during the first half of the book; the second prepares for the second half where the knight under Una is continually sustained by grace until he wields the power to slay the Dragon. 'All the good is Gods', as later in Book II he bears witness : 'his be the praise, that this atchieu'ment wrought, / Who made my hand the organ of his might; / More then goodwill to me attribute nought' (II. i. 33). Until this final adventure, he remains the prostrate figure over whom the cosmic forces of light and darkness, represented in Una and Duessa, battle to possess him. In Book II the two opening stanzas of Canto XI sum its argument :[1]

> What warre so cruell, or what siege so sore,
> As that, which strong affections do apply

[1] Woodhouse selects II. ix. I as the crucial point at which 'the poet pauses to sum up in a single stanza the purport of all that has gone before, and thus to prepare for what is to follow' (p. 208). By my reading this stanza points only to what is to follow. Woodhouse omits the important final line : 'Behold, who list, both one and other in this place', that is, 'mans body . . . kept in sober gouernment' seen in the castle of Alma (Canto IX) and man's body which 'growes a Monster, and incontinent / Doth loose his dignitie and natiue grace', seen in Maleger (Canto XI).

Against the fort of reason euermore
To bring the soule into captiuitie:
Their force is fiercer through infirmitie
Of the fraile flesh, relenting to their rage,
And exercise most bitter tyranny
Vpon the parts, brought into their bondage:
No wretchednesse is like to sinfull vellenage.

But in a body, which doth freely yeeld
His partes to reasons rule obedient,
And letteth her that ought the scepter weeld,
All happy peace and goodly gouernment
Is setled there in sure establishment;
There *Alma* like a virgin Queene most bright,
Doth florish in all beautie excellent:
And to her guestes doth bounteous banket dight,
Attempred goodly well for health and for delight.

The first stanza repeats the argument of Book I in moral terms, that is, the weakness of human nature; but the second declares the strength of the temperate body. Together they assert the power and limitations of natural virtue. Since Guyon manifests its power throughout his journey, he 'euermore himselfe with comfort feedes, / Of his owne vertues, and prayse-worthy deedes' (II. vii. 2). When he sees the damned in Proserpina's garden, he lectures them upon their folly. But the Red Cross Knight whose only strength is to do ill despairs at the memory of 'his deformed crimes, / That all his manly powres it did disperse' (I. ix. 48). And when he sees the damned suffering in hell, he sees himself as one of them. But Guyon's display of the power of natural virtue reveals at the same time its limitations. In meeting his enemies, he cannot slay Furor and Disdain; and though he may subdue Pyrochles and Cymochles, he is prevented in the name of temperance from slaying them. Moreover, though the temperate body may resist temptation, it cannot defeat its besiegers. The image of the besieged body given in the first stanza above is the unifying metaphor of the book. It is expressed in Mortdant and Amavia whose 'raging passion with fierce tyrannie / Robs reason of her due regalitie' (II. i. 57), in Medina surrounded by her two sisters with their warring suitors, in Phedon whose strong affections 'cruell battry bend / Gainst fort of Reason, it to ouerthrow' (II. iv. 34), and culminates in the first half of the book with the image of Pyrochles and Cymochles ready to despoil Guyon's senseless body. The full limitation of natural virtue is seen when Guyon falls, and Arthur must come to rescue him. For though the temperate body is strong, being continually besieged, it stands only by the power of grace.

The significant contrast that we see between the Red Cross Knight's fall and Guyon's, together with the contrast between their rescue by Arthur, defines the scope of each book. The senseless Red Cross Knight dominated by Orgoglio is an emblem of the total depravity of human nature, the death of the spirit. Though he undergoes spiritual death, however, he may be reborn and regenerated through God's grace and finally restored to a higher state. Guyon, prostrate upon the ground under the wrathful Pyrochles and the lustful Cymochles, is an emblem of man's body dominated by the irascible and concupiscent affections. His fall is given in moral, rather than spiritual, terms; and through Arthur's intervention he recovers his natural moral state. He remains, then, upon that natural level which the Red Cross Knight transcends. The cyclical movement of Book I, the spiritual descent and ascent, contrasts with that linear movement upon the natural level described in Book II. In the terms suggested by Professor Woodhouse, we may say that Book I moves upon the level of grace while Book II remains upon the level of nature; but it is important to add that the levels are not exclusive. Though Guyon neither shares the depths of the Red Cross Knight's descent nor rises to his heights, he is not excluded from that knight's regeneration which follows Arthur's rescue: instead, he enjoys its counterpart upon the natural level. From the parallel structure of the second half of both books, it becomes clear that Book I transcends the natural level explored in Book II by including it.

After being rescued by Arthur, each knight must realize the perfection of his own nature in three stages before completing his adventure. Guided by Una, the Red Cross Knight is first purged of sin in the house of Penance; later in the holy Hospital he is taught to frame his life in holy righteousness; and finally he ascends the hill of Contemplation where through a vision of the New Jerusalem he learns his name and nature. Thus fully prepared for his final adventure, he leaves to slay the Dragon. Guyon is not purged, for he need not learn to cherish himself; instead, 'with rare delight' he enjoys immediately the perfection of the temperate body in the castle of Alma. His delight as he moves through the castle, and his feasting, contrast sharply with the Red Cross Knight's agony in a dark lowly place where he diets with fasting until he 'had past the paines of hell, and long enduring night' (I. x. 32). The 'goodly workemanship' of the castle of Alma, its 'wondrous frame' (II. ix. 21, 44), elaborates at some length matter contained in Book I, that 'wondrous workemanship of Gods owne mould' (I. x. 42) which is maintained by the seven bead-men in the holy Hospital. In the final state of his preparation within the castle, Guyon also ascends to see a vision of

> This parts great workmanship, and wondrous powre,
> That all this other worlds worke doth excell,
> And likest is vnto that heauenly towre,
> That God hath built for his owne blessed bowre.   (II. ix. 47)

What is revealed to the Red Cross Knight as his spiritual nature appears to Guyon as his natural body. The Red Cross Knight is taught his future state as Saint George, his present duty to aid Una, and his past history; Guyon is shown the body's power in the three sages who teach the future, the present, and the past. Heavenly Contemplation teaches the Red Cross Knight his 'name and nation': Eumnestes teaches Guyon his country's ancestry. The episodes are clearly parallel upon different levels, the religious and the secular; but again these levels are not exclusive. Man's spiritual nature which is revealed in Book I is embodied in the second book in the perfection of man's natural body governed by temperance and upheld by divine grace.

The spiritual regeneration of the Red Cross Knight, that continual casting out of sin from the time he regains Una as his guide until he slays the Dragon, provides the pattern for Arthur's fight with Maleger and his troops in Book II. The parallel may help us understand the nature of this fight which has become a crux in the allegory. While Guyon voyages to the Bower of Bliss, Arthur confronts Alma's besiegers who are described earlier as that body so 'distempred through misrule and passions bace: / It growes a Monster, and incontinent / Doth loose his dignitie and natiue grace' (II. ix. 1). Maleger is this Monster, the parody of man's body: 'his bodie leane and meagre as a rake, / And skin all withered like a dryed rooke' (II. xi. 22). The pattern for his attack upon the castle of Alma, his counterpart, is given in Book I by the Red Cross Knight's spiritual regeneration, the casting-out of his fallen self. When he first emerges from the dungeon, he looks like Maleger with 'bare thin cheekes . . . his rawbone armes . . . were cleane consum'd, and all his vitall powres / Decayd, and all his flesh shronk vp like withered flowres' (I. viii. 41), for each manifests that state of sin by which our body is totally depraved. Awareness of his sinful state aroused by Despair so pierces the Red Cross Knight's heart that he seeks to pierce his heart: like Maleger, he tries 'to spoyle the Castle of his health' (I. ix. 31). He is saved by Una who leads him to the house of Penance where he undergoes true despair: 'prickt with anguish of his sinnes so sore, . . . he desirde to end his wretched dayes: / So much the dart of sinfull guilt the soule dismayes' (I. x. 21). In the end he is purged of 'inward corruption, and infected sin' (I. x. 25), further instructed by the cardinal virtues and Mercy, and assoiled by Contemplation. Finally, he is regenerated by the three-day battle with the Dragon: twice he is cast to the ground where he is washed in the Well of Life which can cleanse 'guilt of sinfull crimes', and anointed by the Tree of Life which 'deadly woundes could heale' (I. xi. 30, 48). In Book II Alma the soul is similarly besieged by the darts of Maleger so that she was 'much dismayed with that dreadfull sight' (II. xi. 16). She too is saved by divine grace whose instrument is Arthur. From the parallel with Book I we understand that Maleger is the state of sin, both actual and original;[1] it is that state of sin from which the Red Cross Knight must be purged before he may slay the Dragon, and which must be slain before Guyon may overthrow the power of Acrasia. Spenser uses the myth of Antaeus in both books to describe the overthrow of sin. When the Red Cross Knight falls to the ground apparently slain but rises with greater strength, the Dragon is amazed:

> No wonder if he wondred at the sight,
> And doubted, whether his late enemy
> It were, or other new supplied knight.
> He, now to proue his late renewed might,
> High brandishing his bright deaw-burning blade.
>
> (I. xi. 35)

---

[1] Woodhouse (p. 221) identifies Maleger with original sin. V. K. Whitaker has noticed that the baptism at the Tree of Life which delivers the Red Cross Knight from original sin 'seems also to be implied when Arthur kills Maleger by drowning him' ('The Religious Basis of Spenser's Thought', *Stanford Univ. Pub. Lang. and Lit.* vii [1950], p. 50).

And on the second day when the knight arises healed of his wounds, again the Dragon is amazed:

> When now he saw himselfe so freshly reare,
> As if late fight had nought him damnifyde,
> He woxe dismayd, and gan his fate to feare. (52)

When Maleger is cast to the ground but rises 'much stronger then before', Arthur is amazed:

> Nigh his wits end then woxe th'amazed knight,
> And thought his labour lost and trauell vaine,
> Against this lifelesse shadow so to fight:
> Yet life he saw, and felt his mightie maine,
> That whiles he marueild still, did still him paine:
> For thy he gan some other wayes aduize,
> How to take life from that dead-liuing swaine,
> Whom still he marked freshly to arize
> From th'earth, and from her wombe new spirits to reprize.
>
> (II. xi. 44)

There is no paradox in this contrast between the two books. In Book I the knight is Georgos, or Earth; and the ground upon which he falls, Eden, being watered and nourished by the Well and Tree of Life, sustains him. In Book II we see Guyon fall to the ground and rise 'with so fresh hew' once Arthur slays the affections which dominate his body; but the ground belongs to that fallen nature which perverts man because it was perverted by him at the Fall, and so sustains his enemy. Like the Dragon, Maleger is that terrifying image of the enemy whom man in his own power cannot wound or slay.[1] As the Dragon is slain by the knight's baptized hands wielding his 'deaw-burning blade', Maleger is slain by being cast into the standing lake.

The climax to the two books where the knights arrive at the entrance to Eden offers full parallel with contrast. When the Red Cross Knight marries Una, everything serves his pleasure: the posts sprinkled with wine, the great feast, the precious perfumes, the song of love, the heavenly music of the spheres through which he was 'reft of his sences meet, / And rauished with rare impression in his sprite', and above all, Una whose glorious beauty 'his

---

[1] Arthur defeats this enemy not through invoking directly the power of grace, nor through physical strength, but by wisdom. At the moment of his defeat when Maleger rises after each fall to the earth much stronger than before, Arthur 'remembred well, that had bene sayd' (II. xi. 45). What he remembers—this is a nice point —is not Scriptural truth, nor moral doctrine, but the myth of Antaeus.

heart did seeme to melt in pleasures manifold' (I. xii. 39, 40).
These pleasures are parodied in the Bower of Bliss: the wine
offered by its porter, the sweet smells, the song of the rose, the
earthly melody of the birds, waters, and wind, enchant man in
order to enchain him in Acrasia's bower. Her beauty makes her
knight 'quite molten into lust and pleasure lewd' (II. xii. 73). The
heavenly music which lifts man above himself contrasts with the
earthly music which binds him to his senses: the pleasures which
fulfil man for further duties contrast with those which put him to
sleep. The Red Cross Knight 'swimming in that sea of blisfull
ioy', yet who 'nought forgot . . . vnto his Farie Queene backe
to returne' (I. xii. 41), contrasts with the sleeping Verdant who
forgets all honour of arms, 'but in lewd loues, and wastfull
luxuree, / His dayes, his goods, his bodie he did spend' (II. xii.
80). But the Red Cross Knight's final state is parodied earlier,
and it is with this earlier state that the significance of the parallel
with Book II may be realized.

Earlier at the mid-point of his adventure, the Red Cross Knight
yields all to pleasure: disarming himself, he rests by a fountain-
side where he feeds upon the cooling shade of the leaves 'wherein
the cherefull birds of sundry kind / Do chaunt sweet musick, to
delight his mind.' With Duessa in this bower of 'greene boughes
decking a gloomy glade', he 'bathe[s] in pleasaunce of the ioyous
shade' courting Duessa 'both carelesse of his health, and of his
fame'. In just such state is Verdant with the enchantress Acrasia
until Guyon frees him. This parallel between the climax of Book II
and the mid-point of Book I, and the contrast between the climax
of Book II and the climax of Book I, justifies fully the elaborate
paralleling of structure which the poet sets up between the two
books. By destroying the Bower of Bliss, Guyon overthrows all
those forces by which the Red Cross Knight falls into sin. The
overpowering sloth, the carnal lust by which he yields to Duessa,
the great weakness which leaves him helpless before his enemy:
this terrible vision of the noble knight 'forlorne, / And left to losse',
now is set against the power of virtue to release man from enshrouding nature, the womb which imprisons man upon the
level of nature without possibility of rebirth. In terms of their
archetypes which are present at this point, the Red Cross Knight
moves toward man's final state in the Heavenly City when he will
be fully restored to God, while Guyon turns back to man's original

state when he entered Eve's garden and through her enchantments fell from God's grace. The apocalyptic significance of the
Red Cross Knight's slaying the Dragon becomes the pattern for
Guyon's release of man from imprisonment in the Garden of
Eden. As the Red Cross Knight is an image of that second Adam
who harrows hell to redeem mankind from Satan's power, Guyon,
who runs a like race, imitates him to become a new Adam. He is
one who, in Milton's phrase, 'might see and know, and yet
abstain'; one who binds Eve and destroys the Garden that man
may pass successfully through the world towards his final
restoration.

2

It is usual to consider the poet's doctrine as something given him,
something which may be found more logically expressed in moral
or theological treatises. Yet the doctrine to be found in such
'background' material remains background, and not more than
the poet's point of departure. It is something to be realized within
a poetic argument. The usual kind of moral reading of Spenser's
allegory does not satisfy precisely because it ignores the primary
fact of the poet's invention. Of all the books, the second has been
interpreted most thoroughly in moral terms. It is generally in-
ferred from the letter to Ralegh that its subject is the moral virtue
of Temperance as given by Aristotle and the rest. But this inference misreads the letter, besides disregarding the Renaissance
understanding of the poet's subject. More seriously, it reduces the
poem to a succession of exempla illustrating temperance or its
opposite.

The subject of Book II is stated very explicitly in the letter.
After describing the occasion of Guyon's adventure in the Palmer's
story of the bloody-handed Babe whose parents were slain by
Acrasia, Spenser adds: 'which is the beginning of the second
booke *and the whole subiect thereof*'. The term is carefully chosen,
being a key term in Renaissance poetics. To invent his subject
matter was the poet's first task, as Gascoigne writes: 'the first and
most necessarie poynt that euer I founde meete to be considered
in making of a delectable poeme is this, to grounde it upon some
fine inuention'. In a letter to Gabriel Harvey, Spenser speaks of
having written a book which is 'rare for the Inuention'. (It is

a phrase which the reader of *The Faerie Queene* must carefully consider.) In place of the rhetorical term *inuentio*, the critical terms 'fable' and 'fiction' were generally used; Harington, for example, refers to 'inuention or fiction'.[1] The poet's art of imitation was generally defined as the art of creating fiction. Using these terms, we may define the 'whole subiect' of Book II, or its invention, as that fiction which Spenser creates of the bloody-handed Babe whose parents were slain by the enchantress Acrasia. This fiction is the 'cause' of the book, its Idea in Sidney's sense, the significance of which is dramatically realized within the poem itself. The moral virtue of Temperance usually taken as its subject is rather the matter out of which Spenser creates the subject.

The subject of Book II is sufficiently described in the letter to help us read the poem. The parallel set up with the occasion of the Red Cross Knight's adventure where the parents imprisoned in the brazen castle by the huge dragon indicates man's spiritual bondage in the fallen world, suggests that the bloody-handed Babe stands for mankind which from its infancy has been infected by original sin. (Blood upon the hands is the usual token of man's guilty state.) The name of the enchantress reveals that the cause of the Babe's stained hands is Intemperance seen as an enchanting woman. The analogue which inevitably suggests itself is Eve in her Garden of Eden where Adam by submitting to her charms was slain and through him the entire human race stained by original sin. In his quest, then, Guyon seeks to undo the effects of man's first fall, to assert the power of the temperate body over sin. Of course the letter only hints at this subject in terms appropriate to a 'darke conceit' in order to arouse the reader's wonder. But Spenser could depend upon the same response from his reader that Chapman gives to Homer's subject in the *Odyssey*: 'the returne of a man into his Countrie, is his whole scope and obiect; which, in it selfe, your Lordship may well say, is ieiune and fruitlesse enough; affoording nothing feastfull, nothing magnificent. And

---

[1] Gascoigne, 'Certayne Notes of Instruction', in *Elizabethan Critical Essays*, i. 47; Spenser, 'Three Proper . . . Letters', *Works*, ed. Smith and de Selincourt, p. 612; Harington, 'A Brief Apology', in *Elizabethan Critical Essays*, ii. 204. Cf. Gabriel Harvey's praise of Spenser's 'rarenesse of Poetical Inuention', in 'Three Proper . . . Letters', p. 628. Milton uses the term 'whole subiect' in the same way as does Spenser. In the Argument to Book I of *Paradise Lost* he writes: 'this first Book proposes, first in brief, the whole Subject, *Mans disobedience, and the loss thereupon of Paradise wherein he was plac't*'.

yet euen this, doth the diuine inspiration, render vast, illustrous, and of miraculous composure.'[1] Spenser's subject as described in the letter is superbly calculated to excite wonder—the bloody-handed Babe, the parents mysteriously slain, the enchantress Acrasia, the Palmer who complains—and leads the reader into the poem.

After his meeting with the Red Cross Knight Guyon's 'pageant next ensewes' and he seeks an occasion for his adventure. Immediately there follows the episode of the bloody-handed Babe which dramatically expounds the whole subject of the book as given in the letter. It falls into two parts divided between Cantos I and II. In the first part Amavia's 'loues rage' and Mortdant's intemperate lust display 'the image of mortalitie' overcome by the intemperate affections. But Temperance, as the Palmer reveals, 'with golden squire / Betwixt them both can measure out a meane.' Though Mortdant dies through the enchantments of Acrasia 'for he was flesh: (all flesh doth frailtie breed)', Guyon may master this frailty through temperance. (Mortdant's name means one who 'death does giue' by drinking from the charmed cup, even as Milton's Adam ate the fruit 'whose mortal tast / Brought Death into the World.') Since Guyon seeks to overcome the sin by which man has fallen from grace, his quest leads him back to the Garden of Eden which is seen as the Bower of Bliss. There, as the second Adam armed with the power of temperance, he triumphs over Eve.

The occasion of his quest being thus provided, he goes forward to avenge the Babe who is mankind. But it is not within his power to redeem him. The second part of the episode shows Guyon's vain efforts to cleanse the Babe's hands. The Babe being 'in dead parents balefull ashes bred' is, like his parents, the image of mortality: 'such is the state of men: thus enter wee / Into this life with woe, and end with miseree' (II. ii. 2). (The phoenix image suggests renewal, but also identity: the Babe who is 'witnesse of [his] fathers fall' is seen in the image of his father. For this reason he is born at the time when Amavia sets out to find the transformed Mortdant.) When Guyon fails to wash the Babe's 'guiltie hands',

> He wist not whether blot of foule offence
> Might not be purgd with water nor with bath;

[1] Ep. Ded. to *Homers Odysses*, A₄ʳ.

Or that high God, in lieu of innocence,
Imprinted had that token of his wrath,
To shew how sore bloudguiltinesse he hat'th;
Or that the charme and venim, which they druncke,
Their bloud with secret filth infected hath,
Being diffused through the senselesse truncke,
That through the great contagion direfull deadly stunck.

(II. ii. 4)

As exactly as allegorical poetry can, this stanza renders a theological statement of original sin. It may be compared to Article IX of the Thirty-nine Articles which reads in part: 'Original sin . . . is the fault and corruption of the nature of every man, that naturally is engendered of the offspring of Adam, whereby man is very far gone from original righteousness, and is of his own nature inclined to evil, so that the flesh lusteth always contrary to the spirit, and therefore in every person born into this world, it deserveth God's wrath and damnation.'[1] More specifically, the closing lines of Spenser's stanza suggest the Calvinist doctrine of man's total depravity: '. . . haereditaria naturae nostrae pravitas et corruptio in omnes animae partes diffusa, quae primum facit reos irae Dei'.[2] But Spenser describes this infection as a token not only of God's wrath but of man's former righteousness: the Babe's hands 'his mothers innocence may tell . . . as a sacred Symbole it may dwell / In her sonnes flesh' (II. ii. 10). This suggests rather the Christian humanist's emphasis upon man's regenerate nature, that with the aid of grace man's former innocence

---

[1] See E. C. S. Gibson, *The Thirty-Nine Articles of the Church of England* (London, 1897), II. 357. Since Article IX was framed in reply to the Pelagians and Anabaptists who held that infants are born innocent of Adam's transgression, Spenser's choice of the Babe is appropriate. The Babe is infected, though innocent of any actual sin: 'carelesse of his woe, or innocent / Of that was doen' (II. ii. 1). Cf. Donne: 'as soon as wee are any thing, wee are sinners, and there, where there can be no more tentations ministred to us, then was to the Angels that fell in heauen, that is, in *our mothers womb*, when no world, nor flesh, nor Devill could present a provocation to sinne to us, when no faculty of ours is able to embrace, or second a provocation to sin, yet there, in that weaknesse, we are under the weight of Originall sin'. *Donne's Sermons*, ed. L. P. Smith (Oxford, 1919), p. 166. That Guyon cannot cleanse the Babe's hands may suggest Calvin's firm rejection of the false notion that 'by baptism we are delivered and exempted from original sin, and from the corruption which has descended from Adam to all his posterity'.

[2] *Institutes*, II. i. 8. Cited by E. T. Green, *The Thirty-nine Articles* (London, 1896), p. 72. In Norton's translation: '. . . the inheritably descending peruersnesse and corruption of our nature, powred abroad into all the partes of the soule, which first maketh vs guiltie of the wrath of God' (p. 74ʳ).

may be recovered. To be aware of this theological matter, however, is only preliminary to our understanding Spenser's allegory.
The bloody-handed babe whose hands Guyon cannot cleanse is
part of Spenser's invention, an argument to be explored, even
discovered, through its relation to other images in the book.

The two parts of this opening episode which reveal both the
power and limitations of temperance prepare for all that follows.
Later Guyon masters (though only for a time) the intemperate
affections of human nature through which man falls from grace.
In theological terms, what he resists is actual sin. But his power,
limited by the infection of original sin which remains in human
nature, must be supplemented by the power of grace whose
instrument is Arthur.

The intemperate affections are symbolized by Wrath whose
various states are opposed by Guyon to the limit of his own power.
Beyond that limit he needs the power of grace. Guyon's battle
with the suitors in the house of Medina is prevented by Medina
who exclaims:

> Ah puissant Lords, what cursed euill Spright,
> Or fell *Erinnys*, in your noble harts
> Her hellish brond hath kindled with despight,
> And stird you vp to worke your wilfull smarts? . . .
> O fly from wrath, fly, O my liefest Lord.   (II. ii. 29–30)

This *Erinnys* in man's heart causing him 'with bloud guiltinesse
to heape offence' manifests the Babe's 'bloudguiltinesse' which is
God's curse upon man. Though Guyon subdues Wrath displayed
as Furor, he cannot slay him: 'he is not such a foe, / As steele
can wound, or strength can ouerthroe' (II. iv. 10). Phedon, Furor's
victim, may be saved, though not cured, by Guyon. For wrath
'through temperance [may] be easd', as Guyon declares; but the
wound is mortal, as Phedon complains: 'in me yet stickes the
mortall sting, / That during life will neuer be appeasd' (II. iv. 33).
Wrath is further displayed in Pyrochles whom Guyon subdues
and urges to flee 'outrageous anger, and woe-working iarre . . .
which thee to endlesse bale captiued lead' (II. v. 16). But again this
inner wrath may not be cured by Guyon. Pyrochles seeks occasion
to release Furor, and ends in the idle lake seeking vainly to quench
the flames which Furor has aroused: 'yet nought can quench
mine inly flaming syde, / Nor sea of licour cold, nor lake of mire, /
Nothing but death can doe me to respire' (II. vi. 44). 'Water,

water, quench fire: but the fire would not.' According to Padelford's moral interpretation, 'the child of self-indulgence. . . does not
seek relief from anger through reason but through a new form of
indulgence, sensual indolence'; and he finds its source in Aristotle's
Ethics: 'the excesses of pain make people pursue excessive pleasure,
and bodily pleasure generally, as a remedy'. It is such moral reading
which, I believe, the image defies. The image of Pyrochles 'burning in flames, yet no flames can I see, / And dying daily, daily yet
reuiue', plunged in the lake and pleading for help, turns in two
directions. First, to that earlier paradox of the bloody-handed babe
whose stain dwelling in the flesh cannot be removed by water.
Now water cannot quench the indwelling flames which consume
Pyrochles. Earlier it was the innocence of Nature, that water 'chast
and pure, as purest snow,/Ne lets her waues with any filth be dyde, /
But euer like her selfe vnstained hath beene tryde' (II. ii. 9), which is
also the innocence of Amavia. Here it is the corruption of Nature,
of Phaedria's Idle Lake into whose waters Pyrochles has plunged:

> The waues thereof so slow and sluggish were,
> Engrost with mud, which did them foule agrise,
> That euery weightie thing they did vpbeare,
> Ne ought mote euer sinke downe to the bottome there.
>
> (II. vi. 46)

The image of the incurable wound is displayed earlier in Phedon,
and later it is shown in Pilate whose body is covered by the stink-
ing waters of Cocytus

> But both his hands most filthy feculent,
> Aboue the water were on high extent,
> And faynd to wash themselues incessantly;
> Yet nothing cleaner were for such intent,
> But rather fowler seemed to the eye.   (II. vii. 61)

When Archimago enters to help Pyrochles, and by his sage counsel
'him restor'd to health' (II. vi. 51), the image prepares for that
later moment when Arthur enters to help the fallen Guyon. His
appearance as 'one in an auncient gowne, / Whose hoarie locks
great grauitie did crowne' reminds us of Ignaro, that aged man
with 'his reuerend haires and holy grauitie' who bears the keys to
Orgoglio's dungeon, though not to the iron door which encloses
the knight. Like Ignaro who holds the knight imprisoned, Archimago only preserves Pyrochles in his burning state. As such, he

parodies Arthur—he appears 'holding in hand a goodly arming sword' which is Arthur's—who enters to slay him.

The power and limitations of temperance are further displayed in Guyon's passage through Mammon's cave. At the beginning he 'euermore himselfe with comfort feedes, / Of his owne vertues, and prayse-worthy deedes': the irony of the outcome is that he literally consumes his virtues until, with nothing to sustain him, he falls exhausted. Though he resists all the temptations to avarice which the world offers, he is left helpless before the onset of Pyrochles and Cymochles. Paradoxically, though he triumphs, he falls. Through the power of temperance he could subdue, though not destroy, the intemperate affections symbolized by Wrath. He does so by learning how not to act. The Palmer teaches him to avoid occasion to wrath, and restrains him from rescuing Pyrochles. Even his victory over Cymochles is prevented by Phaedria's pleas. His acts cancel themselves: even his release of Pyrochles, where the irony of his remarks later turns against himself: 'great mercy sure, for to enlarge a thrall, / Whose freedome shall thee turne to greatest scath' (II. v. 18). When he is prepared to undergo Mammon's trial, he may be tempted by Atin with charges of cowardice which before had moved him to wrath, but now 'though somewhat moued in his mightie hart, / Yet with strong reason maistred passion fraile, / And passed fairely forth' (II. vi. 40). Within Mammon's Cave he reveals how thoroughly he has learned to resist all temptation to act. Even the desire to act: 'to which if he inclined had at all, / That dreadfull feend, which did behind him wayt, / Would him haue rent in thousand peeces strayt' (II. vii. 64). In the final temptation, when Mammon urges him to eat the fruit and rest upon the silver stool, he is prepared to deny even these natural instincts. But through this victory over himself he reaches that final state of not acting, the state of death. Pyrochles and Cymochles may now enter to disarm and despoil his body; but at this climactic moment Arthur may also enter to save him.

The battle which follows is carefully elaborated in three sections each of seven stanzas, in which each detail is given symbolic significance in order to reveal how this greater Guyon overcomes the irrational part of the soul. That Pyrochles wields Guyon's shield and Arthur's sword shows that man's natural powers both resist and oppose their overthrow. Pyrochles cannot wound in battle; on the other hand, neither can he be wounded. His blows are turned aside, as Arthur's blows against him are turned aside by Guyon's shield. By his nature, being the inner irascible state, he does not fight, nor can be fought against, with force of arms. It is Cymochles who forces Arthur to fight on foot, as Guyon had done; and when he is wounded in the thigh (the sexual wound of concupiscence) not only causes Arthur's spear to break, leaving him helpless, but with his return blow wounds Arthur's right side. (Also the wound of concupiscence, or more correctly, of love to which he is subject, even in his consenting to be Guyon's 'dayesman'.) The first part of the battle (stanzas 32–38) ends with Arthur helpless, himself standing in need of grace. Grace comes in the Palmer who offers him Guyon's sword, that is, the power of reason. In the second stage, stanzas 39–45, there is the same threefold battle which was fought earlier by Guyon against Sansloy and Huddibras, only now it brings not the harmony of the temperate mean—which was all Medina could urge—but the triumph of the rational soul over the concupiscent part of the irrational element. Though Cymochles' blow pierces the skin of Arthur's head (a token wound of his offence against reason which is seen in his earlier wounding), the return blow invades his head to slay him. In the third stage (stanzas 46–52), Arthur's battle against Pyrochles, armour is ineffective. Guyon's sword cannot wound Pyrochles any more than it protected him before against Pyrochles' attack. Arthur wrestles with him, as Guyon was forced to wrestle with Furor whom arms could not wound; only unlike Guyon who was instantly overcome, Arthur wins. His role is now reversed: before he pleads for mercy, now he offers it; but Pyrochles, as before, stands for justice and seeks his death. That his head is cut off expresses his offence against the rational soul. Unlike Archimago who preserves Pyrochles in his wrath, Arthur takes his life. Now Guyon may arise 'with so fresh hew': from this moment of rebirth he acts no longer by his natural power alone, but is guided by reason and aided by grace.

The power of the temperate body is displayed in the house of Alma; its limitations in its besiegers, Maleger with his forces. In his assault upon the temperate body Maleger inflicts wounds which cannot be cured: 'ne was their salue, ne was their medicine, / That mote recure their wounds: so inly they did tine' (ii. xi. 21). What is described in the bloody-handed Babe as 'secret filth'

infecting the body 'that through the great contagion direfull
deadly stunck' is dramatically realized in the monster who manifests that sin in the flesh, that flesh which Arthur may wound but
cannot slay.

> Flesh without bloud, a person without spright,
> Wounds without hurt, a bodie without might,
> That could doe harme, yet could not harmed bee,
> That could not die, yet seem'd a mortall wight,
> That was most strong in most infirmitee.   (II. xi. 40)

As Guyon seeks in vain to cleanse the Babe's hands, 'the which
him into great amaz'ment droue, / And into diuerse doubt his
wauering wonder cloue', Arthur is 'th'amazed knight' whose
'wonder farre exceeded reasons reach, / That he began to doubt
his dazeled sight' (II. ii. 3; xi. 40, 44). Archimago, too, 'wondred
sore' at Pyrochles' 'straunge astonishment' (II. vi. 48, 49) upon
being burned by the flames which cannot be quenched with water.
The element of paradox gathers in the three images until it pre-
cipitates in the riddles which Arthur poses. As we have suggested,
the answer to the riddles is provided by the parallel structure of
the first two books. Maleger is 'the old man, which is corrupt
through the deceyuable lustes' (Ephes. iv. 22), the sin which
overcame mankind when Adam lost his native grace. This answer
may not suggest immediately why Maleger is attended by the two
hags, Impatience and Impotence, but their role is clarified by the
action of the first two books. Impotence is demonstrated by
the complete powerlessness of the Red Cross Knight without the
power of grace, by the limitations upon Guyon's exercise of
virtue, and here by Arthur's inability to defeat Maleger through
the force of arms. Twice he needs the blessing of grace. First,
when he falls to the ground, like Guyon in his trance: only when
the Squire intercedes does he rouse himself

> As one awakt out of long slombring shade,
> Reuiuing thought of glorie and of fame,
> Vnited all his powres to purge himselfe from blame.
>
> (II. xi. 31)

The second time is at the end of the battle when

> he began to faint, and life decay:
> But his good Squire him helping vp with speed,
> With stedfast hand vpon his horse did stay,
> And led him to the Castle by the beaten way.   (II. xi. 48)

Impatience is demonstrated in Book I by the role of Patience, the doctor under whom the knight is purged of sin, and by the battle against the Dragon in which the knight's suffering exceeds all that patience can bear; and in Book II by the impatience of Amavia and Pyrochles, and in Arthur's impatience in seizing the hags. When Spenser writes in the 1590 edition that Arthur fights 'against *his* lifelesse shadow' (II. xi. 44), the error suggests the *psychomachia* behind the whole action. (The reason why the two hags are not more than two is a pretty reason, perhaps deserving Lear's answer; but if we link Maleger and the Dragon, the two hags relate to the two sacraments: the *impotence* of man without the Well of Life, and the *impatience* of seeking godhead before just time had expired which cost him the Tree of Life.) Arthur's victory over Maleger by casting him into the standing lake is, in effect, the cleansing of the Babe's hands through the baptism of grace. By this act man is purged from the guilt of sin.

But the infection of original sin remains in regenerate man. According to Article IX, 'the infection of nature doth remain, yea in them that are regenerated, whereby the lust of the flesh . . . is not subject to the law of God'. Since man's nature is so infected, external Nature becomes a Bower of Bliss tempting him to concupiscence. The emblem upon the gate which leads to the Bower, Medea's 'furious louing fit', Jason's 'falsed faith, and loue too lightly flit', and the 'piteous spectacle' of 'the boyes bloud therein shed', links the classical myth with Spenser's fiction, and both with the Bower where all mankind is perverted by intemperance. Freed from the guilt, but not the infection, of original sin, Guyon confronts the cause of man's fall, Eve within her Garden. He triumphs, and does not fall, but acts in 'the tempest of his wrathfulnesse'. By destroying the Bower, he breaks through enshrouding nature whose harmony seeks to absorb man upon the order of nature. When he approaches the Bower, 'now gins this goodly frame of Temperance / Fairely to rise'; now Guyon becomes this image of temperance, of man guided by reason and aided by grace, standing against all the temptations of the world, the flesh, and the devil. That original sin remains ingenerate in human nature is significantly rendered in the concluding stanza of the book where Guyon denounces Grill who chooses the life of a beast:

> See the mind of beastly man,
> That hath so soone forgot the excellence

Of his creation, when he life began,
That now he chooseth, with vile difference,
To be a beast, and lacke intelligence.[1]

Grill is not the exception, for when the Palmer restores the other beasts to their shape as comely men: 'yet being men they did vnmanly looke, / And stared ghastly, some for inward shame, / And some for wrath, to see their captiue Dame.' Despite all that 'wisedomes powre, and temperaunces might' (II. xii. 43) have achieved, men are still unmanly, still marked by wrath and shame which were the first fruits of the fall. '*Israel* still serves with all his Sons.' This points again to that original sin in human nature which is, upon the theological level, the 'whole subiect' of Book II as described in the fiction of the bloody-handed Babe.

The subject of Book II derives from 'the antique Poets historicall'. Their theme is wrath, as Milton observes when he declares that his argument is more heroic

> then the wrauth
> Of stern *Achilles* on his Foe pursu'd
> Thrice Fugitive about *Troy* Wall; or rage
> Of *Turnus* for *Lavinia* disespous'd,
> Or *Neptun's* ire or *Juno's*, that so long
> Perplex'd the *Greek* and *Cytherea's* Son.
>
> (*P.L.* ix. 14–19)

To the Christian poet, articulating his poem within the heroic tradition, the classical poets treat life upon the order of nature. More specifically, since we are, in Saint Paul's phrase, 'by nature the children of wrath', they treat fallen human nature oppressed by inner wrath (as Achilles) or the wrath of the gods (as Ulysses). Homer contains all poetry, so the Renaissance believed, and his *Iliad* and *Odyssey* provide respectively the pattern for tragedy and comedy.[2] Spenser imitates Homer, then, in order to describe Guyon's fall and restoration.

For the first half of his structure which ends in Guyon's fall, he imitates the *Iliad*. Chapman notes that Homer's first word μῆνιν, *wrath*, contracts the poem's proposition which he calls

---

[1] In the *Hymn of Heavenly Love* Spenser uses the same image of fallen man as one who 'forgetfull of his makers grace . . . wallowest like to filthy swyne / And doest thy mynd in durty pleasures moyle' (120, 219–20).

[2] See Webbe, *A Discourse of English Poetrie*, in *Elizabethan Critical Essays*, i. 234, 249. Cf. Scaliger, *Poetices*, i. 5.

'Predominant Perturbation'.[1] In Renaissance moral terms, revealed by his translation, the story of Achilles' baneful wrath is the story of intemperate man whose irascible affections overcome reason. When he quarrels with Agamemnon, 'his heart / Bristled his bosome, and two waies, drew his discursiue part' (p. 5). Thetis urges him to 'renounce all warre, and feed / Thy heart with wrath', and leaves 'wrath tyring [feeding] on her sonne' (p. 10).

> But *Peleus* sonne at his blacke fleete, sat gyrt in Angers flame,
> Nor to Consults, that makes men wise, nor forth to battail came,
> But did consume his mightie heart in desolate desires.[2]

He remains burning in wrath until at the news of Patroclus' death, 'Griefe darkned all his powres' (p. 254). In despair he recognizes too late that '*Anger* . . . kindles tyrannie / In men most wise . . . And like a pliant fume it spreds through all their breasts; as late / It stole sterne passage thorough mine' (p. 256). When 'farre in rage' he seeks Hector, he has become Wrath itself: 'his teeth gnasht as he stood; his eyes, so full of fire, they warm'd. / Vnsufferd griefe and anger at, the *Troians* so combin'd' (p. 274).

Spenser tells the same story of wrath and grief; but these affections—'both coosen passions of distroubled spright' (III. iv. 12)—are identified with Guyon's antagonists. Achilles' predominant perturbation is opposed by Guyon's temperance.

> Who euer doth to temperaunce apply
> His stedfast life, and all his actions frame,
> Trust me, shall find no greater enimy,
> Then stubborne perturbation, to the same.   (II. v. 1)

In the first half of Book II Spenser shows how Guyon subdues this great enemy. In moral terms he shows how 'griefe and wrath, that be her [feeble nature's] enemies, / And foes of life' (II. vi. 1) may be restrained by the rational soul. First, Guyon subdues Occasion, 'the root of all wrath and despight', and binds Furor in order to rescue Phedon in whom grief and fury have made 'the mortall sting, / That during life will neuer be appeasd' (II. iv. 10, 33). At the end of this episode the Palmer moralizes upon the affections of wrath and grief which 'strong warres . . . make, and cruell battry bend / Gainst fort of Reason, it to ouerthrow' (II. iv. 34). Then Guyon defeats the wrathful Pyrochles (his name may

---

[1] *The Whole Works of Homer*, trans. by Chapman (London, 1616), A₄ʳ.
[2] From his earlier translation, *Seauen Bookes of the Iliades* (1598), p. 16.

have been suggested by Achilles' son Pyrrhus) who has been roused by Atin, and counsels him to 'fly the dreadfull warre, / That in thy selfe thy lesser parts do moue, / Outrageous anger, and woe-working iarre . . . Which thee to endlesse bale captiued lead' (II. v. 16). (Atin corresponds to the role of Ate in the *Iliad*. Agamemnon explains to Achilles that 'all things are done by strife: that ancient seed of *Ioue* / *Ate*, that hurts all' (p. 269).) In the next episode Atin arouses Cymochles, the 'womanish weake knight', from his slumber in the Bower to revenge the death of Pyrochles. In response, 'as one affright / With hellish feends, or *Furies* mad vprore, / He then vprose, inflam'd with fell despight, / And called for his armes' (II. v. 37). Clearly we are meant to see in his anger and grief over Pyrochles' death, Achilles' response to the news of Patroclus' death. (To the Homeric figure of wrath the Renaissance added the 'effeminate man' (Shakespeare's phrase in *Troilus and Cressida*),[1] one who withdraws from fighting because of love.) Guyon subdues these Achillean affections through his own power; but they break out again as Cymochles lapses into lust and Pyrochles burns in the idle lake. When his power is exhausted through resisting Mammon, he falls helpless before them. At the mid-point of the book, Atin and Archimago guide Pyrochles and Cymochles to vent their wrath on his fallen body.

This climactic moment in the first half of Book II reproduces that similar moment in the *Iliad* where the wrathful Achilles meets Hector. Though Hector offers not to shame the body after victory, 'these faire and temperate termes, / Farre fled *Achilles*' who vows that 'now the dogs, and fowles, in foulest vse / Shall teare thee vp, thy corse exposde, to all the *Greeks* abuse' (pp. 304, 305). After slaying Hector, he strips the armour and despoils his corpse. In Spenser, Guyon's antagonist despoils the bodies of his victims, 'whose carkases, for terrour of his name, / Of fowles and beastes he made the piteous prayes' (II. v. 26) while Guyon holds compassionately that 'all so great shame after death I weene, / As selfe to dyen bad, vnburied bad to beene' (II. i. 59) and buries Mortdant and Amavia.[2] When Pyrochles and Cymochles dominate

---

[1] III. iii. 218. Achilles is urged by Patroclus: 'sweete, rouse your selfe; and the weake wanton *Cupid* / Shall from your necke vnloose his amorous fould.'

[2] The Christian basis for Guyon's statement is given in Book I where the sixth bead-man in the holy hospital cares for the dead because they are made in God's image. The significance of the prayer which Spenser adds, 'ah dearest God me graunt, I dead be not defould' (I. x. 42), is not seen until this moment. It is significant

Guyon's 'dead' body, like Achilles they vow to strip his armour
and leave his carcass to 'be entombed in the rauen or the kight'
(ii. viii. 16).

But at this moment the pattern of the *Iliad* is dramatically
reversed. Once Guyon has fallen exhausted, 'and all his senses
were with deadly fit opprest', the funeral march of this final line
of Canto VII ominously announces what seems to be the end.
He has depended upon his own power; with this gone there seems
nothing left. Then the opening lines of the next canto burst
breathlessly upon the reader:

> And is there care in heauen? and is there loue
> In heauenly spirits to these creatures bace,
> That may compassion of their euils moue?
> There is.

(That 'and' suddenly bridges the gap between God and man.)
Since Guyon refuses Mammon's proferred 'grace', and separates
himself from the worldlings who serve this 'greatest god below
the skye', 'highest God, that loues his creatures so' intercedes
directly on his behalf.[1] It is God's one appearance within the action
of the poem: He sends the Angel who guides the Palmer who
urges Arthur who saves Guyon from his enemies. The bridge is
thus complete from God's grace, to the ministering angels, to
'right reason', to the sum of all virtues which may rescue man.
First the Palmer defies the threat to despoil Guyon's body, for
'vile is the vengeance on the ashes cold . . . to spoile the dead of
weed / Is sacrilege, and doth all sinnes exceed' (ii. viii. 13, 16).
(He echoes Hector's plea; but Pyrochles, like Achilles, rejects it.)
Then Arthur enters to plead for Guyon's body, as Priam seeks to
'redeem' Hector's body. But through him all the Achillean virtues
are destroyed. Unlike Achilles in whom 'fit ruth, that now should
draw so deepe / In all the world; being lost in him' (p. 327),
Arthur's immediate response is 'sure I rew his pitteous plight'
(ii. viii. 24). Against the Achillean spirit of revenge, Arthur argues
that vengeance belongs only to God who alone may punish the
dead: 'but gentle knight, / That doth against the dead his hand
vpreare, / His honour staines with rancour and despight' (ii. viii.

that the Palmer wishes at first to bury only Amavia who has been overcome by
anguish, and not Mortdant who has been overcome by crime; but when Guyon
insists that he be buried too, they agree.
[1] ii. vii. 8; viii. 1.

29). Unlike the helpless Priam who pleads prostrate before
Achilles, Arthur confronts the Achillean figures with the sword.
He slays Pyrochles in battle, and when Cymochles refuses grace—
being the unrepentant Achilles—he chops off his head. Finally,
not in the Achillean figures, but in Guyon is true virtue to be
found: 'in [his] dead face he [Arthur] red great magnanimity' (II.
viii. 23). Now Guyon may go beyond this height of virtue: with
the irascible affections destroyed, he arises to begin the second
half of his quest.

Within the structure of the second half of Book II, Spenser
imitates the *Odyssey*. Again Chapman supplies the relevant critical
gloss when he notes that Homer's first word ἄνδρα, *Man*, contracts the poem's proposition: 'the Minds inward, constant, and
vnconquerd Empire; vnbroken, vnalterd, with any most insolent,
and tyrannous infliction'.[1] Spenser displays the form and power
of perfected man in the castle of Alma, and shows how it resists
the tyrannous infliction of the senses under Maleger:

> th'assieged Castles ward
> Their stedfast stonds did mightily maintaine,
> And many bold repulse, and many hard
> Atchieuement wrought with perill and with paine,
> That goodly frame from ruine to sustaine.   (II. xi. 15)

Ulysses as that 'absolute man' (to follow through with Chapman's
orthodox interpretation) does as much; but for the Christian poet,
man may do more than stoically resist the world. He must triumph
over the world, though he may do so only through the aid of
grace. Hence Arthur must free the body from outward infliction
by slaying Maleger. Then Guyon may do more than resist the
Bower of Bliss which he does earlier when he resists Phaedria;
he can destroy it.

Guyon's voyage to the Bower in Canto XII is Spenser's deliberate imitation of Book XII of the *Odyssey*, as the early com-
mentators noted. But the imitation seems no less than the poet's
attempt to overgo Homer. While Ulysses endures four dangers
(the Sirens, the Wandering Rocks, the two rocks of Scylla
and Charybdis, and the island of Thrinacie), Guyon endures
twelve, and these are designed to exhaust all possible dangers and

---

[1] Ep. Ded. to *Homers Odysses*, A₄ʳ.

combination of dangers on sea, land, and in the air.[1] In keeping
with this mechanical design, four stanzas are given to each of the
dangers, except those two in the air which together receive four.
(The Maiden on the island is the exception: she is given three,
but the Palmer has taken her first stanza to dismiss the sea
monsters.) This Homeric material is heavily moralized even for
the Renaissance reader; moreover, it is extravagantly handled.
When Spenser describes the sea monsters as

> All dreadfull pourtraicts of deformitee:
> Spring-headed *Hydraes*, and sea-shouldring Whales,
> Great whirlpooles, which all fishes make to flee,
> Bright Scolopendraes, arm'd with siluer scales,
> Mighty *Monoceroses*, with immeasured tayles,   (II. xii. 23)

he is clearly taking time out. His treatment is comic, and appro-
priately so. The dangers are not real to Guyon. Unlike Ulysses'
companions who are all lost—allegorically interpreted as the perturbations of the soul overwhelmed by adversity[2]—the sober
Palmer and Alma's strong ferryman keep Guyon on a safe course.
The shipwrecked Ulysses is washed up on Calypso's island where
he is held captive in her cave; but Guyon, as that greater Ulysses,
triumphs over the sea and arrives upon Acrasia's island complete
within himself.

By the end of Book II Spenser has absorbed the heroic tradition
as it is contained in Homer. He overgoes it with the figure of
Acrasia, that enchantress

> that with vaine delightes,
> And idle pleasures in her *Bowre* of *Blisse*,
> Does charme her louers, and the feeble sprightes
> Can call out of the bodies of fraile wightes:
> Whom then she does transforme to monstrous hewes,
> And horribly misshapes with vgly sightes,
> Captiu'd eternally in yron mewes,
> And darksom dens, where *Titan* his face neuer shewes.
>
>   (II. v. 27)

---

[1] On the sea: the Gulf of Greediness, the Whirlpool of Decay, the Sea monsters;
on the land: the Rock of Reproch, the Quicksand of Unthriftihed, the wild Beasts;
in the air: the mist, the harmful fowls; on sea and land: the wandering Islands; on
the sea and in the air: Phaedria in her boat seeking to tempt Guyon with her song;
on land and in the air: the maiden on the island pleading for Guyon's aid; on sea,
land, and in the air: the mermaids in the cove of the island singing their enchanting
song.

[2] Comes, *Mythologiae* (Geneva, 1641), p. 940.

Clearly she is Circe, the witch who transforms men into beasts;
and Calypso who lures her victims by promising an immortality
of slothful desire; but more than Circe's victims whose minds
remain unchanged, hers 'turned into figures hideous, / According
to their mindes like monstruous' (II. xii. 85). She is a greater Dido
who keeps the man 'come to paradys / Out of the swolow of
helle'[1] so enthralled that he forever forgets all virtuous action—
a Dido, moreover, whose magic art destroys her escaping lover,
and causes Amavia instead to die for love.[2] Acrasia is all these,
and more.

> And all that while, right ouer him she hong,
> With her false eyes fast fixed in his sight,
> As seeking medicine, whence she was stong,
> Or greedily depasturing delight:
> And oft inclining downe with kisses light,
> For feare of waking him, his lips bedewd,
> And through his humid eyes did sucke his spright,
> Quite molten into lust and pleasure lewd.   (II. xii. 73)

She is the succubus who defiles his body, the lamia who sucks out
his spirit. Her lover, being so enshrouded by her body, forgets
that he is a man. He becomes a child; so goaded by unsatisfied
desire, he becomes beast-like in passion; and yet less than a beast,
for 'greedily *depasturing* delight' he becomes plant-like, one whom
'her lusts did feed'; and finally, laid asleep, he yields his life to
become inanimate as a stone:

> ne for honour cared hee,
> Ne ought, that did to his aduauncement tend,
> But in lewd loues, and wastfull luxuree,
> His dayes, his goods, his bodie he did spend.   (II. xii. 80)

Spenser's image of the enchanting woman who symbolizes all
that stands between the hero and his goal is the same as in the
classical poets: only what is merely implicit in Homer, partly
explicit in Virgil, becomes consciously articulated, fully realized,
and therefore more significant. When Guyon meets Acrasia he
shows no tears such as Ulysses shed before Calypso, but only
'rigour pittilesse', and the tempestuous noise which heralds

---

[1] Chaucer, *Legend of Good Women*, 1103–4.
[2] Upton was the first to note the parallels between Amavia and Dido. See *Var.
Sp. Book II*, pp. 191–2.

Aeneas's yielding to Dido is 'the tempest of his wrathfulnesse' as he destroys the Bower.

With the ending of Book II the formal basis of Spenser's poem is established. The image of the whole poem is rendered in Book I through the image of the knight's adventures, that *Divine Comedy* which includes the tragedy at its centre, being set within the cosmic conflict between Una and Duessa. The states of Holiness and Temperance are preliminary to man's life upon the orders of grace and nature; and beginning with Book III Spenser erects the image of man perfected in all the private virtues. With Book III, then, the structure of the poem formally begins. Or not to be betrayed by an image, the first two books provide not only the foundation but the framework of the poem, both the ensample and the doctrine within which the poem is realized.

IV

The Poem as Fiction

The Fable and Fiction is (as it were) the forme and Soule
of any Poeticall worke.   JONSON

IN the previous chapters of this study I have tried to establish and
illustrate a critical approach to Spenser's allegory which would
focus upon the literal surface while providing for the depth of its
allegorical meanings. In Sidney's *Apology* we found a method by
which to read the poem 'as an imaginatiue groundplot of a
profitable inuention', and have shown how it may be applied to
reading Spenser and Dante. The Idea of the poem we found out-
lined in the letter to Ralegh, and realized in the structure of
Book I. The doctrine of the *ensample* or image we found realized
in the continued allegory of Book II. In the remaining chapters
I shall consider more directly the argument of the whole poem
realized as an image. That involves understanding the continued
allegory as fiction. We have noticed how the fiction in Book I is
consonant with Scriptural truth, and in Book II is rendered within
the tradition of the 'antique Poets historicall'. In Books III and IV,
however, the tradition in which Spenser writes is his own. Here
the fiction can be understood only in terms of the Idea which he
fashions in the whole poem.

The relation of fiction to fact has always been the poet's special
problem, though never so insistently as in the Elizabethan age.
When it is believed that truth is revealed alone in God's Word,
and the cry is that Scripture alone is the religion of Protestants,
the poet is banished from such a Christian Republic except as
Sidney's first kind, the divine poet who sings the praises of God,
never feigning because his subject is truth itself. Sidney's (and
Spenser's!) real enemy was not Gosson and the tribe of *mysomousoi*,
but those who defended divine poetry.[1] The great divine poet

---

[1] For the defence of divine poetry in the sixteenth century, see L. B. Campbell,
'The Christian Muse', *Huntington Library Bulletin*, viii (1935), 29–70.

was, of course, Du Bartas. Though in his first work, the *History of Judith*, he imitates the classical epics, with *Urania* he dedicates himself to divine poetry. As he meditates whether to write poetry after the heroic style, or to sing of wanton Venus, the heavenly Muse reveals herself to him. She urges: 'take me for guyde, lyft vp to heauen thy wing / O *Salust*, Gods immortals honour sing.'[1] Her counsels explain why Sidney was careful to distinguish the divine poet who sings 'the inconceiuable excellencies of GOD' from the right poet. Urania declares that 'all art is learned by art, this art alone / It is a heauenly gift': Sidney notes that poetry has been regarded as 'a diuine gift, and no humaine skill', but cannot agree.[2] To Urania the poet is inspired by a heavenly fury: 'so heauenly fury can / Make man pas man, and wander in holy mist': to Sidney the poet must be 'lifted vp with the vigor of *his owne* inuention', and he must range 'onely *within* the Zodiack of *his owne* wit'.[3] The divine poet sings only God's praise and he scorns those who use dreams and fables:

> Then consecrat that eloquence most rair,
> To sing the lofty miracles and fair
> Of holy Scripture: and of your good ingyne,
> Pour out, my friends, there your fift-essence fyne.
>
> (F_i^r).

Above all, the divine poet must avoid the 'auncient fables' (F_{ii}^r). In this he is opposed to Sidney's right poet who delivers only fiction. Profiting by Urania's counsel, Bartas's next work, the *Sepmaine*, was an extended commentary upon the truth of Holy Scripture. It set the fashion in England for divine poetry. To Protestant England Bartas became 'the Treasurer of Humanity, and the Ieweller of Diuinity for the highnesse of his subiect, and the maiesty of his verse, nothing inferiour vnto Dante, . . . a right inspired and enrauished Poet; full of chosen, graue, profound, venerable, and stately matter; euen in the next Degree to the sacred, and reuerend stile of heauenly Diuinity it selfe'.[4] Against this almost universal praise of the divine poet, there was only the manuscript of Sidney's *Apology* which set forth his Idea of the right poet. Yet profiting by its counsel, Jonson was led to remark

---

[1] *The Vranie, or Heauenly Muse*, 65–66, translated by James VI in *The Essayes of a Prentise* (Edinburgh, 1584), D_3^r.

[2] *Urania*, D_4^r; *Apol.*, p. 50.

[3] *Urania*, E_1^r; *Apol.*, p. 8 (my italics).

[4] *Works of Gabriel Harvey*, ed. Grosart, ii. 103.

that he 'thought not Bartas a Poet but a Verser, because he wrote not Fiction'.[1] Against Harvey's slavish praise quoted above, there is Spenser's ambiguous compliment, as reported by Harvey himself, that he esteems one section of Du Bartas's works, that which treats the heavens 'as the proper profession of Urania'.[2] The proper profession of Urania, indeed!: that muse whom Spenser may serve in his *Hymns* but not in his heroic poem. Though God's Truth is sufficient, the poet may imitate Scripture in his fiction. Precisely because he offers fiction, and does not seek to affirm truth, his work may supplement and does not seek to supplant the Truth. If not in its literal level, then in its Idea and in its end or working. Sidney advocates a kind of poetry which 'deserueth not to bee scourged out of the Church of God' because its fiction with the power of grace seeks man's regeneration. Alone in the age—Shakespeare always excepted—Spenser embodies, as far as any work can, the ideal fiction. Certainly not Ariosto or Tasso, at least in the judgement of Henry Reynolds. Though he approves Spenser's 'exact body of the *Ethicke* doctrine' even while supporting those who wish 'that he had therein beene a little freer of his fiction, and not so close riuetted to his Morall', he praises Tasso's *Gerusalem Liberata* 'so farre as an excellent pile of meerely Morall Philosophy may deserue', and Ariosto 'for the artfull woofe of his ingenious though vnmeaning fables'.[3] Only in Spenser is poetry based upon the Christian vision contained in Holy Scripture, and informed continuously by moral and religious doctrine, while existing most firmly in its own right as fiction.

Invention is one of the two chief requirements of the poet in the Renaissance, the other being the disposition of his matter. Jonson's remark quoted above is the central doctrine of Elizabethan literary criticism which is centred in Sidney's *Apology*, and writings are praised as they are full of rare invention. We have noted before Spenser's boast to Harvey that he has written a book 'rare for the Inuention, and manner of handling [that is, its disposition]'. Even the patron of divine poetry, James VI who translated

---

[1] 'Conversations with Drummond', in *Ben Jonson*, ed. Herford and Simpson, i. 133. Cf. Spenser's teacher, Mulcaster: 'when the *poetes* write sadly and soberly, without counterfeating though they write in verse, yet they be no *poetes* in that kinde of their writing: but where they couer a truth with a fabulous veele, and resemble with alteration' (*Positions* (London, 1581), p. 273).

[2] *Marginalia*, ed. Moore Smith, p. 161.

[3] *Mythomystes*, in *Critical Essays*, ed. Spingarn, i. 146–7.

Bartas's *Urania*, writes: 'sen *Inuention* is ane of the cheif vertewis in a Poete, it is best that ye inuent your awin subiect your self, and not to compose of sene subiectis'.[1] Since invention is not creating out of nothing but discovering what is in the material, it may involve imitation though never in the sense of copying. Nor is it ornament to prettify verse. Since Spenser praises the Muse 'full of high thoughts inuention',[2] we may expect to find an argument which informs and unifies what he writes. He seeks inspiration of the Queen, not to sing her praises or assert her virtues, but 'to *thinke* of that true glorious type of thine'. In the Proem to Book III he tells the Queen that if she wishes to see her self pictured in living colours, she should read Ralegh's *Cynthia*; what he offers instead is her 'glorious pourtraict', not figured plainly but shadowed in coloured shows. His ornament adorns a conception or thought; but to say this suggests wrongly that they are distinct, that he begins with the thought which then he renders poetically. Spenser's own insight into his method of invention is that in writing the poem he finds himself 'rauisht with rare thoughts delight' (VI, Proem i). The phrase is a key to our reading the poem. The delight is taken in the thought, or rather in the process of thinking, for the two are not separable. Delight and understanding are one: what the poet writes, not any hidden doctrine implied beneath what he writes, ravishes him.[3] The phrase should forestall any effort to reduce his thought to commonplace background, or reduce his delight to prettifying a thought, or ever to separate the two.

In the present chapter I shall consider Spenser's invention through his treatment of mythology. As we have seen, in Book I he imitates Holy Scripture, and displays his invention by a point-counterpoint analogy between classical and Christian statements of man's fall and restoration. In Book II he imitates the 'antique Poets historicall', and his invention is displayed through containing them within his own poetic pattern. Since the first two books exhaust all Scripture, both sacred and profane, the transition to the later books is one of the most complex points in his continued allegory. Guyon's act of destroying the Bower does no less than

---

[1] *Ane Schort Treatise*, 1584, in *Elizabethan Critical Essays*, i. 221.
[2] *Colin Clout*, 446.
[3] In Sidney's phrase, he 'exercise[s] to know, [not] as hauing knowne' (*Apol.*, p. 50).

initiate the entire action of the rest of the poem. We will find that the relation between the first two books will help us understand the nature of this transition. In Books III and IV, where he abandons the motif of the knight-hero upon his quest, two classical myths provide the contrapuntal framework for his allegory. Here his invention comes into its own, and he creates his own mythology.

Spenser's treatment of classical mythology has been generally praised, *The Faerie Queene* being viewed, in Douglas Bush's phrase, as 'an endless gallery of mythological paintings'.[1] When Spenser in rendering the myth of Leda and the swan, refers to the 'wondrous skill, and sweet wit of the man, / That her in daffadillies sleeping made', we rightly turn the praise to himself as he writes: 'she slept, yet twixt her eyelids closely spyde, / How towards her he rusht, and smiled at his pryde' (III. xi. 32). But such praise limits our awareness of Spenser's treatment of myth to our enjoying the *elocutio* of his art. Spenser is the English Ovid, but in a more profound way than we have allowed. In the Renaissance the classical poets themselves are praised rather for their fiction than their ornament, as Homer is extolled by Chapman 'for his naked *Vlysses*, clad in eternall Fiction'.[2] Since it was seriously believed that 'the Fable and Fiction is (as it were) the forme and Soule of any Poeticall worke', the greatest demands were made upon the mythopoeic powers of the poet, that he make his fiction his own. In fulfilling these demands Spenser so entirely re-creates traditional mythology that it belongs to the invention of the poem.

I

Book I outlines the poem's pattern. The four stages of the Red Cross Knight's action: (i) his fall through Duessa's witchcraft, (ii) his redemption through Arthur's grace, (iii) his regeneration through Una's faith, and (iv) through slaying the Dragon, his restoration signified by his marriage to Una, contain the action of the whole poem.

The first stage is described in Book II which shows, as we have

---

[1] *Mythology and the Renaissance Tradition in English Poetry* (Minneapolis, 1932), p. 86.

[2] Ded. Ep. to *Odyssey*, in *Works*, A₄ᵛ. Cf. Daniel: 'we admire them [the ancients] not for their smooth-gliding words, nor their measures, but for their inuentions'. *A Defence of Ryme*, in *Elizabethan Critical Essays*, ii. 364.

seen, how virtue aided by grace may prevent the knight's fall.
The second stage is shown in Book III in the redeeming power
of chaste love displayed in the female Arthur, Britomart, who
descends into the dungeon to save Amoret. The third stage is
treated in Books IV and V. In Book IV there is displayed the
'regeneration' of the flesh through love which is preparatory to
marriage: then in Book V the 'regeneration' of England by the
defeat of the enemies who stand between her and her glorious
destiny, and therefore between Artegal and his marriage to Britomart. The fourth stage is reached in Book VI which projects the
vision of the restored lovers joined in delight. If the pattern of
Book I were further fulfilled, Book VII would treat the knight's
next stage when he returns to the world to serve the Faery Queen.
That the cycle of action from fall to restoration may start over
again gives the theme of Mutability.

Book II achieves the first stage of man's ultimate restoration;
and yet it is important to note how limited is the scope of Guyon's
adventure. His first act is to bind an old woman, for which Atin
reproves him:

> Vile knight,
> That knights and knighthood doest with shame vpbray,
> And shewst th'ensample of thy childish might,
> With silly weake old woman thus to fight.
> Great glory and gay spoile sure hast thou got,
> And stoutly prou'd thy puissaunce here in sight.   (II. iv. 45)

His final act is to bind a wanton woman, release her languid lover,
and destroy her Garden. Guyon's reply to Archimago's story of
the knight who raped his lady, 'how may it be . . . that knight
should knighthood euer so haue shent?' might well be turned
against him. He is not one who upholds the traditional order of
chivalric knighthood. 'What is a knyght but whan he is on horse-
backe', Malory's Sir Lamerok asks,[1] and from the beginning of
his adventure—the end of Malory's order of knighthood comes
when the knights free their horses—he walks on foot. It is Braggadocchio, rather, who becomes the traditional knight-errant after
he steals Guyon's horse and spear. It is he, rather, who upholds
the customs of knighthood in his vaunting vow not to use a

---

[1] *Works*, ed. Vinaver (Oxford, 1947), p. 667. At the end when the knights become
clerks, 'their horses wente where they wolde, for they toke no regarde of no worldly
rychesses' (p. 1255).

sword, and in his later vow to assist the distressed Malbecco: 'forth the Boaster marching, braue begonne / His stolen steed to thunder furiously' (III. x. 33).

Guyon does not attack, but rather resists attack; or, more exactly, he endures. Again Book I supplies the pattern for his conduct. The Red Cross Knight falls when 'the eye of reason was with rage yblent', so that he sees Duessa as fair as Una; and in his return journey his vision must be clarified. His restoration begins when he sees Duessa unveiled in all her foulness. Only then he may be placed in the house of Penance where Faith 'opened his dull eyes, that light mote in them shine' (I. x. 18) and he may see the heavenly City. Finally, completely restored, he may see Una unveiled in all her blazing beauty. Guyon must overcome that first moment when the Red Cross Knight falls through Archimago's false vision so that he yields himself to his senses. Against the 'fleshly lustes, which fight agaynst the soule' (1 Pet. ii. 11) physical power cannot avail, and Guyon must endure the attacks of Furor, Pyrochles, and Cymochles, of Phaedria's enchanted isle, of Mammon's call to 'come . . . and see'. This assault upon the senses is rendered symbolically by Maleger's attack upon the five senses of the castle of Alma.

With Maleger defeated, Guyon may approach the Bower of Bliss, that greatest abuse of vision whose 'guilefull semblaunts' (II. xii. 48) flood the senses to make us see as Paradise what actually is the state of hell. They pass through the Bower, seeing all. The repeated injunctions to see: 'ah see, who so faire thing doest faine to see . . . Ah see, the Virgin Rose . . . Lo see . . . Loe see' (II. xii. 74) are represented in the figure of Genius:

> The foe of life, that good enuyes to all,
> That secretly doth vs procure to fall,
> Through guilefull semblaunts, which he makes vs see.
>
> (II. xii. 48)

(In Book I this figure is seen in Archimago, Arch-Imago, the Beast from the sea who forces man to see the image he fashions as a god to be worshipped.) But Guyon rejects Genius when he overthrows his 'guilefull semblaunts' through the power of wisdom. His first enemy was Archimago who 'gan to weaue a web of wicked guile' (II. i. 8); later he met Mammon on whose cave is the emblem of the spider's web: '*Arachne* high did lift / Her cunning web, and spred her subtile net' (II. vii. 28); finally he meets Acrasia

> arayd, or rather disarayd,
> All in a vele of silke and siluer thin,
> That hid no whit her alablaster skin,
> But rather shewd more white, if more might bee:
> More subtile web *Arachne* cannot spin,
> Nor the fine nets, which oft we wouen see
> Of scorched deaw, do not in th'aire more lightly flee.
>
> (II. xii. 77)

Against this enemy, the Palmer weaves a web:

> A subtile net, which onely for the same
> The skilfull Palmer formally did frame . . .
> For that same net so cunningly was wound,
> That neither guile, nor force might it distraine.
>
> (II. xii. 81–82)

This is the web of 'wisedomes powre, and temperaunces might' (II. xii. 43) which sees and knows and yet abstains. At the end Guyon has cast out the power which 'makes vs see', and holds the world in his power: he has the 'gouernall' of the Bower, as Genius had in the beginning. Una's parents 'all the world in their subiection held' until the Dragon expelled them: now Guyon takes that first step towards regaining the lost Eden by holding the world in his subjection.

Guyon sees, knows, and abstains except in that climactic destruction of the Bower. It is a brilliantly conceived stroke by the poet to have his passive hero destroy all:

> their blisse he turn'd to balefulnesse:
> Their groues he feld, their gardins did deface,
> Their arbers spoyle, their Cabinets suppresse,
> Their banket houses burne, their buildings race,
> And of the fairest late, now made the fowlest place.
>
> (II. xii. 83)

Nothing that the reader understands later about the act, how inevitable and necessary it is, ever lessens but only intensifies the shock of a first reading. It is a Dionysian act, and Nietzsche describes one element which is present: 'happiness in becoming is possible only in the *annihilation* of the real, of the "existing", of the beautifully visionary. . . . with the annihilation of the most beautiful phenomena in the world of appearance, Dionysian happiness reaches its zenith.'¹ To realize how destructive and negative his act is, we need only compare the Red Cross Knight's release of Una's parents, how the people shout with joy and crown Una,

> Then all the people, as in solemne feast,
> To him assembled with one full consort,
> Reioycing . . . (I. xii. 4)

with Guyon's release of Verdant who remains 'both sorrowfull and sad', and the other lovers staring in wrath and shame. Guyon himself lacks that joy which is given to the Red Cross Knight when Una appears unveiled in her beauty 'as bright as doth the morning starre appeare / Out of the East' through whose joyous presence he is seen 'swimming in that sea of blisfull ioy'. His comparable vision is of the naked maidens who appear 'as that faire Starre, the messenger of morne' and 'shewd him many sights, that courage cold could reare' (II. xii. 65, 68). The lust which they arouse in him—it is registered in the imagery of the line, and in the word 'courage' with its sense of sexual vigour—must be repressed.

Guyon's final act not only releases, but binds. Acrasia's capture signifies the masculine triumph of reason over the affections which are traditionally feminine. In the perfected temperate body which is described in the Castle of Alma we see

> The frame thereof seemd partly circulare,
> And part triangulare, O worke diuine;
> Those two the first and last proportions are,
> The one imperfect, mortall, fœminine;
> Th' other immortall, perfect, masculine. (II. ix. 22)

Guyon's victory is the triumph of the 'immortall, perfect, masculine'. The feminine is revealed in the passions which are seen as a lovely bevy of ladies 'courted of many a iolly Paramoure' (II. ix. 34) among whom Cupid plays his wanton sports. Yet Cupid has laid his cruel bow aside with which he wounds through love, and the ladies make homage to Alma who remains 'a virgin bright; / That had not yet felt *Cupides* wanton rage' (II. ix. 18). The feminine remains either staunchly virginal in Alma and Belphoebe or blatantly sensual in Acrasia; and all affections, including love, are the enemy of reason.

¹ *The Birth of Tragedy*, trans. W. A. Haussmann (New York, 1924), pp. xxvii–xxviii.

The virginal state of temperance is like the state of man under the Old Law, suffering under wrath, infected by original sin, apparently without hope of redemption. The house of Medina represents the classical view of human nature in which the rational soul must seek the Aristotelian mean, and the Platonic harmony of the affections. But such a mean, and such a harmony, cannot be maintained because of the 'fell *Erinnys*' (II. ii. 29) in man's heart, that foe whom Guyon cannot wound or slay, and to whom he is left finally as the helpless victim. But through the intercession of God, and the entrance of the Angel and Arthur (each being called a 'Child' in order to connect them), the irrational is cast out, and he enters a higher state of temperance than the classical world could allow. When he passes through Mammon's cave he is the type of that greater man who resists the world, the flesh, and the devil. After Arthur slays the forces of Maleger which besiege the temperate body, he is free to move and act. In place of the static picture of Medina's castle 'built on a rocke adioyning to the seas' (II. ii. 12), and the castle of Alma surrounded by enemies who hide all the land under them, we see Guyon moving victoriously over the sea, and through all temptations of the land until he conquers the perverted Nature of the Bower.

Temperance is preparatory to the state of virtue: in Upton's apt phrase, it is 'the foundation of all moral virtue'.[1] Guyon offers Acrasia's victims the choice of virtue, a difficult choice which no one willingly accepts. Theirs is the cry of Saint Augustine when he was called to enter the Christian way: 'O lord, make me chaste, but not yet.' Like the Red Cross Knight with Duessa at the moment before Orgoglio breaks in to bind him, Verdant is seen with Acrasia at that moment before he will be transformed into a beast; only Guyon and the Palmer break in to bind him, and only to release him with the counsel of temperance. It is a painful moment and a rude awakening, precisely because it is a moment of birth.

Throughout Book II there is the struggle to awake out of a dream. Spenser explores that first moment of the Red Cross Knight's fall when the false dream leads him astray. Then the power of Night rules until that final moment when Una as the Dawn arises, the son of Day confronts the Dragon 'awaiting him beside / To haue deuourd, so soone as day he spyde' (I. xi. 52).

---

[1] *Spenser's Faerie Queene* (London, 1758), ii. 512.

(The imagery, we may say, *identifies* the knight with day, and the Dragon with Night.) Night is slain, and the knight awakens to that new day heralded by the morning star who is Una. In Book II the lowest stage of awakening is seen in Guyon's enemy, Cymochles, whom Atin wakes 'out of his delightfull dreame' (II. v. 37) in Acrasia's Bower; but through Phaedria's sensual delight he is soon lulled asleep. When Guyon is rescued from his death-like trance, that state of Cymochles is slain : '*by this* Sir *Guyon* from his traunce awakt, / Life hauing maistered her sencelesse foe.' The Palmer is restored to him, the Angel is ever ready to succour him, and Arthur is present to stead him. But there is a higher state of awakening to be achieved. When Arthur battles Maleger he is overcome by the two hags until his Squire aids him:

> The whiles the Prince prickt with reprochfull shame,
> As one awakt out of long slombring shade,
> Reuiuing thought of glorie and of fame,
> Vnited all his powres to purge himselfe from blame.
>
> (II. xi. 31)

By slaying Maleger he purges the body of that sinful state which threatens to overwhelm the senses; accordingly, when Guyon enters the Bower all his senses are awake. Because of his awakened senses, the Bower becomes a place of intense beauty: he sees all, and yet abstains. When someone sings the song of the Rose, 'the constant paire heard *all*, that he did say, / Yet swarued not' (II. xii. 76). Nothing may overwhelm, or dull, or lull his senses. Opposed to this temperate state is Verdant, fast asleep, enshrouded in the Bower, like Cymochles 'in Ladies lap entombed' (II. v. 36).

When Verdant awakes, man is ready to enter that higher state under the new law of Love. In simple terms, there is the transition from that youthful state of virginity before desire awakens into adolescence. This is that pattern of action described in Arthur. As a youth he scorns love

> in freshest flowre of youthly yeares,
> When courage first does creepe in manly chest,
> Then first the coale of kindly heat appeares
> To kindle loue in euery liuing brest. (I. ix. 9)

He seeks 'those creeping flames by reason to subdew, / Before their rage grew to so great vnrest' until the vision of the Faery Queen makes him yield to 'that fresh bleeding wound, which day

and night / Whilome doth rancle in my riuen brest, / With forced
fury following his behest' (I. ix. 9, 7). Earlier Guyon too had
sought to repress that vision of the young maidens who appear
before him as the morning star. But with the fleeting vision of
the beauty of Florimell in distress

> her faire yellow locks behind her flew,
> Loosely disperst with puffe of euery blast:
> All as a blazing starre doth farre outcast
> His hearie beames, and flaming lockes dispred   (III. i. 16)

he pursues her in full flight. In effect, Alma has now felt Cupid's
rage, and the temperate body is assaulted from above:

> Most sacred fire, that burnest mightily
> In liuing brests, ykindled first aboue,
> Emongst th'eternall spheres and lamping sky,
> And thence pourd into men, which men call Loue;
> Not that same, which doth base affections moue
> In brutish minds, and filthy lust inflame,
> But that sweet fit, that doth true beautie loue,
> And choseth vertue for his dearest Dame,
> Whence spring all noble deeds and neuer dying fame.

(III. iii. 1)

This infusion of grace kindles a fire which must be met by a power
greater than temperance whose scope is limited to suppressing
the fire of lust. This power which must preserve the sacred fire
and make it the source of all noble deeds is, of course, Chastity.

The Nature which Guyon destroys conspires man's fall, its
plenitude tempting man into intemperate lust. Phaedria speaks
for 'nothing enuious nature' which throws flowers 'out of her
fruitfull lap' (II. vi. 15), and she urges man to follow Nature. In
Mammon is seen the 'god of the world' 'that of my plenty poure
out vnto all, / And vnto none my graces do enuye' (II. vii. 8); and
in Acrasia's Bower all the fullness of Nature is manifest. In
Phaedria's 'bounteous boure' (II. vi. 16), Mammon's 'bounteous
baytes' (II. vii. 10), and the 'bounteous smels' (II. v. 29) of the
Bower of Bliss, all fullness seems to belong to the enemies of
Temperance. Another fullness enters, however, when God's 'exceeding grace' brings Arthur 'full of Princely bounty' (II. viii. 51)
to save Guyon. Through grace, temperance becomes 'formerly
grounded, and fast setteled / On firme foundation of true bounti-
hed' (II. xii. 1), and Guyon destroys the false tempting bountihead

of the Bower. It is not Nature which is at fault, however, but man who has abused Nature. When Guyon confronts the god of the world whose offered grace is Nature's plenty tempting man to excess, he defends the antique world:

> The antique world, in his first flowring youth,
>   Found no defect in his Creatours grace,
>   But with glad thankes, and vnreproued truth,
>   The gifts of soueraigne bountie did embrace:
>   Like Angels life was then mens happy cace;
>   But later ages pride, like corn-fed steed,
>   Abusd her plenty, and fat swolne encreace
>   To all licentious lust, and gan exceed
> The measure of her meane, and naturall first need.
>
> (II. vii. 16)

He must tread that narrow path between 'right vsaunce' (II. vii. 7) and abuse, being solicitous about the things of the world but not too solicitous, and so hold the things of the world as not to be held by them.

Guyon's antique world is embodied in Belphoebe. Her entrance into the poem is violent, all the more so because her meeting with Braggadocchio and Trompart in Canto III digresses from Guyon's adventure. A horn shrills through the wood, 'and made the forrest ring, as it would riue in twaine. / Eft through the thicke they heard one rudely rush' (II. iii. 20–21). Suddenly she appears in all her glory.

> Her face so faire as flesh it seemed not,
>   But heauenly pourtraict of bright Angels hew,
>   Cleare as the skie, withouten blame or blot,
>   Through goodly mixture of complexions dew;
>   And in her cheekes the vermeill red did shew
>   Like roses in a bed of lillies shed,
>   The which ambrosiall odours from them threw,
>   And gazers sense with double pleasure fed,
> Hable to heale the sicke, and to reuiue the ded.
>
> (II. iii. 22)

The last line suggests that in the perfection of her nature she is the unfallen Eden watered and nourished by the Well and Tree of Life. Within Book II she is the antithesis of Acrasia, Diana opposed to the lustful Venus. She is seen to rudely rush through the forest: Acrasia lies languorously upon a bed of roses. As Belphoebe flees through the forest, 'in her rude haires sweet flowres themselues did lap, / And flourishing fresh leaues and blossomes did enwrap' (II. iii. 30). The image is startling: not only that the flowers caress her hair, but that the leaves and blossoms are 'flourishing fresh'. Here, we may say, *is* Nature, 'most innocent nature' which Milton's Lady defends against Comus's fallen nature.[1] When we come to Acrasia's Bower, there are no fresh leaves or blossoms, only 'painted flowres' (II. xii. 58) and the plucked flowers upon which Acrasia lies. Belphoebe's presence in the poem shows us that Nature must be redeemed.

In mythic terms, Acrasia is Venus; and the knight wounded by concupiscence over whom she broods is Adonis.[2] The traditional link between Venus and Nature becomes explicit in the description of her Bower, while her lover, as his name *Verdant* suggests, is Spring, the god of vegetation (literally, Ver-dant, one who gives spring). His imprisonment symbolizes the sterility of life upon the order of nature, seen in the eternal summer of the Bower. By destroying the Bower, Guyon shatters that enshrouding nature, *natura naturata*, and releases the regenerative powers of nature, *natura naturans*, what Shakespeare calls 'great creating-Nature'. Since the cycle of the seasons may begin anew, the flight of Florimell immediately follows. Upon the cosmological level of Spenser's allegory, her flight signifies the natural cycle of the seasons. As her name indicates, she is the flower-maiden or Persephone. Accordingly, Spenser surrounds her with images of life, light, and beauty. Clad in 'garments . . . wrought of beaten gold', her golden locks 'in rich circlet . . . enrold', and crowned 'with golden wreath and gorgeous ornament' she appears as the sun dazzling all who look upon her.[3] She is also Beauty itself: 'the surest signe, whereby ye may her know, / Is, that she is the fairest wight aliue' (III. v. 5). And as 'the flowre of womens pride' (III. vii. 31), she is the feminine whose beauty first arouses love. When the knights leave the castle of Alma, first Guyon is overcome by woman's force in

[1] *Comus*, 761.
[2] Cf. Spenser's statement of the myth of Venus and Adonis in III. i. 34–38. Venus enshrouds the sleeping Adonis with her mantle 'colour'd like the starry skyes', as here Verdant is enshrouded by external nature. In each case the sleeping lover is laid in secret shade while the enchantress fixes him with her eyes. Verdant's state—his absorption into Nature—is mythically rendered in the account of Venus changing Adonis into a flower.
[3] III. i. 15, v. 5; vii. 11.

Britomart, and then with the startling vision of woman's beauty in the fleeting Florimell, they are plunged into the chaos of conflicting passions symbolized by the forest.

2

In Books III and IV (which I take to be a unit) Spenser describes the romantic world of lovers. He draws his matter from romance, especially Ariosto and Malory. But such matter could not provide him with the poetic structure which his continued allegory requires. When he announces at the beginning that 'fierce warres and faithfull loues shall moralize my song', he implies that the traditional themes of love and war will be resolved in his poem. For this reason he urges Cupid to 'lay now thy deadly Heben bow apart' and with Venus come to his aid: 'come both, and with you bring triumphant *Mart*, / In loues and gentle iollities arrayd, / After his murdrous spoiles and bloudy rage allayd.' Love and war are at strife not only in the classical heroic tradition, as we might expect, but also in the romances. In Ariosto Cupid and Venus reduce the hero to madness; in Malory adulterous love destroys the order of chivalry. Neither an episodic nor an organic treatment of earlier fiction could provide Spenser with the means of bringing the two themes into harmony. He was able to do so, and reduce the nightmare world of romance to the ordered dream of faery land by treating thematically two classical myths, Venus and Adonis, and Cupid and Psyche. They provide the pattern for the diverse action within the two books.

The two myths are definitively rendered in the Garden of Adonis. Within this 'first seminarie / Of all things' (III. vi. 30) the 'efficacie of Nature' (to use Sidney's term)[1] is expressed through the love between Venus and Adonis: 'she her selfe, when euer that she will, / Possesseth him, and of his sweetnesse takes her fill' (III. vi. 46). Only he is not 'dead' as Verdant is:

> All be he subiect to mortalitie,
> Yet is eterne in mutabilitie,
> And by succession made perpetuall,
> Transformed oft, and chaunged diuerslie:
> For him the Father of all formes they call;
> Therefore needs mote he liue, that liuing giues to all.
>
> (III. vi. 47)

[1] *Apol.*, p. 9.

He lives 'in eternall blis, / Ioying his goddesse, and of her enioyd.'
This myth is extended into the legend of Cupid and Psyche. Even
as Adonis enjoys his love, Psyche is restored to Cupid:

> And his true loue faire *Psyche* with him playes,
> Faire *Psyche* to him lately reconcyld,
> After long troubles and vnmeet vpbrayes,
> With which his mother *Venus* her reuyld,
> And eke himselfe her cruelly exyld:
> But now in stedfast loue and happy state
> She with him liues, and hath him borne a chyld,
> *Pleasure*, that doth both gods and men aggrate,
> *Pleasure*, the daughter of *Cupid* and *Psyche* late. (III. vi. 50)

What the former myth expresses upon the cosmic level, this
expresses upon the human or psychological: Psyche is herself the
pattern of 'true feminitee' who may teach Amoret 'all the lore of
loue, and goodly womanhead' (III. vi. 51).

This last line suggests Spenser's reading of the Cupid and
Psyche myth. 'However, in the outward bark and title thereof, it
appear painted with vanity', writes Marmion, 'yet is that but as
a light garment to cover more deep and weighty mysteries'.[1] It
was traditionally interpreted as an allegory of the human soul.
According to Boccaccio's anagogic reading, Psyche is the rational
soul which is separated from God through mortality, purified by
suffering, and restored to immortal glory. But the myth is capable
of many meanings: 'if we should wish to lay open this sublime
fiction to its precise meanings, it would certainly turn into a huge
book' ('si huius tam grandis fabulae ad unguem sensum enucleare
uoluerimus: in ingens profecto uolumen endaret').[2] Capella treats
the myth apocalyptically as the soul married to divine love; Fulgentius interprets it tropologically as the soul's fall into the state
of concupiscence; and there are any number of allegorical read-
ings.[3] Treatments of the myth range from the literal rendering of
the sensuous state of Psyche's marriage in Renaissance art, to its
religious rendering by Calderon in an *auto sacramentale*, and by
Joseph Beaumont in his *Psyche, or Love's Mystery in XXIV Cantos*:

---

[1] Ep. Ded. to 'The Legend of Cupid and Psyche', in *Minor Poets of the Caroline
Period*, ed. G. Saintsbury (Oxford, 1906), ii. 6.

[2] *De Genealogie Deorum Gentilium* (Venice, 1494), v. xxii (pp. 43^r, 43^v).

[3] Capella, *De Nuptiis Philologiae et Mercurii*, ed. Eyssenhardt (Leipzig, 1866), pp.
41–42; Fulgentius, *Mythologiarum*, ed. Helm (Leipzig, 1898), pp. 67–70; and see
Apuleius, *Opera*, ed. Hildebrand (Leipzig, 1842), pp. xxviii–xxxviii.

Displaying the Intercourse betwixt Christ and the Soul. Or quite differently, Chaucer treats Psyche's labours in his tale of the patient
Griselda, and Shakespeare treats her labours in more sophisticated
fashion in *All's Well* where Helena performs the miracles through
which she is finally translated, socially at least, to her husband's
'sphere'. A later treatment, and one close to Spenser's, is Hey-
wood's *Love's Mistress* in which the cosmological significances of
the myth are realized. Psyche is a Persephone figure: with her
fall the golden age is succeeded by the state of winter; she is
released from hell with Persephone; and both are translated to
heaven where Ceres holds her annual feast. We may expect Spenser
in his treatment of the myth to exploit this range of significance.
It is not surprising, of course, that he should be the first English
poet to render the myth.[1] Apuleius's Platonism would appeal
strongly to him. That from love 'spring all noble deeds and neuer
dying fame' (III. iii. 1) is his central faith, and it is the centre too
of his poem. Like Psyche, Arthur enjoys that brief vision of his
love which leads him to wander throughout the world:

> From that day forth I lou'd that face diuine;
> From that day forth I cast in carefull mind,
> To seeke her out with labour, and long tyne,
> And neuer vow to rest, till her I find. (I. ix. 15)

What appeals most strongly to Spenser's imagination is the quest
of the beautiful and virtuous woman seeking her lover, for

> Nought is there vnder heau'ns wide hollownesse,
> That moues more deare compassion of mind,
> Then beautie brought t'vnworthy wretchednesse
> Through enuies snares or fortunes freakes vnkind. (I. iii. 1)

Its poignancy is first realized in Una's search for her lover: 'for-
saken, wofull, solitarie mayd / Farre from all peoples prease, as
in exile, / In wildernesse and wastfull deserts strayd, / To seeke
her knight' (I. iii. 3). In Books III and IV Psyche's quest provides
a definitive myth for shaping the matter of romance. She is the
image of feminine virtue, and the pattern for the female knights.

The Adonis theme is expressed in the male knights, all of whom
are wounded. Timias's story renders the theme in erotic terms.
Since he forgoes woman's love for Arthur, he does not follow
Florimell, but pursues instead the lustful Foster. Like Adonis who

[1] D. C. Allen has demonstrated that the legend provides a key to the allegory of
Muiopotmos. See his article in *S.P.*, liii (1956), 141–58.

leaves Venus for the boar hunt, he is wounded in the left thigh
by the Foster's 'bore-speare':

> His locks, like faded leaues fallen to grownd,
> Knotted with bloud, in bounches rudely ran,
> And his sweete lips, on which before that stownd
> The bud of youth to blossome faire began,
> Spoild of their rosie red, were woxen pale and wan.
>
> (III. v. 29)

The imagery of these lines links him with the god of nature. Only
his 'sinfull wounds' (III. v. 35) are tended not by Venus—here is
Spenser's significant adaptation of the myth—but by the chaste
Belphoebe. She cures only to wound again through love, and will
not cure him by yielding the flower of her virginity. Similarly,
Marinell who is 'loues enimy' is wounded in the left side. Not the
boar, but woman's force in Britomart's enchanted lance inflicts
his wound; and he must languish until the end of Book IV where
he too is cured only to be wounded again by love. Like Adonis,
he was warned 'to forbeare / The bloudie battell' (III. iv. 24), but
all in vain; and like Venus, Cymoent comes to lament his death.
Arthur, the Witch's son, the Squire of Dames, the Fisherman,
Proteus, Malbecco, Paridell: they display in turn the diverse
pageants of love. Arthur's love for the Faery Queen; the Witch's
son who so lusts after Florimell that 'closely the wicked flame his
bowels brent, / And shortly grew into outrageous fire' (III. vii. 16);
and the Squire of Dames bound hand and foot by feminine lust
seen in the giantess Argante. When the Fisherman sees Florimell,
'the sight whereof in his congealed flesh, / Infixt such secret sting
of greedy lust' (III. viii. 25); Proteus seeks to win Florimell to his
liking; Malbecco is torn between Cupid and cupidity; Paridell
lusts after the wanton Hellenore. 'Wonder it is to see, in diuerse
minds', the poet exclaims, 'how diuersly loue doth his pageants
play, / And shewes his powre in variable kinds' (III. v. 1). The
wounding rises to a crescendo with the pageant of Cupid's wars
displayed in the house of Busyrane which shows all the world
wounded by his darts:

> to declare the mournfull Tragedyes,
> And spoiles, wherewith he all the ground did strow,
> More eath to number, with how many eyes
> High heauen beholds sad louers nightly theeueryes.
>
> (III. xi. 45)

His power is represented in Busyrane's power over Amoret; and once this power is destroyed by Britomart's chastity, the way is open in Book IV for the knights to be cured.

At the beginning of Book III, as a symbolic statement of the pageant of love, Spenser places the traditional story of Venus and Adonis. The tapestries in Castle Joyeous reveal all the stages of love, from Venus's 'bitter balefull stowre . . . when first her tender hart was with his beautie smit' (III. i. 34) until she changes him into a flower. The story serves to 'define' the nature of the women knights. Venus's love is seen in Malecasta, the 'sighes, and sobs, and plaints, and piteous griefe' (III. i. 53) which overcome her when she sees Britomart's beauty:

> Her fickle hart conceiued hasty fire,
> Like sparkes of fire, which fall in sclender flex,
> That shortly brent into extreme desire,
> And ransackt all her veines with passion entire.
>
> (III. i. 47)

Such 'in burning fire' and 'fleshly flame' (III. i. 53, 50) is the sin of concupiscence, that original sin which is manifest earlier in Guyon's enemies. In contrast, Britomart reveals herself as light: 'such was the beautie and the shining ray, / With which faire *Britomart* gaue light vnto the day' (III. i. 43). When she leaves the bed which Malecasta has defiled, she separates herself literally from lust. But not as Diana—Virgil's name for her—for she has been wounded by love, as she reveals in her 'hart-thrilling throbs and bitter stowre' (III. ii. 5) when she speaks of her love to the Red Cross Knight. Later we learn how her tender heart was smitten by the vision of Artegall's beauty in Venus's looking-glass. She is wounded by the sting that

> hath infixed faster hold
> Within my bleeding bowels, and so sore
> Now ranckleth in this same fraile fleshly mould,
> That all mine entrailes flow with poysnous gore,
> And th'vlcer groweth daily more and more.   (III. ii. 39)

Before she glances into the mirror, she did not lust after any 'for she was pure from blame of sinfull blot' (III. ii. 23)—Spenser's description of her love may point to menstruation—now through the wound of concupiscence she seeks Artegall's bed. In Malecasta she meets one similarly overpowered through a vision of a beautiful face, one who also seeks a stranger's bed. Only Malecasta's vision arouses lust which is offered to any stranger. The parallel only enforces the contrast between them. If we may return for a moment to relent our pace with Guyon before those two charming girls in the Bower, we see that their fault is not that they wish to be seen in their nakedness—for they are as beautiful as the morning star—but that they do not hide their nakedness 'from vew of any, which them eyde' (II. xii. 63). Though love forces Britomart to 'seeke an vnknowne Paramoure, / From the worlds end, through many a bitter stowre' (III. iii. 3), it is love for one stranger alone. Her awakening to find Malecasta beside her parallels the Red Cross Knight's sight of the false Una coming to his bed, and with the same holiness of affections that made him 'thought haue slaine her in his fierce despight', she sought 'to gride / The loathed leachour.'[1] Though she may be wounded in the side by Gardante—for her sight is wounded once she looks in Venus's looking-glass—with her power of chastity aided by Holiness she rejects Malecasta's passive lust, and with it the whole order of romantic love in Malecasta's knights. Castle Joyeous is Malory's Joyous Gard where Launcelot takes Guinevere, thereby destroying the Round Table. Romantic love as described by Malory ends either in adultery or the rejection of love when the lovers retire to the cloister. (The law of Castle Joyeous enforces adultery: the knight who successfully defends his lady gains Malecasta's love.) But Britomart, the female Arthur, seeks to establish a new order of the Round Table, an order of chivalry founded on chastity.

When Britomart leaves the castle to seek her unknown paramour whom she has seen in a vision, it becomes clear why Spenser extends the Venus-Adonis myth into the legend of Cupid and Psyche. Psyche, rather than Venus, is his pattern for woman. Underlying the whole poem, and central to the vision which it projects, is Arthur's vision of the Faery Queen, and the long search for 'that face diuine' through which he reveals himself as the image of a brave knight. His vision enters the poem through Britomart, through her vision of the knight whose 'manly face . . . lookt foorth, as *Phœbus* face out of the east' (III. ii. 24). In her long labours for her love, faithful always to the vision she has seen, she is Psyche.

[1] I. i. 50; III. i. 62.

So much the more her griefe, the more her toyle:
Yet neither toyle nor griefe she once did spare,
In seeking him, that should her paine assoyle.   (IV. v. 30)

At the mid-point of her journey, in her rescue of Amoret from the house of Busyrane, she enters Love's Palace, a room 'abounding with all precious store', and sees Cupid in his glory:

That wondrous sight faire *Britomart* amazed,
Ne seeing could her wonder satisfie,
But euermore and more vpon it gazed,
The whiles the passing brightnes her fraile sences dazed.

(III. xi. 49)

The symbol of Cupid under whom 'a wounded Dragon . . . did ly, / Whose hideous tayle his left foot did enfold' (III. xi. 48) is found in Apuleius where Psyche is brought to believe through her wicked sisters that Cupid is a serpent.[1] At night a very different Psyche awaits Cupid, one armed with the invincible power of chastity.

Britomart's role as Psyche is also treated indirectly through the fortunes of Belphoebe, Amoret, and Florimell. As the titular heroes are aspects of Arthur, these women are different revelations of this female Arthur's complex role in the allegory. Roughly speaking, Belphoebe represents the power of her chastity; Amoret's story embodies the fortunes of her love for Artegall; and Florimell symbolizes its cosmic significances. In terms of the legend of Psyche, Belphoebe represents her state before being sacrificed; Amoret shows her marriage and suffering through love; and Florimell expresses the labours which end in her deification.

Belphoebe's role is the simplest of the three. She lives in that state of innocence in which her fresh flowering virginity is proof against all human affection. In Apuleius Psyche is first worshipped as the chaste Venus born of the land: 'by fresh heavenly dew, the land, not the sea, budded to have brought forth another Venus gifted with the flower of virginity'.[2] Belphoebe is such a chaste

[1] The same symbol is treated psychologically in Book V where Britomart dreams that she is the goddess Isis and the Crocodile under her feet threatens to eat her until she subdues it.

[2] 'novo caelestium stillarum germine non maria, sed terras Venerem aliam, virginali flore praeditam, pullulasse' (Loeb ed., p. 186). Adlington in his translation adds: 'by a newe concourse and influence of the celestiall Planetes' (*The xi Bookes of the Golden Asse* [London, 1566], p. 43ᵛ), a phrase which may be reflected in Spenser's

Venus whose 'berth was of the wombe of Morning dew, / And her conception of the ioyous Prime', one who tenders so carefully her virginity, 'that dainty Rose, the daughter of her Morne' (III. v. 51; vi. 3). Her mother's immaculate conception shows that her birth is free from original sin. Such, too, is Britomart's state before she glances into Venus's mirror.

Belphoebe and Amoret together express the image of a virtuous woman:

> These two were twinnes, and twixt them two did share
> The heritage of all celestiall grace.
> That all the rest it seem'd they robbed bare
> Of bountie, and of beautie, and all vertues rare.   (III. vi. 4)

Belphoebe is trained 'in all chast vertue, and true bounti-hed / Till to her dew perfection she was ripened'; Amoret is trained 'in true feminitee . . . in all the lore of loue, and goodly womanhead' (III. vi. 3, 51). Together they are expressed in Britomart: that inviolability of her chaste virtue through which she overthrows all who attack her, and the true femininity which she reveals in her love for Artegall. Belphoebe in the strength of her chastity remains a huntress in the forest; Amoret through her chaste love remains helpless in the house of Busyrane; but Britomart makes that love the source of all virtuous deeds. She has what each lacks. Spenser's phrase 'virgine wife' (IV. i. 6) expresses her state exactly: wedded, in that she has vowed her love to one man, but still unbedded. It is a state of womanhood poised in perfection which also fascinated Shakespeare in Helena, Imogen, and Perdita. Yet the phrase expresses Britomart's dilemma, and it is this which the allegory of Books III and IV explores.

Amoret, too, is a Psyche figure. Upon her marriage she becomes the victim of womanly fears which lead to her being cursed by Cupid.[1] Unlike Psyche, however, who is finally rescued by Cupid, Amoret cannot be rescued by '*Cupids* man' (IV. x. 54). Neither force nor wisdom can release her from Busyrane's power:

account of Belphoebe's birth when 'the heauens so fauourable were and free, / Looking with myld aspect vpon the earth' (III. vi. 2).

[1] Spenser anticipates the Jungian interpretation offered by Erich Neumann, *Amor and Psyche, the Psychic Development of the Feminine, A Commentary on the Tale by Apuleius* (New York, 1956). Unlike the Renaissance interpreters, Neumann sees Psyche's original state with Cupid as fallen: 'a rapture of sexual sensuality which may fittingly be characterized as a being devoured by a demon, a monster' (p. 74).

> powre of hand, nor skill of learned brest,
> Ne worldly price cannot redeeme my deare,
> Out of her thraldome and continuall feare.   (III. xi. 16)

In his helplessness Scudamour prays to God to intervene: in answer Britomart enters. She urges 'if that heauenly grace some good reliefe / You send, submit you to high prouidence', and vows to deliver Amoret from prison, or die: 'life is not lost, (said she) for which is bought / Endlesse renowm, that more then death is to be sought' (III. xi. 14, 19). What she proposes, then, is to submit her body as ransom or sacrifice, even as Psyche was forced to do. This requirement to accomplish her quest distinguishes her from the earlier titular heroes. Through might aided by grace the Red Cross Knight slays the Dragon: we witness his 'rigorous might', and 'his late renewed might', until his sword 'ran through [the Dragon's] mouth with so importune might'[1] and in the closing and climactic words of the canto, Una praises him for 'so great a conquest by his might'. Guyon learns the limits of might, and only by 'bridling his will, and maistering his might' (II. xii. 53) does he pass through the Bower. He defeats Acrasia through wit, that is, 'wisedomes powre, and temperaunces might' (II. xii. 43). But neither might nor wit avails against the unquenchable fire which guards Busyrane's house:

> for neither may
> This fire be quencht by any wit or might,
> Ne yet by any meanes remou'd away,
> So mighty be th'enchauntments, which the same do stay.
>
> (III. xi. 23)

After Britomart submits her body to the flames, and endures the power of Night which brings the vision of Cupid, she finds Amoret sacrificed to Cupid's power. She receives the wound which Busyrane intends for Amoret:

> From her, to whom his fury first he ment,
> The wicked weapon rashly he did wrest,
> And turning to her selfe his fell intent,
> Vnwares it strooke into her snowie chest,
> That little drops empurpled her faire brest.   (III. xii. 33)

The wound is a token of her sharing love's suffering, for she too is wounded by love. She endures the charms which sought to

[1] I. xi. 16, 35, 53.

make Amoret yield, but without faltering. By submitting her body to Busyrane's enchantment, that is to Cupid's power, she frees love from love's palace:

> those goodly roomes, which erst
> She saw so rich and royally arayd,
> Now vanisht vtterly, and cleane subuerst
> She found, and all their glory quite decayd.

(III. xii. 42)

That moment was the beginning of Psyche's wanderings in search of her love; and in the 1590 version Spenser rounds out the legend by having Britomart restore Amoret to Scudamour.

> Lightly he clipt her twixt his armes twaine,
> And streightly did embrace her body bright,
> Her body, late the prison of sad paine,
> Now the sweet lodge of loue and deare delight:
> But she faire Lady ouercommen quight
> Of huge affection, did in pleasure melt.

The terms remind us of Psyche's restored state in which she has borne Cupid a child Pleasure.

The chief Psyche figure is Florimell. Her appearance at the beginning of Book III is explained by Boccaccio's statement that the rational soul is born of Apollo and Endelichia, or perfect age, because in the perfect age we truly begin to act from reason.[1] Florimell appears when the rational soul, Alma, has come of age: her enemies defeated, and both Guyon and Arthur are her guests. Psyche's birth brings her fall into the world stained by concupiscence, and when Florimell appears she is pursued by the lustful Foster. The significance of her flight is given by Arthur when he contrasts the golden age with the present iron one:

> Then beautie, which was made to represent
> The great Creatours owne resemblance bright,
> Vnto abuse of lawlesse lust was lent,
> And made the baite of bestiall delight:
> Then faire grew foule, and foule grew faire in sight,
> And that which wont to vanquish God and man,
> Was made the vassall of the victors might;
> Then did her glorious flowre wex dead and wan,
> Despisd and troden downe of all that ouerran.   (IV. viii. 32)

Florimell is that 'glorious flowre' whose bright beauty reflects

[1] *De Gen. Deor.*, p. 43.

God's image, but is abused now by lawless lust. The story of her
flight which ends with her imprisonment under the sea contains
the whole action of Books III and IV, and her release brings their
resolution. When 'faire grew foule, and foule grew faire in sight',
her place is taken by the snowy Florimell.[1] Like Psyche 'cruelly
exyld' by Cupid, Florimell endures her troubles for Marinell who
scorns her love. But as with Psyche, the gods intervene at last,
and she is translated to the company of the sea gods. Then no
longer 'did her glorious flowre wex dead and wan', but she is again
recognized as excelling all creatures in her beauty. At her appearance Marinell revives, even as Cupid is cured of his wound:

> As withered weed through cruell winters tine,
> That feeles the warmth of sunny beames reflection,
> Liftes vp his head, that did before decline
> And gins to spread his leafe before the faire sunshine.

> (IV. xii. 34)

For she is that Sun, Psyche, the daughter of Apollo, whose return
restores the golden age. Earlier in his poem we may say that
Spenser *uses* the Psyche legend. When Guyon, like Psyche,
descends to the garden of Proserpina he is tempted to eat and
rest, and upon leaving falls asleep. Psyche is rescued by Cupid
who relents her punishment through love, while Guyon is rescued
by the Angel. But such an Angel, Spenser tells us in rapturous
terms unique in Book II, 'of wondrous beautie, and of freshest
yeares', whose face 'diuinely shone', and whose wings were
'decked with diuerse plumes, like painted Iayes': 'like as *Cupido*
on *Idæan* hill, / When hauing laid his cruell bow away, / And
mortall arrowes . . .' (II. viii. 5, 6). By now, however, he has
rendered the Psyche legend his own, so entirely is it *there* within
his poem.

The story of Florimell is the most ambitious myth which
Spenser renders in his poem. The story is told for its own sake
while being the most explicitly didactic:

> what so my feeble Muse can frame,
> Shall be t'aduance thy goodly chastitee,
> And to enroll thy memorable name,
> In th'heart of euery honourable Dame,

---

[1] Northrop Frye relates Florimell to the myth of Proserpine in *Anatomy of Criticism* (Princeton, 1957), p. 138.

> That they thy vertuous deedes may imitate,
> And be partakers of thy endlesse fame. (III. viii. 43)

It has the strongest analogy to the myths of Psyche and Proserpina while being most original to Spenser. By contrast, in the story of Amoret bound to the brazen pillar, the repeated references to Britomart as the Virgin refer the reader obliquely to the myth of Andromeda. While the same myth is 'present' in Florimell being sacrificed to the sea, that oblique reference is not made. Spenser's allegorical technique reminds one most strongly of Shakespeare's method of portraying Perdita by surrounding her with images of flowers, life, and light, so that the central human figure becomes a matrix of meaning. Spenser's Florimell is most humanly rendered —the fearful woman in flight, her suffering at the hands of the fisherman, the sight of her 'blubbred face with teares of her faire eyes' (III. viii. 32), her distress at the sight of the sea god, the pure pathos of her lament in the dungeon with the revealing feminine accent of her appeal to Neptune:

> if ye deeme me death for louing one,
> That loues not me, then doe it not prolong,
> But let me die and end my daies attone,
> And let him liue vnlou'd, or loue him selfe alone.
>
> (IV. xii. 9)

At the same time Spenser surrounds her with images and associations which make her richly symbolic within his allegory. We have noticed how her name suggests the flower-maiden, Persephone, and that her description suggests the Sun. When Arthur wishes 'that Lady faire mote bee / His Faery Queene, for whome he did complaine : / Or that his Faery Queene were such, as shee' (III. iv. 54) she is linked with glory itself. His extremely compassionate remark to the Dwarf that he would rather know where Florimell was 'then ransome of the richest knight, / Or all the good that euer yet I gat' but that darkness 'fro me reft both life and light attone' (III. v. 7) links her with all goodness, even with life itself. That she was fostered by the graces upon Mount Acidale, the source of all life in the Garden of Adonis, links her with 'great creating-Nature'. It is within this context that we must understand her flight from the lustful Foster.

Our understanding of her cosmic significance is intensified during the progress of her flight. First she flees from Lust, the sin of concupiscence in the Foster. Her next enemy is the Witch's Monster: 'likest it to an *Hyena* was, / That feeds on womens flesh, as others feede on gras' (III. vii. 22). Spenser invokes classical mythology to indicate the significance of her plight:

> Not halfe so fast the wicked *Myrrha* fled
> From dread of her reuenging fathers hond:
> Nor halfe so fast to saue her maidenhed,
> Fled fearefull *Daphne* on th' *Ægæan* strond,
> As *Florimell* fled from that Monster yond,
> To reach the sea. (III. vii. 26)

The tearing and loss of her 'broken girdle' (III. viii. 2) is the loss of her maidenhead. Spenser's similes suggest this significance, but later it is spelled out when we learn that this girdle while tied about the loins preserves chastity:

> That girdle gaue the vertue of chast loue,
> And wiuehood true, to all that did it beare;
> But whosoeuer contrarie doth proue,
> Might not the same about her middle weare,
> But it would loose, or else a sunder teare. (IV. v. 3)

(The interpretation is later repeated: 'vnlesse that she were continent and chast, / . . . it would lose or breake' [v. iii. 28].) This loss of maidenhead is dramatically expressed in the Monster feeding upon her milk-white Palfrey: the monster which feeds upon woman's flesh feeds upon her horse, which is her body according to traditional Renaissance symbolism. Like Maleger, this monster cannot be wounded. When Satyrane engages it,

> Full many wounds in his corrupted flesh
> He did engraue, and muchell bloud did spend,
> Yet might not do him dye, but aye more fresh
> And fierce he still appeard, the more he did him thresh.
>
> (III. vii. 32)

The link with Maleger suggests the sin of concupiscence which the monster symbolizes. As such, the significance of the encounter remains upon that level explored in Book II. But the pressure of myth is so intense at this point that the romantic narrative is broken by a striking simile which carries the significance of the action into the cosmological terms explored in Books III and IV. Satyrane holds the Monster

As he that striues to stop a suddein flood,
  And in strong banckes his violence enclose,
  Forceth it swell aboue his wonted mood,
  And largely ouerflow the fruitfull plaine,
  That all the countrey seemes to be a Maine,
  And the rich furrowes flote, all quite fordonne:
  The wofull husbandman doth lowd complaine,
  To see his whole yeares labour lost so soone,
For which to God he made so many an idle boone.

(III. vii. 34)

'So him he held, and did through might amate', Spenser continues; but on the romantic level, the simile is meaningless. While Satyrane holds the monster, the one who seeks to hold the flood only forces the water to overflow the land. Upon the level of allegory, however, the simile illuminates what follows: in Proteus's rape of Florimell we see the sudden flood overwhelm the fruitful plain, 'that all the countrey seemes to be a Maine'.

The Ovidian metamorphosis, suggested in the references to Myrrha and Daphne, prepares for that greater metamorphosis when Florimell commits herself to the sea. She escapes on the boat with the sleeping Fisherman, and the apparently innocent line that she was driven to great distress 'and taught the carefull Mariner to play' (III. viii. 20) leads into an elaborate erotic allegory. She calls him father—which links the episode with the Myrrha simile—and urges him to 'guide the cock-bote well' which he is well prepared to do now that the sight of her beauty 'infixt such secret sting of greedy lust, / That the drie withered stocke it gan refresh' (III. viii. 25). At the end when he throws her down, her gay garments become foully arrayed with the scales of fish: in this we see the beginning of her metamorphosis. Earlier Spenser speaks of Fortune which 'did heape on her new waues of weary wretchednesse' (III. viii. 20), and this cliché is extended into the description of her floating on the water. 'And with the tide droue forward careleslie' (III. viii. 21) is the first expression of her yielding to the sea; and when heaven does not answer her prayers she calls upon the sea: 'and the wide sea importuned long space / With shrilling shriekes' (29) which answers in the form of Proteus. The appearance of the Old Man of the Sea, 'an aged sire with head all frory hore, / And sprinckled frost vpon his deawy beard', overcomes her inwardly:

> For her faint heart was with the frozen cold
> Benumbd so inly, that her wits nigh fayld,
> And all her senses with abashment quite were quayld.
>
> (III. viii. 34)

This inward change precedes the embrace through which she is overcome by age, winter, and the sea:

> Her vp betwixt his rugged hands he reard,
> And with his frory lips full softly kist,
> Whiles the cold ysickles from his rough beard,
> Dropped adowne vpon her yuorie brest. (35)

The cliché at the beginning is then literally realized: new waves of wretchedness are heaped upon her, and she falls to the bottom of the sea.

This myth of the fall of Florimell provides an enveloping structure of myth for the action of Books III and IV. Her appearance plunges the knights in a chaos of conflicting emotions; her disappearance occasions the creation of the false Florimell who reduces the knights and their ladies to discord; and only after chastity and concord are once more established, is she redeemed from the power of the sea. Her marriage to Marinell brings that cosmic harmony which prepares for the great heroic theme of Book V. Spring returns to the earth, and the flowering of England, to be seen in her victories over the Church of Rome, heralds the coming of the Apocalypse.

3

Within this surrounding myth, the Temple of Venus is the focus towards which the action moves, and from which the action begins. Here we see nature, art, and human nature in its perfected state. Nature and art are one:

> For all that nature by her mother wit
> Could frame in earth, and forme of substance base,
> Was there, and all that nature did omit,
> Art playing second natures part, supplyed it. (IV. x. 21)

When Scudamour enters the Island which contains the Temple, he enters Paradise: 'in such luxurious plentie of all pleasure, / It seem'd a second paradise to ghesse, / So lauishly enricht with natures threasure', where lovers enjoy 'endlesse happinesse':

'being free from feare and gealosye, / Might frankely there their
loues desire possesse.'[1] It is this state which the Bower of Bliss
parodies, that false paradise which is

> goodly beautifide
> With all the ornaments of *Floraes* pride,
> Wherewith her mother Art, as halfe in scorne
> Of niggard Nature, like a pompous bride
> Did decke her, and too lauishly adorne,
> When forth from virgin bowre she comes in th'early morne.
>
> (II. xii. 50)

Nature niggarded by art; Art as mother, and not nature, beautify-
ing the earth to entrap man; the pompous Bride decked by art in
scorn of nature: these are the symbols which Guyon destroys so
that out of the chaos, they may be redeemed. They appear in their
perfection in that vision which Scudamour gains of Amoret
'shyning with beauties light, and heauenly vertues grace' (IV. x.
52), whom he may claim as his bride. The gap between Guyon's
vision in the Bower and Scudamour's vision in the Temple is the
subject of Books III and IV.

But the harmony achieved here is also the source of all the
discord treated in the two books. When Scudamour through his
manhood boldly claims the shield of love and passes into the
inner Temple, he hears one sing a paean of praise to 'great *Venus*,
Queene of beautie and of grace', to whose sight all nature responds
with joy:

> Then doth the dædale earth throw forth to thee
> Out of her fruitfull lap aboundant flowres,
> And then all liuing wights, soone as they see
> The spring breake forth out of his lusty bowres,
> They all doe learne to play the Paramours;
> First doe the merry birds, thy pretty pages
> Priuily pricked with thy lustfull powres,
> Chirpe loud to thee out of their leauy cages,
> And thee their mother call to coole their kindly rages.
>
> Then doe the saluage beasts begin to play
> Their pleasant friskes, and loath their wonted food;
> The Lyons rore, the Tygres loudly bray,
> The raging Buls rebellow through the wood,
> And breaking forth, dare tempt the deepest flood,

[1] IV. x. 23, 28.

To come where thou doest draw them with desire
So all things else, that nourish vitall blood,
Soone as with fury thou doest them inspire,
In generation seeke to quench their inward fire.

(IV. X. 45–46)

This paean of praise is dramatically realized in the action of the two books. When Scudamour claims Amoret, Womanhood blames him for seeking to take Venus's maid; but when he sees Venus herself 'with amiable grace / To laugh at me, and fauour my pretence' (IV. x. 56) he becomes more bold and leads Amoret away despite all her attempts to woo her freedom. This is the moment when, at the sight of Venus, love enters the world. The 'amiable grace' with which she laughs upon Scudamour's act is the 'smyling looke' which makes the 'heauens laugh, and al the world shews ioyous cheare' (IV. x. 44). His seizing Amoret is that moment when love enters the world. Yet his act is a rape through which Amoret is bound. In narrative terms, Amoret is later raped by Busyrane and imprisoned in his dungeon; but on the level of the allegory this is the consequence of the present moment when Womanhood is left 'astonisht staring' (IV. x. 56), quelled by shame and terror at Scudamour's seizing Amoret against her will. It is the shield of love which Scudamour gains through his manhood which forces Womanhood to yield. Until this moment Cupid's love was absent from the Temple. Not Cupid, but 'a flocke of litle loues' fly about the Idol of Venus, that is, Amoretta whom Venus in her search accepts in place of Cupid. Now the state of 'goodly womanhead' which Amoret embodies is overcome, leaving her bound by iron bands to a brazen pillar in the house of Busyrane. There she appears with 'deathes owne image figurd in her face', her breast naked,

And a wide wound therein (O ruefull sight)
Entrenched deepe with knife accursed keene,
Yet freshly bleeding forth her fainting spright,
(The worke of cruell hand) was to be seene,
That dyde in sanguine red her skin all snowy cleene.

(III. xii. 20)

Her lover cannot save her because he is the cause of her imprisonment. When he wields his shield to assail the flames about Busyrane's house, he only increases their fierceness, for it is just the assertion of his manhood which has bound Amoret, and produces the flames, her womanly fears, which prevent the consummation of their marriage.

This moment when Venus's love enters the world is also dramatically realized at the beginning of Book III. In the song of praise to Venus we are told that when all living creatures see 'the spring breake forth out of his lusty bowres', then 'all doe learne to play the Paramours'. After Verdant breaks out of the lusty Bower of Bliss, there follows at the beginning of Book III that appearance of Florimell through which all the knights follow 'beauties chace' and seek 'Ladies Loue', that is, they 'all doe learne to play the Paramours'. It is at this point, as we have noted already, that the virgin Alma now feels '*Cupides* wanton rage'. When Nature is inspired by Venus, 'the Lyons rore, the Tygres loudly bray, / The raging Buls rebellow through the wood': and this is the setting in which the knights see Florimell:

> a forrest wyde,
> Whose hideous horror and sad trembling sound
> Full griesly seem'd: Therein they long did ryde,
> Yet tract of liuing creatures none they found,
> Saue Beares, Lions, and Buls, which romed them around.
>
> (III. i. 14)

The whole action of Books III and IV is carefully placed within Nature aroused by Venus.

But the entrance of love is again the moment of its bondage. We have noticed earlier that Guyon's victory over Acrasia is the victory of masculine reason over the affections which are traditionally feminine. To translate this into the terms of Book III, we may say that the binding of Acrasia binds Amoret; or in less paradoxical terms, binding Venus binds Venus's maid. (I do not find that Spenser uses the traditional concept of the two Venuses, any more than he allows that love and lust differ in their cause however much they do in their effects. There is only one Venus whose Idol is revealed in the Temple; and there is only one Cupid though he may wield or lay aside his bow. Venus appears according to man's inner condition: to the intemperate she appears as the lustful Acrasia; to married lovers she appears as that hermaphroditic union of male and female; to the royal Britomart she appears as Isis with Osyris beneath her feet.) The overall movement of the allegory in the two books is to free Venus, to free love so that it may become 'the root of all that ioyous is' (IV. x. 47), the source of all virtuous deeds.

4

We are in a position now to consider more generally the relation of Spenser's treatment of mythology to the structure of Books III and IV.

Book III displays the wounds of love. The emblem of its action is given in the story of Venus's love for Adonis which is portrayed on the walls of Castle Joyeous: 'the bitter balefull stowre' when she sees his beauty:

> And whilst he slept, she ouer him would spred
> Her mantle, colour'd like the starry skyes,
> And her soft arme lay vnderneath his hed,
> And with ambrosiall kisses bathe his eyes;
> And whilest he bath'd, with her two crafty spyes,
> She secretly would search each daintie lim,
> And throw into the well sweet Rosemaryes,
> And fragrant violets, and Pances trim,
> And euer with sweet Nectar she did sprinkle him.

(III. i. 36)

This is that vision which Guyon sees of Acrasia: the starry mantle here signifies the order of nature which blankets man in the Bower. The agony of Venus's passion when his beauty is destroyed contrasts with that smiling triumphant Venus who is lauded in her Temple: they are the two poles of the action in the two books. The lovers in Castle Joyeous which is walled with beds,

> Some for vntimely ease, some for delight,
> As pleased them to vse, that vse it might:
> And all was full of Damzels, and of Squires,
> Dauncing and reueling both day and night,
> And swimming deepe in sensuall desires,
> And *Cupid* still emongst them kindled lustfull fires

(III. i. 39)

parodies that final state of lovers' bliss which Scudamour sees in the Temple. The difference between the two states is rendered precisely in the absence here of the word 'joy'.

With the rape of Florimell, Book III gathers into diverse images of concupiscence. First, the witch's Monster whose corrupted flesh Satyrane cannot wound, one who becomes only more fresh through strife. After this monster who feeds on woman's flesh, comes Argante who, 'not content so fowly to deuoure / Her natiue flesh' by committing incest with her brother in the womb,

> Did wallow in all other fleshly myre,
> And suffred beasts her body to deflowre:
> So whot she burned in that lustfull fyre,
> Yet all that might not slake her sensuall desyre.
>
> (III. vii. 49)

From the cosmic treatment of the great mother Venus in the previous canto we descend to this monstrous earthly Venus. Spenser's treatment of her is, accordingly, broadly comic. As Shakespeare's Venus handles Adonis, 'couragiously to plucke him from his horse', this Venus man-handles the Squire of Dames, 'out of his wauering seat him pluckt perforse, / Perforse him pluckt, vnable to withstand' (III. vii. 43). Like Venus who retires into a secret shade to reap her pleasure of Adonis, this monster

>   ouer all the countrey she did raunge,
> To seeke young men, to quench her flaming thrust,
> And feed her fancy with delightfull chaunge:
> Whom so she fittest finds to serue her lust,
> Through her maine strength, in which she most doth trust,
> She with her brings into a secret Ile,
> Where in eternall bondage dye he must,
> Or be the vassall of her pleasures vile,
> And in all shamefull sort him selfe with her defile.   (III. vii. 50)

The third image of concupiscence is the witch's False Florimell, created out of snow to seem like Florimell, 'and in the stead / Of life, she put a Spright to rule the carkasse dead' (III. viii. 7). The dead carcass is the body of Florimell's horse, her body, which we next see benumbed with the frozen cold from Proteus's embrace, and the wicked Spright

>   yfraught with fawning guile,
> And faire resemblance aboue all the rest,
> Which with the Prince of Darknesse fell somewhile,
> From heauens blisse   (III. viii. 8)

Milton rightly made the source for his figure, Sin. Here is the true image of concupiscence. That first figure of Lust, the Foster, may be slain by Timias; the witch's Monster may be bound by the girdle of chaste virtue though he later escapes; Argante must flee from the chaste Palladine; but the false Florimell triumphs over all. She is the Duessa figure who seems to be what she is not; and in the coy titillation which makes her lover 'thinke him selfe in heauen, that was in hell', and in her constant change, she most mocks that true state of lovers seen in the Temple of Venus. The final image of concupiscence is seen in Malbecco and Hellenore.[1] In their story we see how love may transform both lover and beloved into beasts: Malbecco's jealous love transforms him into a fowl with crooked claws, Hellenore's adulterous love transforms her body into the antithesis of the chaste body, a female Grill content to serve beasts.

All these woundings through love gather into a climactic series of visions which show Cupid's victory over love. That victory is emblematically described in Ovidian mythological terms in the account of Cupid's wars against the gods and all mankind which is woven in the arras of Busyrane's house. It is symbolically represented in medieval allegorical terms in Cupid's masque which shows Amoret, true love itself, pierced by Cupid's dart. Finally it is dramatically realized in Spenser's own invention of Amoret bound by iron bands to the brazen pillar, while that enchanter hovers over her seeking to gain her love through his incantations. Here we see what Amoret has become, as later we learn what she once was. Here the house with the idol of Cupid at the centre; there the temple with the idol of Venus at the centre. Here the girdle of flames, the cruelty of Cupid's wars, the pageant of wounded love, and at the centre Amoret bound: there the encircling paradise, the lovers' endless happiness, the pageant of true lovers, and at the centre the bevy of damsels in a round with Amoret at the centre upon the lap of Womanhood. One who was placed in the world 'to be th'ensample of true loue alone, / And Lodestarre of all chaste affectione' is here sacrificed. When Britomart submits her chaste body as a sacrifice, love is freed from all bondage:

[1] I do not include such secondary images of concupiscence, such as Malbecco's sight of Trompart 'yclad in garments light, / Discolour'd like to womanish disguise' (III. x. 21) whom he takes for his lady. In the anatomy of perversion given in the two books, I assume that the reference is to homosexuality or perhaps to transvestism.

The cruell steele, which thrild her dying hart,
  Fell softly forth, as of his owne accord,
  And the wyde wound, which lately did dispart
  Her bleeding brest, and riuen bowels gor'd,
  Was closed vp, as it had not bene bor'd,
  And euery part to safety full sound,
  As she were neuer hurt, was soone restor'd:
  Tho when she felt her selfe to be vnbound,
And perfect hole, prostrate she fell vnto the ground.

(III. xii. 38)

With the curing of Love's wounds, all the woundings through
love may be cured. At the beginning of Book III Britomart entertains Malecasta through their common wound of love, but rejects
her from the bed which, through her lust, she defiles. Now at the
beginning of Book IV, as a defining 'statement' of its theme, we
see Britomart enter a Castle with a similar custom where she gains
Amoret for her love. When Amoret comes to her bed, she 'found
right safe assurance theare' (IV. i. 15).

The theme of Book IV is the contest between Amoret and Ate.
Love, 'most sacred fire . . . ykindled first aboue, / Emongst
th'eternall spheres and lamping sky, / And thence pourd into
men' (III. iii. 1) opposes Ate, 'firebrand of hell first tynd in
Phlegeton, / By thousand furies, and from thence out throwen /
Into this world, to worke confusion' (IV. ii. 1). Ate seeks to preserve that state of chaos to which the sword of temperance reduces
nature, art, and human nature; while out of that chaos love seeks
to create a new order which will redeem them.

Of the twin passions, grief and wrath, revealed as the 'foes
of life' in Book II, the grief of wounded lovers is displayed in
Book III. Book IV treats lovers' wrath: the false friends quarrelling
over the false Florimell, the brothers' battle for Canacee, the
knights' wrath at the tournament in Martian field, the ladies'
wrath at the tournament for beauty's prize, Scudamour's jealous
wrath, and Artegall's rage against Britomart. Though the two
tournaments are designed to establish order and degree, as
Scudamour explains,

    And of them all she that is fayrest found,
    Shall haue that golden girdle for reward,
    And of those Knights who is most stout on ground,
    Shall to that fairest Ladie be prefard. (IV. ii. 27)

they end in the greatest discord. Mars's tournament is won by a woman knight. In Venus's tournament the fairest is found to be the False Florimell who is awarded the golden girdle, but cannot wear it. Nor can any of the ladies: all remain 'vngirt vnblest', lowering in shame while their knights laugh in scorn. Though the fairest lady should prefer the stoutest knight, the False Flori-mell chooses Braggadocchio: 'which when they all beheld they chaft and rag'd, / And woxe nigh mad for very harts despight, / That from reuenge their willes they scarse asswag'd' (IV. v. 27).

When the jealous Scudamour and the angry Artegall together plan 'to wreake their wrathes on *Britomart*' (IV. vi. 8), Ate would seem to have won. But when Britomart enters 'soft ryding towards them'—how carefully Spenser chooses that term *soft* to contrast the knights' violent wrath!—love wins. In their plighted troth is the first promise of that concord which through their posterity will bear fruit in Elizabeth's reign. Neither triumphs over the other: but love triumphs over both when each yields to the vision of the other's face. Through their reconciliation, Mars and Venus, man-hood and womanhood, reason and the affections, are at last coming into accord. In Book II they are opposed, as Phaedria, Acrasia's servant, declares:

> *Mars* is *Cupidoes* frend,
> And is for *Venus* loues renowmed more,
> Then all his wars and spoiles, the which he did of yore.
>
> (II. vi. 35)

In the climactic vision of the Bower, we see how Verdant in the service of Venus leaves the service of Mars. His warlike arms hang idly upon a tree. When Spenser came to treat 'louers deare debate' in Books III and IV, his premise is that from love 'spring all noble deeds and neuer dying fame' (III. iii. 1), that 'loue does alwayes bring forth bounteous deeds, / And in each gentle hart desire of honour breeds' (III. i. 49). (That *all* and *alwayes*, italicized through their stress, are said almost defiantly.) But in Book III the knights who are wounded by love are unable to act virtuously. The only male knight who triumphs without himself being mortally wounded is Braggadocchio who defeats the Witch's son! Well he deserves the False Florimell, as the only undefeated male knight in Faeryland. But in Book IV we begin to understand how love

of honor and all vertue is
The roote, and brings forth glorious flowres of fame,
That crowne true louers with immortall blis,
The meed of them that loue, and do not liue amisse.

(iv, Pr. 2)

It is seen first in the heroic battle of the three brothers whose love
unites their spirits in one; and then in the exemplum of friendship
of Cambell and Cambina, Triamond and Canacee where 'vertue is
the band, that bindeth harts most sure' (iv. ii. 29). It is seen again
in the union of Britomart and Artegall. Love which is the source
of her bounteous deeds, now sustains him.

Yet at this moment Amoret is again seized and bound, this time
by Lust who imprisons her in his cave. Again Scudamour is left
helpless, and Britomart vows to restore her to him. It seems that
the entire cycle of action will be repeated. (The reason why she
is raped at this moment becomes clear, as we shall see later, in
Book V where the lovers' dear debate extends into a marriage
debate. In general terms we understand here that with the plight-
ing of marriage in which womanhood submits to manhood,
Amoret is again bound as before at her marriage to Scudamour.)
Amoret's story develops into an elaborately erotic allegory. There
is the broad comedy of her horror when she sees Lust masturbat-
ing, 'spredding ouer all the flore alone, / Gan dight him selfe vnto
his wonted sinne' (iv. vii. 20)—the true image of Lust in action—
and her flight:

> Which when as fearefull *Amoret* perceiued,
> She staid not the vtmost end thereof to try,
> But like a ghastly Gelt, whose wits are reaued,
> Ran forth in hast with hideous outcry . . .
> Full fast she flies, and farre afore him goes,
> Ne feeles the thorns and thickets pricke her tender toes.

(iv. vii. 21)

The bawdy significance of the second line, and the delightful
comedy of the last, are typical of Spenser's humour in these books.
Like Æmylia she remains 'vntouched'—the word has its erotic
significance as in Braggadocchio's monstrous complaint when
Belphoebe flees before his advances: 'what foule blot / Is this to
knight, that Ladie should againe / Depart to woods vntoucht'
(ii. iii. 43)—until she is caught again by Lust and confronted by
Timias. At the beginning of his adventure Timias follows the

Foster rather than Florimell, that is he seeks lust rather than love. When he is wounded by concupiscence—the Foster's boar-spear pierces his left thigh—Belphoebe finds him by pursuing the chase of a wild beast

> which with her arrowes keene
> She wounded had, the same along did trace
> By tract of bloud, which she had freshly seene,
> To haue besprinckled all the grassy greene.   (III. v. 28)

The beast she has wounded is Timias who has overcome Lust but is himself wounded. His wound may be cured only by 'devouring' her virginity, which she refuses him. When he comes upon Amoret overcome by Lust, her body is used as the shield to bear the power of his strokes:

> Which subtill sleight did him encumber much,
> And made him oft, when he would strike, forbeare;
> For hardly could he come the carle to touch,
> But that he her must hurt, or hazard neare:
> Yet he his hand so carefully did beare,
> That at the last he did himselfe attaine,
> And therein left the pike head of his speare.
> A streame of coleblacke bloud thence gusht amaine,
> That all her silken garments did with bloud bestaine.
>
> (IV. vii. 27)

With Amoret wounded, Lust overcomes Timias so that 'scarse the Squire his hand could once vpreare'. For readers of Shakespeare's bawdy, the allegory does not need translating. Nor should it be translated, for as an erotic allegory it provides sophisticated pleasure rather than crude laughter. In realistic terms, Belphoebe's anger when she finds the Squire 'handling soft the hurts, which she did get. / For of that Carle she sorely bruz'd had beene, / Als of his owne rash hand one wound was to be seene' (IV. vii. 35), would be reduced to jealousy that her sister would grant her suitor a cure for his concupiscence which she denied him. In its own terms as an allegory of sexual intercourse, it is surely unique in English poetry.

Within the allegory we see Belphoebe through the power of her virginity slay Lust, and then threaten to slay the lustful pair with the same arrow. Timias lapses into the state of brutishness when he retires into a cabin—his long hair is the symbol of his

state of lust—and after he is forgiven, remains within the forest.
He displays the pageant of love which Spenser describes in

> The baser wit, whose idle thoughts alway
> Are wont to cleaue vnto the lowly clay,
> It stirreth vp to sensuall desire,
> And in lewd slouth to wast his carelesse day.

(III. v. 1)

By contrast, the brave spirit such as Arthur never suffers 'vncomely idlenesse, / In his free thought to build her sluggish nest'
(Timias's forsaking Arthur for a life of idleness in the forest), nor
suffers 'thought of vngentlenesse, / Euer to creepe into his noble
brest' (his rape of Amoret). The contrast does not, of course,
prevent our seeing Timias as Arthur's romantic self.

   In the episodes which show how Amoret is restored from her
present fallen state, I find the images blurred. In their conception
we may understand how grace must intervene in three areas of
love and friendship. Once Amoret is separated from the protection
of Britomart's chastity and Belphoebe's virgin power, only Arthur
may guard her from Sclaunder until she is united to Scudamour.
He must slay Corflambo, the lust in the heart, before love may
flourish in the heart. Then he may achieve the concord of married
love by joining Pœana and Placidas. Finally, only the power of
grace may resolve that discord in love and war aroused among the
knights by the tournaments. All the diverse pageants of love in
Books III and IV are represented in the grand battle in which
Britomart and Scudamour oppose the combined forces of Druon
or single life, Claribell or intemperate love, Blandamour or
changeable love, and Paridell who lusts after all. These kinds of
love have been seen respectively in Marinell and Belphoebe,
Timias and Amoret, the Squire of Dames and Claribell, Paridell
and Pœana. They have been symbolically expressed in the Foster
or intemperate love, Lust or changeable love—he devours a
woman a day—and Corflambo who lusts after all. Such discord
cannot be resolved by might, but only by Arthur's presence. At
the close of the ninth canto, if the concluding stanzas to the 1590
edition belong here as they would seem to, Arthur restores
Amoret to Scudamour. All this prepares for the grand series of
resolutions in the three closing cantos of Book IV.

   Yet some shadow seems to have fallen over this pattern. When
Spenser can write such a line as 'that she vneath discerned, whether

whether weare' (IV. ix. 10) something has gone wrong. The restoration of love to Timias in his reconciliation with Belphoebe remains pure narrative. Corflambo is superbly drawn, and one sees in him a Maleger figure whom grace must slay. But to me there is confusing ambiguity in his blow which strikes Arthur's shield with such force

> that hard vnto his crowne
> The shield it droue, and did the couering reare,
> Therewith both Squire and dwarfe did tomble downe
> Vnto the earth, and lay long while in senselesse swowne.

(IV. viii. 42)

Do these lines mean that the blow knocked the Squire and dwarf off Arthur's horse? or that the blow tears the covering of Arthur's shield, as earlier Orgoglio's blow loosed the covering of the shield? The meaning may be unravelled only later when we see Corflambo tumble down, as the Squire and dwarf do here. I suspect that the episode remains complicated, rather than complex. The actual execution is less interesting than the conception behind it. The story of Amyas and Placidas where Spenser claims a moral to be 'approued plaine' certainly does not turn out that way. An explanation for this failure, if it is one and not in my reading, may be that the pattern of the book calls for a climactic resolution rather than a central allegorical core to which episodes before may converge and out of which succeeding episodes arise. Or it may be that the final cantos themselves where Spenser achieves one of the greatest triumphs of his allegory cast a shadow on what comes before. Or the explanation may be technical. The triumphant concluding stanzas of the 1590 edition which describe the hermaphroditic union of Scudamour and Amoret belong as the climax to the story of Amoret, and so placed at the end of Canto IX would precede the image of the hermaphroditic Venus. But the stanzas do not belong once Spenser had planned Book VI where Amoret's story is extended into Serena's.

Scudamour's gaining of Amoret in the Temple of Venus is both the triumph of love and the triumph over love. The characteristic motion of Spenser's allegory is a moving ever inward, penetrating ever more deeply until we achieve some vision of perfection at the centre. This motion determines the kind of reading which I have tried to follow in this study. It is not a narrative movement in which we leave one part for another, but one towards a centre

which unifies the whole. It is characteristic also of Dante where
the pilgrim at the centre of the *Inferno* bears the whole weight of
the descending circles, and where his later ascent brings a vision
of the whole climb below. In this episode Scudamour overcomes
the knights on the plain before the Castle, and passes the perils of
the bridge to come to an island. The island is paradise, where
lovers 'being free from feare and gealosye, / Might frankely there
their loues desire possesse' (IV. x. 28). Within the island he comes
to the temple whose 'goodly workmanship' (29) shows the
triumph of art, and passes from the porch with its vision of Concord flanked by Love and Hate to the inmost temple with its
hundred pillars, the hundred altars with the hundred cauldrons
'to bath in ioy and amorous desire' (38) each with a damsel as a
priest, and 'right in the midst the Goddesse selfe did stand' (39).
At her feet he sees a bevy of damsels in a round, and in the centre
of all, Amoret.

> Thus sate they all a round in seemely rate:
>   And in the midst of them a goodly mayd,
>   Euen in the lap of *Womanhood* there sate,
>   The which was all in lilly white arayd,
>   With siluer streames amongst the linnen stray'd;
>   Like to the Morne, when first her shyning face
>   Hath to the gloomy world it selfe bewray'd,
>   That same was fayrest *Amoret* in place,
> Shyning with beauties light, and heauenly vertues grace.
>
> (IV. x. 52)

(The curious reader will find that this inward motion is carefully
patterned in groups of four stanzas: 4–7, introduction; 8–11, the
plain before the bridge; 12–15, Doubt and Delay at the first gate;
16–19, Danger at the second gate; 21–24, the description of the
island; 25–28, the lovers; 32–35, the allegory of Love and Hate;
39–43, the Idol of Venus; 44–47, the address to Venus; 49–52, the
bevy of maidens; 55–58, the actual rape of Amoret.) At the centre
is a vision which is seen in its concrete reality; and if Womanhood
is an abstraction, Amoret is real enough, the timid virgin who fears
her lover's boldness. If her name suggests Love, it does not turn
us to some particular love, as when we see Boethius's vision of
Philosophy as the love of Wisdom; but Love itself seen as a
woman. The vision first communicates itself, and he is a barren
reader indeed who cannot win through with Scudamour to

contemplate that vision for its own sake. But only for the moment: action must follow, or the lover would become like Verdant, hypnotized by his vision.

Scudamour triumphs over love, and Amoret becomes his 'spoile' (IV. x. 3, 55, 58). His actions are patterned after Britomart's when she invades the house of Busyrane. Over the door which she must go through, she reads the injunction '*be bold*':

> she oft and oft it ouer-red,
> Yet could not find what sence it figured:
> But what so were therein or writ or ment,
> She was no whit thereby discouraged
> From prosecuting of her first intent,
> But forward with bold steps into the next roome went.
>
> (III. xi. 50)

But she had already obeyed when she boldly drew her weapon to divide the flames, and now she goes through that door 'with bold steps'. Within, she again confronts the God's mysterious injunction:

> she did behold,
> How ouer that same dore was likewise writ,
> *Be bold, be bold*, and euery where *Be bold*,
> That much she muz'd, yet could not construe it
> By any ridling skill, or commune wit.
> At last she spyde at that roomes vpper end,
> Another yron dore, on which was writ,
> *Be not too bold*; whereto though she did bend
> Her earnest mind, yet wist not what it might intend.
>
> (III. xi. 54)

But this injunction, '*be not too bold*', she does not obey. When that iron door opens, 'in went / Bold *Britomart* . . . neither of idle shewes [Cupid's mask], nor of false charmes [the inscriptions] aghast' (III. xii. 29). For her too great boldness she is wounded by Busyrane, but frees love from his enchantments. When Scudamour invades the Temple of Venus he obeys the injunction of his manhood, '*be bold*'. He explains to the company of knights how 'I boldly thought (so young mens thoughts are bold)' (IV. x. 4) to conquer sweet love, and how he 'boldly' encounters the knights defending the shield (10), and passes through dangers that made other bold knights become cowards (18). But when he attempts to seize Amoret, Womanhood rebukes him 'for being ouer bold'

(IV. x. 54). But this injunction, *be not too bold*, like Britomart, he does not obey. Through Venus's consent, he becomes 'emboldned with more confidence', and leads the reluctant Amoret from the Temple. However much his later grief exceeds the glory of his present conquest, he gains 'that glorious spoyle of beautie' (58) for his own. And however much his freeing Amoret binds her womanhood, through Britomart's chaste power, Belphoebe's virgin power, and Arthur's grace, she will be restored to his sight.

After Scudamour tells his story of how he 'by the lilly hand her labour'd vp to reare' (53), he compares his perils to those of Orpheus who 'did recoure / His Leman from the Stygian Princes boure' (58). The reference mocks the story, for, like Orpheus, he did not recover his beloved but through his over-boldness brings her imprisonment. But the reference also prepares for the climactic episode where we see Florimell in her Stygian bower, imprisoned within the body of the Dragon, that rocky dungeon walled

> with waues, which rag'd and ror'd
> As they the cliffe in peeces would haue cleft;
> Besides ten thousand monsters foule abhor'd
> Did waite about it, gaping griesly all begor'd.
>
> (IV. xi. 3)

This sea must be tamed before she can be recovered. But more than a lover's power, though aided by all human virtue, is needed to make the sea relent. The power of this sea is described at the beginning of Britomart's adventures, when she sits upon the rocky shore and laments her plight:

> Huge sea of sorrow, and tempestuous griefe,
>   Wherein my feeble barke is tossed long,
>   Far from the hoped hauen of reliefe,
>   Why do thy cruell billowes beat so strong,
>   And thy moyst mountaines each on others throng,
>   Threatning to swallow vp my fearefull life?
>   O do thy cruell wrath and spightfull wrong
>   At length allay, and stint thy stormy strife,
> Which in these troubled bowels raignes, and rageth rife.
>
> For else my feeble vessell crazd, and crackt
>   Through thy strong buffets and outrageous blowes,
>   Cannot endure, but needs it must be wrackt
>   On the rough rocks, or on the sandy shallowes,
>   The whiles that loue it steres, and fortune rowes;

> Loue my lewd Pilot hath a restlesse mind
> And fortune Boteswaine no assuraunce knowes,
> But saile withouten starres gainst tide and wind:
> How can they other do, sith both are bold and blind?
>
> (III. iv. 8–9)

The sea is both within and without: her 'bleeding bowels' (III. ii. 39) through the wound of love and the sea's 'troubled bowels'; and the chaos within her expresses the chaos of fallen nature in which she now begins to seek her lover. The sea of sorrow upon which she sees her feeble bark being tossed is literally rendered in the story of Florimell when she jumps into the boat and drifts with the tide, her 'lewd Pilot' being that 'old leachour' who tries to rape her, until she is imprisoned below the waves. Florimell echoes her lament when she complains that the 'greedy seas doe in the spoile of life delight' (IV. xii. 6). Britomart's first act is to wound Marinell who represents the power of the sea which extends to the land in his Rich Strond. (He is the son of a sea-nymph and a knight.) This is the occasion of Florimell's flight which brings her imprisonment under the sea. Once the sea conquers the land, there seems no escape from the 'huge sea of sorrow' against which Britomart complains. She ends her lament with a prayer to Neptune that he will calm the waters. The power which can calm the seas is Venus

> That with thy smyling looke doest pacifie
> The raging seas, and makst the stormes to flie;
> Thee goddesse, thee the winds, the clouds doe feare,
> And when thou spredst thy mantle forth on hie,
> The waters play and pleasant lands appeare,
> And heauens laugh, and al the world shews ioyous cheare.
>
> (IV. x. 44)

At the marriage of the Thames and the Medway, all the seas' posterity gather for the bridal feast. In the Garden of Adonis Spenser recounts 'the endlesse progenie / Of all the weedes' (III. vi. 30) in the birth of life: now he counts 'the seas abundant progeny' (IV. xii. 1) in marriage. In these two vast pageants we see that power behind nature on land and sea, that creative power of love which sustains and restores all life. Together they prepare for the union of the sea and land in the marriage of Marinell and Florimell. He is the sea which overwhelms her:

Yet loe the seas I see by often beating,
Doe pearce the rockes, and hardest marble weares;
But his hard rocky hart for no entreating
Will yeeld, but when my piteous plaints he heares,
Is hardned more with my aboundant teares.   (IV. xii. 7)

When her love wounds him to the death, and his mother is forced
to yield him to his fate, Apollo reveals that he is afflicted by love
'that leads each liuing kind' (25). Here is the final affirmation of
Venus's power. When Florimell is released from the sea's dungeon
by the power of Neptune to which Britomart appeals, and appears
in all her beauty, we see '*Venus* of the fomy sea' (IV. xii. 2) emerg-
ing from the calm waters. Like Psyche, she is the new Venus born
of the land, that daughter of Apollo through whose power she is
released to restore Marinell to life; but a greater Psyche whose
marriage to Marinell brings the concord of land and sea, all Nature
reduced to the harmony of love.

V

This Antique Image

I could never thinke the study of *Wisdome* confin'd only
to the Philosopher: or of *Piety* to the *Divine*: or of *State* to
the *Politicke*. But that he which can faine a *Common-wealth*
(which is the *Poet*) can governe it with *Counsels*, strengthen
it with *Lawes*, correct it with *Iudgements*, informe it with
Religion, and *Morals*; is all these.   JONSON

I

SPENSER'S fiction seems to break down in Book V. Probably for
this reason the book is the least popular. C. S. Lewis finds part of
its unpopularity in our changed concept of Justice;[1] yet Spenser
forms all his virtues according 'to the antique vse':

> For that which all men then did vertue call,
> Is now cald vice; and that which vice was hight,
> Is now hight vertue, and so vs'd of all.   (v, Pr. 4)

Surely it is that we are here more aware of the virtue itself than
in the other books. When Spenser introduces an episode with the
remark that 'so much as to my lot here lights, / That with this
present treatise doth agree, / True vertue to aduance, shall here
recounted bee' (v. iii. 3) his didacticism takes over the fiction.
Professor Lewis considers Artegall to be one of the most disagreeable characters in the whole poem,[2] and most readers would
agree with him. I know that it does not make him less disagreeable
to remind ourselves of Spenser's special problem with him; but
for the first time among his titular heroes, the virtue must be
separate from the man. In the Proem Spenser declares that he will
treat the Queen's great justice whose instrument is Artegall.
Justice must be impersonal. While the Red Cross Knight learns
to frame his life in holiness, Guyon displays temperance, Britomart's chastity is her self, and Calidore's courtesy is as natural to
him as breathing, Artegall must stand apart from the virtue which

[1] *The Allegory of Love*, p. 347.   [2] Ibid., p. 348.

he administers. Though he wields the sword of justice, he may use it only once in the book, and that is in his final battle against Grantorto. (Earlier he chops off Pollente's head with the sword, but he has already won the battle through physical encounter.) Talus is his executive power—and with the poet's stubborn literalness, this becomes simple execution—while he stands aside. When he confronts the women who attack Terpine, he draws back:

> Yet though him selfe did shame on womankinde
> His mighty hand to shend, he *Talus* sent
> To wrecke on them their follies hardyment. (v. iv. 24)

The true gentleman! one may want to interject; yet no judge should serve as his own hangman. Further, the virtue of justice itself imposes limitations upon the amount of sympathy which the titular hero may generate. For this reason many readers would find the most disagreeable character in Shakespeare to be Henry V.

Moreover, the theme of justice commits the poet to the fallen world. All its action is circumscribed by the starry heavens which are described in the Proem. While Book II is also committed to the order of nature, its *psychomachia* throws up subliminal images which always appeal. Justice treats most directly the iron world of what must be, rather than that ideal world of what should be. Characters and events in the poem are almost too close to our world, almost appearing at times like actors who have dropped their roles and speak in their own persons. Florimell, who evokes the most profound poetic meanings in the earlier books, appears as an embarrassed young lady when Braggadocchio prefers another before herself.[1] The noble Britomart who has overwhelmed all who look upon her with awe and dread of her royal presence, throws herself upon a bed when she learns of Artegall's imprisonment, and weeps 'like as a wayward childe'. Clarinda, the deceitful maid whose love for Artegall 'boyld / Her inward brest, and in her entrayles fryde' (v. v. 53) could not appear earlier in the poem; her confusion when Radigund questions her, 'so soone / As she her face had wypt, to fresh her blood' (45) could not happen earlier. There is the 'realism' of Britomart's battle against Radigund, the first battle in the poem in which both contestants are caught in wild fury:

[1] v. iii. 16.

> Their dainty parts, which nature had created
> So faire and tender, without staine or spot,
> For other vses, then they them translated;
> Which they now hackt and hewd, as if such vse they hated.

(v. vii. 29)

Such a cat-fight! Spenser rightly compares them to a lioness and a tigress fighting over a beast (Artegall!) whom the lioness (Britomart) claims because she got it first.

Even when we allow the nature of the theme, however, there is a general thinness in the matter. For example, the opening canto which has always been such a complex allegory of the unfolding argument is here, in thirty stanzas, a poor imitation of the judgement of Solomon. Sanglier and the Squire each claims the lady as his own, and accuses the other of murdering the beheaded lady. Artegall decides that

> this doubtfull causes right
> Can hardly but by Sacrament be tride,
> Or else by ordele, or by blooddy fight.

(v. i. 25)

Or else by asking the lady herself, the reader wants to add. But Artegall knows that the lady might not tell the truth, and so frustrate the working of justice. He decides to divide the lady equally between them, and whoever dissents from his judgement shall be forced to carry the dead lady's head. Again the reader wants to interject that all this is monstrously unjust to the lady herself, and that though the Squire is the one who dissents, it is Sanglier who is punished. And is it just that one who committed such a brutal murder of an innocent woman should get off so lightly? But Artegall is not concerned with the dead lady. When Sanglier rode off, she 'rather of his hand besought to die', and got what she wanted; and it is a magnificent gesture with which he 'at one stroke cropt off her head with scorne' (v. i. 18). Neither is he trying to discover who murdered the lady, nor is he concerned with discovering to whom the living lady rightfully belongs. Rather he wants to assert the lore of justice by discovering which knight is worthy to have the living lady, and which the dead. When the Squire dissents, he decides: 'thine I deeme / The liuing Lady, which from thee he reaued: / For worthy thou of her doest rightly seeme' (v. i. 28). And Sanglier is forced to

carry the dead lady's head, not because he is a murderer, but
because he lightly esteems love:

> And you, Sir Knight, that loue so light esteeme,
> As that ye would for little leaue the same,
> Take here your owne, that doth you best beseeme,
> And with it beare the burden of defame. (v. i. 28)

At the end 'much did that Squire Sir *Artegall* adore, / For his
great iustice.' Rightly so; yet it is the justice we adore, not the
image of a just man. The fiction itself here fails Spenser.

Throughout Book V the reader is aware of fact pressing down
upon the fiction.[1] There is the pressure of contemporary events in
Canto IX, the trial of Duessa in Mercilla's palace which renders
Mary Queen of Scots' trial before Elizabeth. James VI was rightly
offended at the slander of his dead mother. Anyone who has
exposed himself to other contemporary records of the trial will
admire the delicacy and tact with which Spenser treats Elizabeth's
conduct, but not the excellence of the poetry. The pageant of
prosecutors reads like a good imitation of Spenser, but not much
more than that. The poet is more true to himself earlier when he
chooses to praise Britomart's warlike power rather than Elizabeth's wisdom. There is the pressure of historical fact again in
Canto VIII, where Arthur's defeat of the Souldan in his iron
chariot renders England's defeat of the Spanish Armada. One
effect of this pressure may be shown by comparing two similar
stanzas. When Arthur and the Souldan meet in battle,

> Thus goe they both together to their geare,
>   With like fierce minds, but meanings different:
>   For the proud Souldan with presumpteous cheare,
>   And countenance sublime and insolent,
>   Sought onely slaughter and auengement:
>   But the braue Prince for honour and for right,
>   Gainst tortious powre and lawlesse regiment,
>   In the behalfe of wronged weake did fight:
> More in his causes truth he trusted then in might.
>
> (v. viii. 30)

Earlier in the poem there is that similar stanza which describes
the Red Cross Knight and Sansjoy meeting in battle:

---

[1] The historical allegory is treated in the *Var. Spenser, Book V*, pp. 299–335.

> The Sarazin was stout, and wondrous strong,
>> And heaped blowes like yron hammers great:
>> For after bloud and vengeance he did long.
>> The knight was fiers, and full of youthly heat:
>> And doubled strokes, like dreaded thunders threat:
>> For all for prayse and honour he did fight.
>> Both stricken strike, and beaten both do beat,
>> That from their shields forth flyeth firie light,
> And helmets hewen deepe, shew marks of eithers might.
>
> (I. v. 7)

This earlier stanza is an elaborate dance, the pattern of the first three lines being repeated in order in the next three, until it is finely locked in the seventh line. The reader extends this pattern of movement into the whole episode when he sees the Red Cross Knight becoming at the end what he fights against. But with the later stanza there is only the moral pose. There is no conflict to be realized in the action. It is true that fact is transmuted in the conception of the episode. The Tyrant's chariot 'with yron wheeles and hookes arm'd dreadfully . . . drawne of cruell steedes, which he had fed / With flesh of men' (v. viii. 28) turns the Armada into an image of the burning sun. We see the contrast between 'the infants sunlike shield' (41) and the Tyrant as Phaeton in his fall, 'as when the firie-mouthed steeds, which drew / The Sunnes bright wayne to *Phaetons* decay' (40). But the conception never becomes an allegory of action. Talus is present 'to th'end / He should his flale to finall execution bend' (29): but he does not act because 'slaughter and auengement' which seem to belong to his iron flail belong rather to the Souldan's 'yron wheeles and hookes'. The image of that enemy who cannot be wounded is truly terrifying, but his battle against Arthur is not translated into action. For the first time Arthur lifts the veil from his shield; and he does so not because the act is inevitable within the allegory, but because England defeated the Armada not by might but through God's deliberate intervention on her behalf.

More obviously, there is the pressure of fact in the climactic episodes, Arthur's defence of Belge and Artegall's freeing Irena, where there is little more than an allegory of contemporary events. Fact is not transmuted, sometimes hardly translated, and its thread may be traced throughout. Spenser relies upon his earlier invention. Gerioneo, the threefold giant, is another Orgoglio. Arthur's battle with Gerioneo's Dragon imitates the Red Cross Knight's battle with Error. While the imitation is appropriate since the Dragon is the Inquisition, which meant wandering in a labyrinth of doubt and theological error, it remains ingenious. One effect is that the complexity of the allegory is reduced to one level of meaning. In Canto XI where Artegall succours Burbon from the peasants who oppress him and restores the lady Flourdelis to him, this allegory of contemporary events in France becomes a treatise against temporizing in matters of faith. The emphasis upon the knight's shield which must not be thrown away, no matter how battered, irritated me to the point of counting thirteen repetitions of the word 'shield' in one canto. No wonder it is battered. Earlier when Arthur throws away his shield in order to defeat Maleger through physical force, we are not meant to interpret his action as temporizing with his faith. Here, despite Artegall's lecturing Burbon upon not losing his shield:

> That is the greatest shame and foulest scorne,
> Which vnto any knight behappen may
> To loose the badge, that should his deedes display,
>
> (v. xi. 52)

Spenser does not exploit the irony of his defeating Grantorto only when 'loosing soone his shield, did it forgoe' (v. xii. 22) and while the Giant is encumbered with it, strikes off his head. Since he does exploit that earlier moment when Artegall lectures Terpine for running 'so fondly far astray, / As for to lead your selfe vnto your owne decay' (v. iv. 26) by submitting to Radigund's power, only to lead himself to the same decay, here the allegorical reference impoverishes the fiction.

In Book V Spenser subjects his fiction to very great strain, perhaps the kind of strain which no heroic poem should meet. His model was Virgil who, in his *Georgics*, expresses his patriotic ambition to sing the triumphs of Augustus; following him, Spenser proposes, in the October eclogue of the *Calender*, to sing of Elizabeth and her knights. Yet while the *Aeneid* fulfils Virgil's ambitions only very obliquely,[1] Spenser treats the triumphs of Elizabeth directly in Book V. With Spenser as his model, Milton may have learned that the poet's abilities to sing 'the deeds and triumphs of just and pious Nations doing valiantly through faith against the enemies of Christ, to deplore the general relapses of

[1] See E. M. W. Tillyard, *The English Epic and its Background* (London, 1954), p. 70.

Kingdoms and States from justice and Gods true worship', should be written in 'the cool element of prose' where the poet writes with his left hand.[1] In the body of his writings there is that sharp division between the heroic poem which treats divine matters and the prose which treats his patriotic ambitions. Yet if the task of writing a patriotic heroic poem was ever possible, and should have been attempted, it was in the 1580's when God's Will seemed to guide England, making her His instrument to overthrow Antichrist. 'Methinks I see in my mind a noble and puissant Nation rousing herself like a strong man after sleep, and shaking her invincible locks: Methinks I see her as an Eagle muing her mighty youth, and kindling her undazl'd eyes at the full midday beam; purging and unscaling her long abused sight at the fountain it self of heav'nly radiance': how much more strongly Milton's apocalyptic faith in England could be held in Spenser's time. To celebrate the triumphs of Elizabeth would be to celebrate the ways of God to England. Yet the task was peculiarly not Spenser's. Always he avoids the deliberate assault, the playing out of his powers. It is characteristic of him that he places the climax of the whole poem in the second twelve books which treat the political virtues in King Arthur. Here, presumably, we should see Elizabeth's glory mingle with the glory of Christ's second coming. Instead he writes of Prince Arthur; and yet not of Arthur directly but of the twelve knights who are phases of him. Further, when he writes of the Red Cross Knight's adventure, it is not that final pilgrimage to the heavenly City but his serving Una by slaying the Dragon. But even this adventure is only preliminary to his serving the Fairy Queen. At the end he goes back to the Queen 'her to serue six yeares in warlike wize, / Gainst that proud Paynim king, that workes her teene' (I. xii. 18). When Spenser describes his battle against the Dragon, he appeals to the muse not to come with that mighty rage which inspires the great heroes:

> Faire Goddesse lay that furious fit aside,
> 　Till I of warres and bloudy *Mars* do sing,
> 　And Briton fields with Sarazin bloud bedyde,
> 　Twixt that great faery Queene and Paynim king,
> 　That with their horrour heauen and earth did ring,
> 　A worke of labour long, and endlesse prayse:

---

[1] *Reason of Church Government*, in *Columbia Milton*, iii. 235, 238.

> But now a while let downe that haughtie string,
> And to my tunes thy second tenor rayse,
> That I this man of God his godly armes may blaze.

(I. xi. 7)

Similarly, the story of Britomart's love for Artegall prepares for that time when she will bring him back to Britain 'strongly to aide his countrey, to withstand / The powre of forrein Paynims, which inuade thy land' (III. iii. 27). The whole poem is a Prelude, the Growth of a Hero's Mind, except here in Book V where Spenser anticipates his final patriotic theme.

That delicate balance in allegory between the extrinsic meaning which relates the poem to our world and the intrinsic meaning which relates it to its own, is seriously disturbed in Book V. But if we, as readers, focus upon the world of fact we will only tilt that balance further. Instead, I shall focus upon the fiction, to see how the poet shapes his matter into that 'antique Image' which is his poem.

Britomart's vision in the Temple of Isis is the allegorical core of Book V, both the focus and radiating centre for its action. Here the theme of justice gives way to the relation of mercy to justice which, through Britomart's vision, is revealed in her relation to Artegall. Earlier the poem treats of Justice which Artegall administers by Talus's iron flail. We have noticed that moment when he sits apart and sends Talus against Radigund's women 'to wrecke on them their follies hardyment: / Who with few sowces of his yron flale, / Dispersed all their troupe incontinent' (V. iv. 24). Now Spenser treats of Equity in Isis which 'restraines those sterne behests, and cruell doomes' (V. vii. 22) of Osiris. Immediately after this episode we have that corresponding moment when Britomart engages Radigund's forces. Now when Talus begins 'a piteous slaughter', he is restrained by Britomart:

> And now by this the noble Conqueresse
>   Her selfe came in, her glory to partake;
>   Where though reuengefull vow she did professe,
>   Yet when she saw the heapes, which he did make,
>   Of slaughtred carkasses, her heart did quake
>   For very ruth, which did it almost riue,
>   That she his fury willed him to slake:
>   For else he sure had left not one aliue,
> But all in his reuenge of spirite would depriue.   (V. vii. 36)

That clemency or mercy administers justice is emblematically expressed in the episode of Mercilla's Palace where the Queen is flanked by Artegall and Arthur. Arthur's tender heart is so impassioned for Duessa 'that for great ruth his courage gan relent' (v. ix. 46); Artegall 'with constant firme intent, / For zeale of Iustice was against her bent' (49); while Mercilla unites both:

> But she, whose Princely breast was touched nere
> With piteous ruth of her so wretched plight,
> Though plaine she saw by all, that she did heare,
> That she of death was guiltie found by right,
> Yet would not let iust vengeance on her light;
> But rather let in stead thereof to fall
> Few perling drops from her faire lampes of light.
>
> (v. ix. 50)

Besides the perling drops, the rough axe must also fall, for mercy never departs from justice. Mercy is the greater power and art, Spenser explains, because it preserves not only the right but also the subject:

> So much more then is that of powre and art,
> That seekes to saue the subiect of her skill,
> Yet neuer doth from doome of right depart:
> As it is greater prayse to saue, then spill,
> And better to reforme, then to cut off the ill.   (v. x. 2)

Accordingly, in the climactic episodes Spenser does not focus upon the triumphs of Elizabeth's reign, but through them to the triumph of mercy which fulfils justice. Arthur slays Gerioneo and his Monster in order to release Belge's people who 'gan shout aloud, that vnto heauen it rong; / And all the damzels of that towne in ray, / Came dauncing forth, and ioyous carrols song' (v. xi. 34). (We may contrast this moment with that earlier occasion when Artegall slays the Giant only to have the people become a mutinous crowd which must be dispersed with Talus's flail.) When Artegall restores Burbon to Flourdelis, Talus drives the rascal rout into the sea until he 'commaunded him from slaughter to recoyle' (v. xi. 65). In his final adventure he does not seek vengeance against Grantorto but rather goes to save Irena. When Talus scatters Grantorto's forces, '*Artegall* him seeing so to rage, / Willd him to stay, and signe of truce did make' (v. xii. 8); and after he slays Grantorto, there is no 'piteous slaughter', but instead his efforts 'to reforme that ragged common-weale' (v. xii. 26).

Historical fact is translated, at least in part, into a moral theme, the relation of justice to mercy.

This thematic structure which is expressed symbolically in the statue of Isis is embodied in the relation of Britomart to Artegall. In a vision Britomart sees herself transfigured into Isis wearing her scarlet robe and crown of gold. While she enjoys her state, a tempest fans the flames about the altar causing her great perplexity, until the Crocodile under her feet awakes and devours both the flame and tempest. It threatens to eat her until she beats it back with her rod; but when it seeks her love, she accepts and gives birth to a lion. This vision is interpreted by the heavenly-inspired priest as a prophecy of her future:

> For that same Crocodile doth represent
> The righteous Knight, that is thy faithfull louer,
> Like to *Osyris* in all iust endeuer.
> For that same Crocodile *Osyris* is,
> That vnder *Isis* feete doth sleepe for euer:
> To shew that clemence oft in things amis,
> Restraines those sterne behests, and cruell doomes of his.

> That Knight shall all the troublous stormes asswage,
> And raging flames, that many foes shall reare,
> To hinder thee from the iust heritage
> Of thy sires Crowne, and from thy countrey deare.
> Then shalt thou take him to thy loued fere,
> And ioyne in equall portion of thy realme.
> And afterwards a sonne to him shalt beare,
> That Lion-like shall shew his powre extreame.
> So blesse thee God, and giue thee ioyance of thy dreame.
>
> (v. vii. 22–23)

It points forward to that time which Merlin has foretold when she will bring him 'firmely bound with faithfull band, / To this his natiue soyle' (III. iii. 27); it points to the present in which the sleeping crocodile represents Artegall 'forlorne in womens thraldome' (v. vii. 21); but also, more significantly, it points to the past. Britomart's love for Artegall which is given here in psychological terms has been rendered previously in the story of Amoret. Her great perplexity when the tempest kindles the outrageous flames which threaten to destroy the temple has been seen in her dismay before the flames which surround the house of Busyrane, that house in which a stormy whirlwind closes the iron door that imprisons Amoret. The tempest which comes from below (v. vii. 14) is the power of Artegall to arouse in Britomart love's 'cruell flame' (III. ii. 52). But though love's 'deepe wound more deepe engord her hart' (III. iv. 6), Merlin taught her not to dismay 'the hard begin, that meets thee in the dore, / And with sharpe fits thy tender hart oppresseth sore' (III. iii. 21). Consequently through the power of her chastity she enters the door of Cupid's Palace and endures the fantasies which imprison Amoret:

> an hideous storme of winde arose,
> With dreadfull thunder and lightning atwixt,
> And an earth-quake, as if it streight would lose
> The worlds foundations from his centre fixt;
> A direfull stench of smoke and sulphure mixt
> Ensewd, whose noyance fild the fearefull sted,
> From the fourth houre of night vntill the sixt;
> Yet the bold *Britonesse* was nought ydred,
> Though much emmou'd, but stedfast still perseuered.
>
> (III. xii. 2)

In terms of the later vision, her chaste love 'devours' the flames and tempest. In the next stage of her love Britomart fights Artegall; in the end they plight their troth, and she submits to him. At this moment we learn that Amoret is raped by Lust who threatens to eat her. This encounter is clearly reproduced in psychological terms in Britomart's vision of the crocodile swollen with pride of its own power, threatening to eat her.[1] Her vision of herself as the goddess beating the crocodile back with her rod is rendered dramatically in Belphoebe, who slays Lust with her arrow. The consummation of her love in the vision points to the future, and so is not rendered in Amoret's story, but it fulfils even such a precise detail as the crocodile's wreathed tail enfolding Isis's middle.

From this vision it becomes clear that Spenser is treating the relation between the sexes, that problem of 'maisterie' which forms the unifying subject of the marriage group in Chaucer's *Canterbury Tales*. The 'louers deare debate' of Books III and IV expands into a marriage debate in Book V, and it is resolved in the central episodes which treat of Radigund. This debate becomes

---

[1] See A. S. P. Woodhouse's perceptive comments on the vision as a 'wonderful piece of dream psychology and symbolic art', in *E.L.H.* xvi (1949), p. 216.

Spenser's chief means for rendering Book V as part of his 'antique Image'.

The debate opens at the beginning of Book III when Britomart defeats Malecasta's knights who try to force the Red Cross Knight to forgo his love for Una. 'Truth is strong, and true loue most of might', she declares,

> Ne may loue be compeld by maisterie;
> For soone as maisterie comes, sweet loue anone
> Taketh his nimble wings, and soone away is gone. (III. i. 25)

These lines are Spenser's closest imitation of Chaucer, in fact they seem drawn from memory of a close reading:

> Love wol nat been constreyned by maistrye.
> Whan maistrie comth, the God of Love anon
> Beteth his wynges, and farewel, he is gon![1]

(Chaucer's source is probably Apuleius's legend: when Psyche sought the 'maisterie', the God of Love flew from her; and Spenser certainly would recognize this source.) That love may not be compelled by 'maisterie' is repeated by Arthur at the end of Book IV when he ends the discord among the knights who attack Britomart and Scudamour. They admonish her for beguiling them of their love, that is, Amoret; she replies that her love had been left to her own liking; and Arthur concludes:

> Certes sir Knight, ye seemen much to blame,
> To rip vp wrong, that battell once had tried;
> Wherein the honor both of Armes ye shame,
> And eke the loue of Ladies foule defame;
> To whom the world this franchise euer yeelded,
> That of their loues choise they might freedom clame,
> And in that right should by all knights be shielded:
> Gainst which me seemes this war ye wrongfully haue wielded.
>
> (IV. ix. 37)

His words resolve the discord among the knights, and prepare for the story of its beginning. There follows immediately Scudamour's conquest of 'sweet loue' (IV. x. 3) which brings Womanhood's rebuke for his 'vnseemely shame' and Amoret's plea for her freedom:

---

[1] *The Franklin's Tale*, 764–6.

> She often prayd, and often me besought,
> Sometime with tender teares to let her goe,
> Sometime with witching smyles : but yet for nought,
> That euer she to me could say or doe,
> Could she her wished freedome fro me wooe.   (IV. x. 57)

Once he leads her into marriage, she becomes bound in the house of Busyrane : 'for soone as maisterie comes, sweet loue anone / Taketh his nimble wings, and soone away is gone.' This rape of Amoret is the occasion of the two books, and manifests in human terms, as we have seen, Britomart's relation to Artegall.

In her first vision of her lover Britomart loses the 'maisterie'. Upon seeing his portly person, his 'honorable gest', and his crest,

> Thenceforth the feather in her loftie crest,
> Ruffed of loue, gan lowly to auaile,
> And her proud portance, and her princely gest,
> With which she earst tryumphed, now did quaile.
>
> (III. ii. 27)

In the first stage of her adventure to bring him bound back to Britain, she must free sweet love, Amoret, from the womanly fears of masculine 'maisterie' by which she is bound. In the next stage, at the beginning of Book IV, she cherishes the love which before had led her to despair. In the tournament she conquers Artegall's manhood, but thereby arouses the wrath which leads to the climactic battle between them. Her spear—the power of her chastity—unseats him from his horse, but his return blow which wounds her horse's hind parts forces her to fight on foot without the spear. The wound represents the wound of concupiscence, her love for Artegall through which she must fight without her enchanted spear. There is a similar sexual significance in her stroke that 'shew'd all his bodie bare vnto the cruell dent' (IV. vi. 15). His own counter-blow defeats him by bringing the vision of her face whose beauty awakens love. When she fails to return the blow but grants him a truce, the vision of his face overcomes her. It may seem at first that Artegall has yielded her the 'maisterie' in humbly bowing before her, seeking her pardon. Only she has not forced him to yield : he yields of his own accord, through his own blow. Moreover, he does not yield to her, but to woman's beauty; or more exactly, he yields to his own will which has been overcome by woman's beauty. (His moral state at the moment is not much better than Verdant's; only her chastity 'his ranging fancie did refraine, / And looser thoughts to lawfull bounds withdraw' [IV. vi. 33].) He does not submit to Britomart's will, but retains the 'maisterie' to himself. Britomart, on the other hand, has already yielded the 'maisterie' to him, earlier and now again when she cannot strike that blow which will make him yield to her. The violence of the battle expresses that rape of her love, Amoret, by Lust, that brutal masculine power. His passion which 'grew more fierce and faine, / Like to a stubborne steede whom strong hand would restraine' (IV. vi. 33) when he woos her only to be restrained by her chaste presence is shown, upon the psychological level of woman's fantasies, in that battle in which Lust causes Amoret to be wounded by Timias but later is slain by Belphoebe's virgin power.

That masculine power which refuses to yield the 'maisterie' is shown in cosmic terms in Marinell's stubborn refusal to submit to woman's love, even though he must yield to woman's force in Britomart's enchanted spear. Psychologically, his state is expressed in his obedience to his mother. Upon the natural level, he expresses the power of the sea: that chaotic element in nature into which Britomart plunges in her search for Artegall, the brute force of nature which imprisons the creative powers of the land expressed in Florimell. Once Marinell yields to love, and land and sea are joined in the harmony of marriage, the way is open for Britomart and Artegall to establish the true harmony of marriage in the fallen world.

Since Artegall submits to woman's beauty and power of his own will, his meeting Britomart is a fall. When Spenser writes in the argument to the canto that Artegall 'doth fall in loue', he means just that. Consequently, when he meets woman's beauty and power again in Radigund, he is ready to submit to her. Her conditions for the battle between them,

> That if I vanquishe him, he shall obay
> My law, and euer to my lore be bound,
> And so will I, if me he vanquish may;
> What euer he shall like to doe or say.   (v. iv. 49)

pose the problem of 'maisterie', one sex claiming to dominate the other. By yielding to her conditions Artegall begins to yield to her. Her words to the messengers, 'and bid him eate' (v. iv. 49), suggest Eve's temptation; and his accepting them

> Which he accepting well, as he could weete,
> Them fairely entertaynd with curt'sies meete,
> And gaue them gifts and things of deare delight,
>
> (v. iv. 51)

is a prelude to his fall. There is the same sexual wounding as before: his blow shears her armour 'that halfe her side it selfe did naked show', while her return blow 'glauncing downe his thigh, the purple bloud forth drew' (v. v. 9). (His wound is no more than a token, such as that given Britomart by Gardante and later by Busyrane; otherwise he would be totally overcome by concupiscence, like Timias.) Though he defeats her in battle, the sight of woman's beauty overwhelms his manhood as it did before. Before his sword had fallen from his fingers of its own accord: now he deliberately throws it away. Helpless before her renewed onslaught, he delivers his shield and submits himself to her law:

> So was he ouercome, not ouercome,
> But to her yeelded of his owne accord;
> Yet was he iustly damned by the doome
> Of his owne mouth, that spake so warelesse word,
> To be her thrall, and seruice her afford.
> For though that he first victorie obtayned,
> Yet after by abandoning his sword,
> He wilfull lost, that he before attayned.   (v. v. 17)

By voluntarily submitting to woman's will ('not deceav'd, / But fondly overcome with Femal charm' is Milton's expression of Adam's fall in *Paradise Lost*), he is justly damned: 'left to her will by his owne wilfull blame' (v. v. 20)

> in wretched thraldome, weake and wan,
> Not by strong hand compelled thereunto,
> But his owne doome, that none can now vndoo.
>
> (v. vi. 16)

Like Hercules he is dressed in woman's attire to spin a distaff, a state which Sidney describes as producing both delight and laughter. 'For the representing of so strange a power in loue procureth delight: and the scornefulnes of the action stirreth laughter.'[1] Laughter is evoked in the power of love which reduces

---

[1] *Apol.*, p. 55. Cf. Musidorus's outburst against love: 'this effeminate love of a woman, doth so womanish a man, that (if he yeeld to it) it will not onely make him an *Amazon*; but a launder, a distaff-spinner; or what so ever other vile occupation their idle heads can imagin, & their weake hands performe'. *Arcadia*, in *Works*, ed. Feuillerat (Cambridge, 1922), i. 78.

him to become 'a womans slaue'; but delight is aroused by the power of love to endure this state, for unlike Terpine he does not seek death:

> Yet he it tooke in his owne selfes despight,
> And thereto did himselfe right well behaue,
> Her to obay, sith he his faith had plight,
> Her vassall to become, if she him wonne in fight.
>
> (v. v. 23)

When he does not forgo Britomart's love for Radigund, he proves himself to be, in the priest's words, 'the righteous Knight, that is thy faithfull louer' (v. vii. 22). Mars and Venus, the 'fierce warres and faithfull loues' which is Spenser's theme in the whole poem, are truly in conjunction.

When Artegall remains faithful to Britomart, he offers the 'maisterie' to her. Consequently, Britomart rejects all conditions for the battle with Radigund, and though the reproach that Artegall would take her life for his is wounding, her return blow slays Radigund. 'Lewdly thou my loue deprauest' (vii. 32) is her response to the reproach: at once claiming him as her faithful lover and a righteous knight. Since Radigund expresses Britomart's womanly pride to which Artegall submits, they are both freed. When she breaks open the iron prison in which 'her wretched loue was captiue layd', and 'sought with ruth to salue his sad misfortunes sore' (v. vii. 38), we see her in the role of Arthur who before had succoured her fallen love, Amoret, and protected her from shame. When she dresses him in his armour, she restores the manhood which she had taken from him. Now they have achieved the true marriage state in which each yields the 'maisterie' to the other. He is the faithful lover, yet free from woman's pride; she submits to Artegall, yet retains her supremacy. Now she *becomes* Isis ruling Radigund's kingdom with true justice:

> The liberty of women did repeale,
> Which they had long vsurpt; and them restoring
> To mens subiection, did true Iustice deale:
> That all they as a Goddesse her adoring,
> Her wisedome did admire, and hearkned to her loring.
>
> (v. vii. 42)

This final appearance of Britomart in the poem—like Una restored to her kingdom—fulfils that vision of herself as Isis, and the two parts of Canto VII as the allegorical centre of Book V render the whole book within Spenser's 'antique Image'.

The marriage of Britomart and Artegall is the means through which the fallen world may be redeemed. Artegall stands for Justice, that virtue which seeks to impose heavenly harmony on earth:

> th'heuens themselues, whence mortal men implore
> Right in their wrongs, are rul'd by righteous lore
> Of highest Ioue, who doth true iustice deale
> To his inferiour Gods, and euermore
> Therewith containes his heauenly Common-weale:
> The skill whereof to Princes hearts he doth reueale.　(v. vii. 1)

Britomart stands for Mercy, that greater virtue which was first bred 'in th'Almighties euerlasting seat . . . from thence pour'd down on men, by influence of grace' (v. x. 1). Their union unites the two virtues, and the two states of the Old Law and the New in the harmony of marriage. This higher state is expressed in a pattern of imagery which extends through Books III and IV until it is resolved in Book V.

Artegall first appears to Britomart as the sun: his manly face

> Lookt foorth, as *Phœbus* face out of the east,
> Betwixt two shadie mountaines doth arize.　(III. ii. 24)

Britomart first appears as the moon:

> As when faire *Cynthia*, in darkesome night,
> Is in a noyous cloud enueloped,
> Where she may find the substaunce thin and light,
> Breakes forth her siluer beames, and her bright hed
> Discouers to the world discomfited;
> Of the poore traueller, that went astray,
> With thousand blessings she is heried;
> Such was the beautie and the shining ray,
> With which faire *Britomart* gaue light vnto the day.
>
> 　　　　　　　　　　　　　　　　　(III. i. 43)

When Artegall first enters the poem as the '*Saluage* Knight' in the tournament, he appears in the image of the burning sun as he

> Far'd like a lyon in his bloodie game,
> Hewing, and slashing shields, and helmets bright,
> And beating downe, what euer nigh him came,
> That euery one gan shun his dreadfull sight,
> No lesse then death it selfe, in daungerous affright.
>
> 　　　　　　　　　　　　　　　　　(IV. iv. 41)

In his sole manhood he rules the day, until Britomart enters:

> So he continued all that day throughout,
> Till euening, that the Sunne gan downward bend.
> Then rushed forth out of the thickest rout
> A stranger knight, that did his glorie shend.   (IV. iv. 43)

'His glorie': that is, the sun's glory and Artegall's; for he is the sun in its destructive power. Britomart's defeat of Artegall and all the knights is described, not through action, but through a simile:

> Like as in sommers day when raging heat
> > Doth burne the earth, and boyled riuers drie,
> > That all brute beasts forst to refraine fro meat,
> > Doe hunt for shade, where shrowded they may lie,
> > And missing it, faine from themselues to flie;
> > All trauellers tormented are with paine:
> > A watry cloud doth ouercast the skie,
> > And poureth forth a sudden shoure of raine,
> That all the wretched world recomforteth againe.

> So did the warlike *Britomart* . . .   (IV. iv. 47–48)

The image is a striking one, significantly placed at this climactic moment. Artegall in his manhood is linked with the destroying sun: Britomart is linked with the rain which renews the world.

When she meets Marinell, another symbol of manhood on the cosmic level, she changes from grief of love into wrath:

> As when a foggy mist hath ouercast
> > The face of heauen, and the cleare aire engrost,
> > The world in darkenesse dwels, till that at last
> > The watry Southwinde from the seabord cost
> > Vpblowing, doth disperse the vapour lo'st,
> > And poures it selfe forth in a stormy showre;
> > So the faire *Britomart* hauing disclo'st
> > Her clowdy care into a wrathfull stowre,
> The mist of griefe dissolu'd, did into vengeance powre.
>
> > > > (III. iv. 13)

When she reveals her beauty to Amoret, she appears as 'the shining skie in summers night, / What time the dayes with scorching heat abound' (IV. i. 13). In the battle against Artegall her face appears 'like to the ruddie morne' (IV. vi. 19). Through these images she is revealed as Nature which restores life: the moon

which comforts lost travellers, the rain which comforts the burning earth, the shower which dispels the fog which shrouds the
world in darkness, the beauty of the night sky after the scorching
heat of day, and early morning which brings the new day. We
have already noticed that with the marriage of the sea and land,
in the marriage of Marinell and Florimell, nature is renewed and
the apocalypse which is the theme of Book V becomes possible.
When Florimell revives Marinell through her return, 'as withered
weed through cruell winters tine, / That feeles the warmth of
sunny beames reflection', for the first time, the sun as light renews
the world.

In Book V this pattern of imagery is resolved. In the first part
of the book Artegall is the sun, and Talus with his iron flail
represents his destructive rays. His chief foe is Radigund who
wears the emblem of the moon upon her shield, and he falls into
her power at that moment when her face appears 'like as the
Moone in foggie winters night, / Doth seeme to be her selfe,
though darkned be her light' (v. v. 12). (The simile is carefully
phrased to distinguish her from Britomart who gives light to the
world.) When Britomart seeks him, 'she to a window came, that
opened West, / Towards which coast her loue his way addrest'
(v. vi. 7), for he is the sun which has been devoured by the west,
and in his stead rules Radigund or the moon.

This imagery is definitively expressed in the Temple of Isis
where the priests who serve the goddess wear mitres 'shaped like
the Moone, / To shew that *Isis* doth the Moone portend; / Like
as *Osyris* signifies the Sunne' (v. vii. 4). That the moon controls
the sun expresses the control of the mutable world over the sun's
destroying power. In the Garden of Adonis we see the sun and
moon in conjunction, the sun serving life:

> Great father he of generation
> Is rightly cald, th'author of life and light;
> And his faire sister for creation
> Ministreth matter fit.   (III. vi. 9)

But this symbol is transformed through Britomart's vision. When
she sees herself as Isis with the crocodile sleeping at her feet, the
priest interprets this part of her vision as showing her lover in
woman's power. This is the state of night when the sun's power
is replaced by the moon, or winter when the sun is no longer

'th'author of life and light'. When Britomart sees herself changed
from a priest into Isis, her moon-like mitre changes to a crown
of gold which signifies 'that she had powre in things diuine' (v.
vii. 6). In terms of the allegory she changes from her role as
Radigund—one who occasions Artegall's fall—to one who restores
his power. Later he is separated from that destroying power of
the sun through the intervention of Arthur.[1] We have already
noticed that the Souldan's chariot 'with yron wheeles and hookes
arm'd dreadfully' is a symbol of the burning sun, and that his
defeat by the light from Arthur's sun-like shield is compared to
the death of Phaeton. In terms of the moral allegory Artegall is
separated from the rough justice of Talus's iron flail, and in the
second half of the book the rule of justice gives way to mercy.

It is through the moral pattern, the marriage debate, and the
cosmic imagery that Spenser seeks to render Book V within his
antique Image. They provide the fiction, and the context within
which we read his allegory of historical events in the climactic
episodes of the book. In the first part of the book he avoids treating the triumphs of Elizabeth's reign, and treats instead the justice
which directs those triumphs. Artegall's first act is to achieve
harmony between the sexes, the basic unit of society, when he
grants the lady to the worthy squire and shames the knight who
abuses love. In Guizor and Pollente he punishes those who despoil
the poor and tyrannize over the rich: that is, those who destroy
the class order in society. In Munera he overthrows the love of
money: the source of discord in society. In the Giant with the
Scales he defeats that satanic endeavour to destroy God's divine
order in society. Then he establishes the perfected society at
the spousals of Florimell. Braggadocchio claims the honour of
chivalry, the False Florimell claims the prize of woman's beauty,
and it would seem that the tournaments would again bring that
discord among the knights and shame to their loves. But by
revealing himself, Artegall uncases Braggadocchio and places the
false Florimell beside the true Florimell whose sun 'her snowy
substance melted as with heat' (v. iii. 24). Now Mars and Venus,
the fierce wars and faithful loves, are joined in that happy society
revealed earlier in the Temple of Venus:

---

[1] Thus it is significant that he triumphs at the tournament through wearing
Braggadocchio's shield 'which bore the Sunne brode blazed in a golden field'
(v. iii. 14).

> in pleasure and repast,
> Spending their ioyous dayes and gladfull nights,
> And taking vsurie of time forepast,
> With all deare delices and rare delights,
> Fit for such Ladies and such louely knights.   (v. iii. 40)

His act corresponds to Arthur's stripping Duessa of her 'borrowed light': as the restored Red Cross Knight now may see and choose rightly, the restored human society is purged of discord. Within this context we may read the events of the second half of the book as fiction.

In the elaborate metamorphoses of Malengin until he is destroyed by Talus there may be the pressure of fact, namely, Essex's massacre of 600 of the wild Irish in their caves. If we focus upon the fact we infer that Spenser seeks to justify the massacre; but in the fiction all that he 'justifies' is the destruction of guile. Guile has been practised earlier by the enemies of the just society, notably by Braggadocchio and the false Florimell; now guile itself is overthrown, that power of metamorphosis which is the source of Archimago's power, and Duessa's. In the second part of the canto guile is displayed in Duessa; and if the pressure of fact, that she is Mary Queen of Scots, breaks through the fiction, at least it is balanced by the elaborate artifice of the trial. The episode is one of the most ornate in the poem, and the pageantry in which Mercilla appears as Isis the most excessive. In its intent, at least, it is not Elizabeth's trial of Mary, but Mercy trying to save the enemies of society while fulfilling all justice. The last three cantos are distanced from fact by the increasing element of fairy tale—the final episode is pure fairy tale—and the obvious emphasis upon the ideal. One editor of the book has observed that the hard facts are that Prince Arthur retired with dishonour from the fight with the Seneschal, and Belge was glad to be rid of him, that Gerioneo and Grantorto were scotched, not killed. He concludes that 'as an idealized version of history a great part of Cantos x and xi would be ridiculous'.[1] Such, surely, is the point which Spenser deliberately makes. The contradiction between the hard facts and what seems to be the poet's allegorical reference to them, removes his poem into the ideal, into fiction. He sees the present as an antique Image.

---

[1] *The Faerie Queene*, Book *V*, ed. A. B. Gough (Oxford, 1918), p. 289. See also his Introduction, p. xlix.

2

Book VI is the triumph of Spenser's fiction. In the enormous range of his poem he includes the 'antique Poets historicall', and also the moderns. Holy Scripture is included in Book I; Homer and Virgil in Book II; Ariosto is overgone in Books III and IV, and Tasso in Book V. Later Milton moves broadly in the area defined by Book I; earlier Dante moves within that area which Spenser leaves undefined at the end of Book I. But Book VI is what Spenser contributes uniquely to tradition. Here he comes into his own; it is both a fresh beginning and the crown of his whole work.

The virtue of courtesy is the most inclusive of the virtues while it remains most natural to man. When Arthur shows himself to be the image of a brave knight in Book I, one who expresses Holiness in his role as the knight's Redeemer, Temperance in his restraint on meeting Ignaro, Chastity in his love for the Faery Queen, Friendship in the bond he pledges with the Red Cross Knight, and Justice in his treatment of Duessa, his defining virtue above all these is his Courtesy. We *see* him as a goodly knight, gently persuading Una to reveal the cause of her grief, then because 'entire affection hateth nicer hands' (I. viii. 40) willing to endure long pains to rescue a fellow knight. Spenser defines courtesy as the gentle heart revealing itself 'in doing gentle deedes with franke delight' (VI. vii. 1). Such is revealed in the 'louely court' (I. vii. 38) with which Arthur entertains Una in her grief, the 'eger greedinesse' (I. viii. 6) with which he encounters Orgoglio, the 'greedie great desire' (29) with which he enters the castle. It is revealed also in Belphoebe in whom steadfast chastity

> was so curteous and kind,
> Tempred with grace, and goodly modesty,
> That seemed those two vertues stroue to find
> The higher place in her Heroick mind. (III. v. 55)

Of course it is revealed, too, in Britomart when she promises to deliver Amoret from prison:

> Ah gentlest knight aliue, (said *Scudamore*)
> What huge heroicke magnanimity
> Dwels in thy bounteous brest? (III. xi. 19)

This natural desire to do good, to act 'with franke delight', is here rightly named *magnanimity* which Spenser defines as the perfection of all the virtues.

Since courtesy approaches the perfection of all the virtues, Book VI resolves the arguments of the previous books, as their fulfilment or consummation. We have noticed before how Book I provides the basis and structure for the whole poem, in its scope embracing man's entire life seen *sub specie aeternitatis*, from an original state of innocence, through fall, redemption, and regeneration, to its final restoration expressed in human terms through the Red Cross Knight's marriage to Una. One central theme of the whole poem is that love which Una bears the Red Cross Knight. She reveals to Arthur 'how I him lou'd, and loue with all my might, / So thought I eke of him, and thinke I thought aright' (i. vii. 49). At first that love only wounds. When her knight believes her disloyal, he becomes defiled by Duessa. This wounding power of love is explored in Book III. Later in Book I Una's love is redemptive: she brings Arthur to his rescue, saves him from despair, succours him in the house of Penance until he is fully restored and she 'him dearely kist' (i. x. 29), and at the end marries him. This redeeming power of love is explored in Book IV. Towards the end of that book, when Arthur resolves the discord among all the knights and ostensibly restores Amoret to Scudamour, the perfected society stands ready to be achieved. In its closing cantos the vision of that perfection of art, nature, and human nature which it seeks is given in the paradise of lovers within the island which contains the Temple of Venus, and the cosmic harmony which may allow that perfection to enter the world is shown in the marriage of Marinell and Florimell. In terms of the pattern of Book I this is that moment when Una's parents and all the people watch Una bring her knight to slay the Dragon who keeps them out of Eden. Book V treats that heroic action which will release mankind from the Dragon, an action which Spenser treats in political terms of Elizabeth's reign because he believed that England was God's instrument to achieve the Apocalypse.

Book VI explores the moment of the Red Cross Knight's restored state when he is married to Una. When their troth is plighted, Duessa blames the knight for 'shamefull iniury' to her, and claims him as her own. Adam,

> When he these bitter byting words had red,
> The tydings straunge did him abashed make,
> That still he sate long time astonished
> As in great muse, ne word to creature spake.
> At last his solemne silence thus he brake,
> With doubtfull eyes fast fixed on his guest.   (I. xii. 29)

But the knight clears himself from the charge, and Una defends him. Their marriage proceeds, and the knight's love is consummated:

> Thrise happy man the knight himselfe did hold,
> Possessed of his Ladies hart and hand,
> And euer, when his eye did her behold,
> His heart did seeme to melt in pleasures manifold.

> Her ioyous presence and sweet company
> In full content he there did long enioy,
> Ne wicked enuie, ne vile gealosy
> His deare delights were able to annoy.   (I. xii. 40–41)

This is that moment before when in his imagination, abused by Archimago, Una was brought to his bed. Then it was the occasion of his fall into Duessa's power. Now he denies Duessa's right to him; Una exposes Archimago's duplicity; and he accepts Una as his bride. We have noticed how this moment is parodied by Verdant as he lies drowned in sensual bliss, forgetful of all virtuous action. It is also the moment of Amoret's marriage whose psychic shock (the shock, that is, to Psyche) brings her imprisonment in the house of Busyrane until the powers of chastity in Britomart, of virginity in Belphoebe, of grace in Arthur restore her to her lover. This moment of fulfilled love is seen in the Garden of Adonis where

> Without fell rancor, or fond gealosie;
> Franckly each paramour his leman knowes,
> Each bird his mate, ne any does enuie
> Their goodly meriment, and gay felicitie;   (III. vi. 41)

only in time their love is cut down, their paradise 'fowly mard'. Within the island which contains the Temple of Venus, the lovers 'ne euer for rebuke or blame of any balkt' but enjoy 'endlesse happinesse . . . that being free from feare and gealosye, / Might frankely there their loues desire possesse' (IV. x. 25, 28).

In Book VI Spenser focuses upon this image of the restored

state, as though deliberately to force the alignment of those who fulfil this state and those who turn it into a fall. His dominant symbol is woman in love, as Una appears in her glory before the Red Cross Knight, or Acrasia before Verdant, or Amoret in her frightened womanhood before Scudamour, or Britomart before Artegall—all of which are aspects of that vision of the Faery Queen which appeared to Arthur.

The antagonists of the lovers' state are, like Duessa, the off-spring of Deceit and Shame. There is the cruelty of Crudor in rejecting Briana who then attacks the lovers' state—expressed in her shearing the knights' beards and their ladies' locks—until Calidore forces Crudor to forgo his cruelty and accept her. Such discourtesy, we understand, may be reformed. But the second antagonist, the envy of that unnamed knight who, upon seeing Priscilla and Aladine 'ioying together in vnblam'd delight' (vɪ. ii. 43), wounds him and beats his own lady, must be slain by Tristram.[1] But the third antagonist, the Blatant Beast, cannot be reformed, wounded, or slain. As Calidore pursues his quest,

> He chaunst to come whereas a iolly Knight,
> In couert shade him selfe did safely rest,
> To solace with his Lady in delight:
> His warlike armes he had from him vndight:
> For that him selfe he thought from daunger free,
> And far from enuious eyes that mote him spight.
> And eke the Lady was full faire to see,
> And courteous withall, becomming her degree. (vɪ. iii. 20)

When the two knights talk of their adventures, Serena is bitten by the Blatant Beast. 'What is that Blattant Beast?' Artegall earlier asks Calidore; and his answer is that it is a monster

> fostred long in *Stygian* fen,
> Till he to perfect ripenesse grew, and then
> Into this wicked world he forth was sent,
> To be the plague and scourge of wretched men:
> Whom with vile tongue and venemous intent
> He sore doth wound, and bite, and cruelly torment.
>
> (vɪ. i. 8)

---

[1] I do not pretend that this logical connexion redeems the Tristram episode: it remains as boring in Spenser as it is in his source, Malory. The true discourtesy, it would seem, is not in the knight but in his lady who remarks of Priscilla: 'faire was the Ladie sure, that mote content / An hart, not carried with too curious eyes' (vɪ. ii. 16).

Elsewhere we learn that this monster serves Envy and Detraction, and also Defetto, Decetto and Despetto (Malice, Deceit, and Detraction),

> A wicked Monster, that his tongue doth whet
> Gainst all, both good and bad, both most and least,
> And poures his poysnous gall forth to infest
> The noblest wights with notable defame:
> Ne euer Knight, that bore so lofty creast,
> Ne euer Lady of so honest name,
> But he them spotted with reproch, or secrete shame.
>
> (VI. vi. 12)

If any, that last word 'shame' defines his nature.[1] But he cannot be defined further than to say that he is Antichrist: with his thousand defaming, blaspheming tongues he is that total perversion of the Word against the Word.

Only Calidore stands between the monster and its power to infect the whole world. In the first defining episode he resists the repeated charges of 'vncomely shame' which Briana's blatant tongue heaps upon him:

> Much was the Knight abashed at that word;
> Yet answerd thus; Not vnto me the shame,
> But to the shamefull doer it afford.
> Bloud is no blemish; for it is no blame
> To punish those, that doe deserue the same;
> But they that breake bands of ciuilitie,
> And wicked customes make, those doe defame
> Both noble armes and gentle curtesie.
> No greater shame to man then inhumanitie. (VI. i. 26)

This reply defends the virtue of Justice; and it explains why Calidore, like Artegall, cannot be wounded by the Blatant Beast. He goes beyond the power of Justice when he shows mercy to the defeated Crudor, and reforms Briana:

> For his exceeding courtesie, that pearst
> Her stubborne hart with inward deepe effect,
> Before his feet her selfe she did proiect,
> And him adoring as her liues deare Lord. (VI. i. 45)

[1] In Milton the first invader of the Garden after the fall is Shame, 'the last of evils; of the first / Be sure then' (*P.L.* ix. 1079–80): Adam seeks to clothe himself 'that this new commer, Shame, / There sit not, and reproach us as unclean' (1097–8). In Bunyan Shame assaults Faithful with the defaming tongues of the Blatant Beast.

Such is that virtue 'that seekes to saue the subiect of her skill, / Yet neuer doth from doome of right depart' (v. x. 2). From the perfection of his nature, the Blatant Beast must flee.

Yet even Calidore cannot prevent the Beast from wounding Serena; in fact, it is through his interrupting the lovers' delight that she is left alone to wander where the Blatant Beast seizes her. Consequently his quest contains the story of Serena and Calepine, of her wounding by the Beast and his wounding by Turpine. This inner story reveals the depravity of human nature. First, in Serena's wound which leaves her helpless. Her wounded state brings the wounding of her lover, and though she is sustained by the Salvage Man and later by Arthur who takes her to the Hermit, she cannot be cured: 'for by no art, nor any leaches might / It euer can recured be againe' (VI. vi. 1). When she is healed enough to continue her journey with Timias, Disdain which overcomes him through Mirabella's foes, brings her flight which ends in her capture by the Savages. The second part of this inner story is Turpine's inhumanity, that 'baser mind' which displays itself

> In cancred malice and reuengefull spight.
> For to maligne, t'enuie, t'vse shifting slight,
> Be arguments of a vile donghill mind,
> Which what it dare not doe by open might,
> To worke by wicked treason wayes doth find,
> By such discourteous deeds discouering his base kind.
>
> (VI. vii. 1)

His baseness reduces Calepine to that nightmare of fleeing from him, chased like a wild goat until he seeks refuge behind his lady's back. Even though Arthur reduces him to a similar plight of seeking protection under the garment of his lady, and shows the mercy which he had denied, not even the power of grace can reform him. In his further efforts to bring others to take Arthur's life he shows, if the pun may be allowed, that baseness has no bottom. He *is* the Blatant Beast in human form.

Within this inner story, and at the centre of the whole book, is the story of Mirabella. This series of inner movements, though complicated by the tale of Sir Bruin and Matilda, Arthur's rescue of Timias, and the life of the Hermit, is carefully patterned to focus upon three separate emblems. The first is the pageant of Mirabella flayed by Disdain. The desecration of the woman's body is

displayed in the opening episode where Maleffort is seen 'with
hand vnblest / Hayling that mayden by the yellow heare, / That
all her garments from her snowy brest, / And from her head her
lockes he nigh did teare' (VI. i. 17), then in that Lady 'in foule
array' (VI. ii. 4) beaten by her envious knight, in Priscilla who is
left 'nigh dead' (VI. ii. 43) with grief and shame, and in Serena
who is bitten by the Blatant Beast and left 'in dolorous dismay
and deadly plight, / All in gore bloud there tumbled on the
ground, / Hauing both sides through grypt with griesly wound'
(VI. iii. 27). Now we see Mirabella

> in such misseeming foule array;
> The whiles that mighty man did her demeane
> With all the euill termes and cruell meane,
> That he could make; And eeke that angry foole
> Which follow'd her, with cursed hands vncleane
> Whipping her horse, did with his smarting toole
> Oft whip her dainty selfe, and much augment her doole.
>
> (VI. vii. 39)

'The greatest shame that euer eye yet saw' (VI. viii. 6) is Sir
Enias's comment. Though in her first youth, as she declares,
'nature me endu'd with plenteous dowre, / Of all her gifts' (VI. viii.
20)—except modesty, surely—through her disdain and scorn of
love for the sake of her liberty, she is now so shamefully subjected
to Disdain and Scorn. Now when Arthur offers her liberty, she
chooses bondage. Upton has noted, and I believe rightly, that she
is the cruel Rosalind of the sonnets, in her pride and insolence
towards love.[1] Arthur 'hearkned wisely to her tale' (VI. viii. 25),
as we are meant to do: in this elaborate medieval pageant we see
how woman may shamefully desecrate her body through her
discourtesy towards love.

The second half of Canto VIII brings the second emblem of
desecration in the vision of Serena bound naked upon the altar.
The one is brought to her present plight through rejecting love,
the other through accepting it. In the beginning she shows
courtesy to her lover as they lie in the shade enjoying 'their quiet
loues delight'; but through Calidore's entrance, she is left 'loosely
wandring here and there':

---

[1] *Spenser's Faerie Queene*, i. xiv.

> Allur'd with myldnesse of the gentle wether,
> And pleasaunce of the place, the which was dight
> With diuers flowres distinct with rare delight,
> Wandred about the fields, as liking led
> Her wauering lust after her wandring sight,
> To make a garland to adorne her hed.   (VI. iii. 23)

This setting in which she is raped by the Blatant Beast suggests the myth of Proserpine, or within Spenser's poem, the myth of Florimell: through her we see how woman's love which should renew the world is brought to shameful bondage. Her wound by the Beast is incurable: though she is sustained by the Salvage Man, aided by Arthur, counselled by the Hermit to abstain from pleasure, at the end in full circle, she is again deprived of her knight who becomes the victim of Mirabella's foes, and is left at the mercy of the 'saluage nation'.

Her adventure may be seen to extend Amoret's, in which Calepine's helplessness to aid her corresponds to Scudamour's, and in which Timias and Arthur play a similar role. When Amoret, like Serena later, walks through the wood she is seized by lust, and afterwards desperately wounded by Timias. When he flees through shame at Belphoebe's appearance, she is left 'almost dead and desperate / Through her late hurts, and through that haplesse wound, / With which the Squire in her defence her sore astound' (IV. viii. 19). She is aided by Arthur whose precious liquor 'vnto strength restor'd her soone anew' (IV. viii. 20) but the attack of Sclaunder brings such 'great feeblesse . . . that scarcely she could ryde' (37). Even with Arthur, she is overcome with fear of shame:

> in feare of shame she more did stond,
> Seeing her selfe all soly succourlesse,
> Left in the victors powre, like vassall bond;
> Whose will her weakenesse could no way represse,
> In case his burning lust should breake into excesse.
>
> (IV. ix. 18)

Like Amoret, then, who was the victim first of womanly fears which left her bound in the house of Busyrane, and then of that Monster who sought to despoil and then devour her, Serena is bound naked upon an altar, surrounded by savages who intend to despoil and then devour her. The moment of her waking to find herself despoiled of her rich array, the priest with his knife raised, and the howling savages waiting to devour her flesh, gathers all the sexual phantasies of woman in love. This ironic vision is broadly comic in tone. The savages debate whether to 'her eate attonce; or many meales to make' but decide to let her sleep and then 'of her dainty flesh they did deuize / To make a common feast, and feed with gurmandize' (VI. viii. 37–38). There are the comic details of the savages whetting their knives and stripping their elbows bare—not too far removed from the comic detail of Shylock whetting his blade in the sacrifice of *The Merchant of Venice*—and the savages flocking around her 'like many flies, / Whooping, and hallowing on euery part' (40) (the comma hardly saves the simile). The tone is almost that of burlesque. If Spenser's poem should reach a paperback edition, underneath the title will be a picture of Serena

> her bellie white and clere,
> Which like an Altar did it selfe vprere,
> To offer sacrifice diuine thereon,

the priest with his knife poised 'readie to launch her brest', surrounded by leering savages waiting to devour her. What delicious horror she must feel, this reluctant Hellenore among the satyrs. This is Spenser's Epithalamion in reverse, much like Donne's in which the nuptial bed is love's altar, on which the bride lies at the bridegroom's approach 'like an appointed lambe, when tenderly / The priest comes on his knees t'embowell her.'[1] Even when rescued by her lover, 'inward shame of her vncomely case / She did conceiue' (the bawdy sense is in keeping with the whole tone of the episode) until day 'made her knowen to him at last' (VI. viii. 51).

The third and climactic emblem of woman is Calidore's vision of the graces. After the separate images of the women in foul array, the pageant of Mirabella led by Disdain and whipped by Scorn, the nightmare of Serena despoiled of her array bound upon the altar as a sacrifice, comes Calidore's ecstatic vision of the dancing graces. The image of Serena naked before the savages' lustful eyes,

---

[1] 'Epithalamion made at Lincolnes Inne', 89–90, in *Poems*, ed. H. J. C. Grierson (Oxford, 1912), i. 144.

> Those daintie parts, the dearlings of delight,
> Which mote not be prophan'd of common eyes,
> Those villeins vew'd with loose lasciuious sight,
> And closely tempted with their craftie spyes,
>
> (VI. viii. 43)

consolidates all those separate images of woman's body desecrated through love which have filled the poem since that image of the lustful Acrasia, and before that to the Red Cross Knight's vision of the false Una as 'a loose Leman to vile seruice bound' in the opening canto. Like Calepine, Calidore is led by the sound of bagpipes to see a vision of a woman naked: not one, but a hundred; not bound in terror and shame, but dancing in delight; and not the leering savages who surround the woman despoiled of her rich array, but naked maidens who surround the muses who dance and also sing to one in the midst of them who is decked with all the graces. But it is a vision, too, 'which mote not be prophan'd of common eyes': like Faunus peering at Diana in great joy but unable to resist forcing his presence upon her—

> a foolish *Faune* indeed,
> That couldst not hold thy selfe so hidden blest,
> But wouldest needs thine owne conceit areed, (VII. vi. 46)

is Spenser's remark in the Mutability Cantos—Calidore seeks to understand his vision. Thereupon it vanishes.

Calidore's vision of the graces is the allegorical centre of the book, and the whole poem; and it is one of the most complex episodes, and the most perplexing, in the poem. When Calidore comes to that hill bordered by the trees which 'did all winter as in sommer bud' (VI. x. 6) and at whose foot flows the stream whose waves cannot be defiled, we know that we have reached at last the true Eden. When he reaches the plain at the top which is called Mount Acidale, he has reached that place where Florimell 'in her first ages flowre / Was fostered by those *Graces*' (IV. v. 5). There he sees

> An hundred naked maidens lilly white,
> All raunged in a ring, and dauncing in delight.

> All they without were raunged in a ring,
> And daunced round; but in the midst of them
> Three other Ladies did both daunce and sing,
> The whilest the rest them round about did hemme,
> And like a girlond did in compasse stemme:

And in the midddest of those same three, was placed
Another Damzell, as a precious gemme,
Amidst a ring most richly well enchaced,
That with her goodly presence all the rest much graced.

(VI. x. 11–12)

There have been other visions such as this, the Red Cross Knight's
vision of Una in 'the blazing brightnesse of her beauties beame, /
And glorious light of her sunshyny face', or Scudamour's vision
of the hundred damsels with the bevy of ladies surrounding
Amoret who appears 'shyning with beauties light, and heauenly
vertues grace', or Arthur's vision of 'that face diuine'. Of the
damsel whom Calidore sees,

Who can aread, what creature mote she bee,
Whether a creature, or a goddesse graced
With heauenly gifts from heuen first enraced?
But what so sure she was, she worthy was,
To be the fourth with those three other placed:
Yet was she certes but a countrey lasse. (VI. x. 25)

All those heavenly significances gather in one who remains a
country lass, a woman of flesh and blood, one who is the poet's
beloved. When we first see this damsel at the centre, our gaze is
suddenly directed ecstatically to the heavens: 'looke how the
Crowne, which *Ariadne* wore . . . Such was the beauty of this
goodly band . . . but she that in the midst of them did stand, /
Seem'd all the rest in beauty to excell' (13–14). Our gaze gathers
the heavenly vision and turns it back to the simple maiden.

A curtain is suddenly drawn, and for a moment we see that
sacred nursery of virtue which inspires the poet to fashion his
image of a brave knight perfected in all the virtues. Colin Clout
('who knowes not *Colin Clout*?') sits in the midst of the dancing
maidens where he leads 'ioyous dayes . . . in this goodly merry
make, / Frequented of these gentle Nymphes alwayes' (19). In the
Proem to the book Spenser seeks inspiration to guide him in
Faery land, 'in these strange waies, where neuer foote did vse, /
Ne none can find, but who was taught them by the Muse', and
here we see that vision at the centre which the Muses grant to the
poet. Once Calidore seeks to know what he has seen, the maidens
vanish. Colin breaks his pipe, and tells him:

> Not I so happy, answerd then that swaine,
> As thou vnhappy, which them thence didst chace,
> Whom by no meanes thou canst recall againe,
> For being gone, none can them bring in place,
> But whom they of them selues list so to grace.   (IV. X. 20)

We may see in Calidore's desire to know, a repetition of the Fall,
Adam's act of eating from the tree of knowledge through which
he lost the vision of paradise. But what choice has Spenser's hero?
Arthur wakens to pursue his vision, the Red Cross Knight leaves
his vision of Una to re-enter the service of the Faery Queen,
Britomart does not seek to gaze again into the mirror but puts
on the armour so that she may know her lover, and Scudamour
conquers his vision of Amoret. Only Verdant remains frozen
before his vision, and Faunus nourishes his desire. Moreover, it
is not Calidore's vision, but the poet's. It is as difficult not to see
the poet intruding himself into the poem, as it is not to see Shakespeare in the role of Prospero with the breaking of the pipe, the
dissolving of the vision, and our awareness (but surely the poet's
too) that his work is being rounded out. Yet *we* are the intruders
in our desire to understand the poet's vision. We want to see the
vision of faery land, and to seize it; and though this brings an
end to the vision, it is meant to be only preliminary to action.
The vision reminds us that the end of the poet's antique Image
is to fashion a gentleman or noble person in virtuous and gentle
discipline.

Before the poem releases us from its vision it turns back to
Calidore's own vision: that 'faire damzell, which did weare a
crowne / Of sundry flowres, with silken ribbands tyde, / Yclad
in home-made greene that her owne hands had dyde', whom he
has seen also sitting upon a hill 'enuiron'd with a girland, goodly
graced, / Of louely lasses' while round about the shepherds praise
this 'miracle of heauenly hew' (VI. IX. 7–8). In Calidore's relation
to Pastorella courtesy extends into a whole way of life. That
virtue which reveals itself 'in doing gentle deedes with franke
delight' is shown through all phases of courtship, from the humble
acts of the lover to his heroic action against the pirates. Moreover,
that state of lovers' bliss which is either fallen, as Verdant with
Acrasia, or has led to a fall, as Scudamour with Amoret, now
triumphantly prepares him for his fierce war against the Blatant
Beast, even as the Red Cross Knight's marriage prepares him for

his great service. When Calidore forgoes his quest of the Blatant
Beast throughout the world, and chooses to pursue his love of
Pastorella, he 'falls'. At the beginning,

> So sharply he the Monster did pursew,
> That day nor night he suffred him to rest,
> Ne rested he himselfe but natures dew,
> For dread of daunger, not to be redrest,
> If he for slouth forslackt so famous quest. (vi. ix. 3)

But he does rest himself when he enters the pastoral world, and
there his contentment at the shepherd's praise of the shepherd's life
merges into the vision of Pastorella:

> That he was rapt with double rauishment,
> Both of his speach that wrought him great content,
> And also of the obiect of his vew,
> On which his hungry eye was alwayes bent;
> That twixt his pleasing tongue, and her faire hew,
> He lost himselfe, and like one halfe entraunced grew.
>
> (vi. ix. 26)

That last line reminds us of the Red Cross Knight wandering in
the Wood, or of Verdant lost in the Bower; and we almost expect
to see Pastorella reveal her serpentine form, or hear the thundering
tread of Orgoglio. When he doffs his bright arms and puts on
shepherd's weeds, Spenser adds:

> who had seene him then, would haue bethought
> On *Phrygian Paris* by *Plexippus* brooke,
> When he the loue of fayre *Oenone* sought,
> What time the golden apple was vnto him brought.
>
> (vi. ix. 36)

That is, he would have thought of Paris's fall; and also of Artegall's fall when he puts off his bright arms for woman's weeds.
When 'that enuenimd sting . . . deepe fixed in his hart . . . now
gan afresh to rancle sore' (x. 31), we see that fatal wound of love
which overcomes all the knights in Books III and IV. Only
Calidore does not fall. He does not become that wandering knight
of Book I, nor the sleeping knight of Book II, nor the languishing
lover in Books III and IV, nor the effeminate knight of Book V.
Through his courtesy, the perfection of human nature, external
Nature is redeemed. Hence Nature herself may appear in the
projected Book VII. Earlier in the poem the Red Cross Knight's

retreat from his quest brought the vision of the monster Error, and later of Orgoglio; Verdant's retreat brought that overwhelming vision of the great enchantress; Scudamour's retreat gained him Amoret but his hopelessness to rescue her; and Artegall's retreat brought his bondage as woman's slave. Calidore's retreat brings his vision of the naked damsels, and knowledge of the graces which sustain human nature; and his vision of Pastorella allows him to display all virtuous action. In short, he triumphs over his vision.

The story of Pastorella is the consummation of Spenser's fiction. By this I mean that the romantic narrative maintains its serene surface at the same time that it suggests many levels of allegorical meaning. It accommodates these meanings without strain, and without yielding to any. Moreover, they are realized upon the narrative level by the story itself. In short, what the image means, it is. Where previously Spenser's rendering of myth helps our understanding the allegory, now the myth and its allegory become the same thing. One name for this kind of treatment would be 'romantic', that is, the dark conceit is embodied in the romantic fiction. 'Literal' would be an adequate term provided that it is seen as anagogic in Dante's sense, whereby the universal significance is realized upon the literal level.

The Pastorella story uses the typical romance elements: the baby girl who is exposed, then adopted by shepherds, later becoming a pattern of beauty and virtue, and being courted by a knight by whom she is restored to her rightful parents. Without violating this story, rather by intensifying its romance elements, Spenser conveys the larger meanings of his allegory. While Pastorella is the simple shepherdess, she is also the flower-maiden who wears 'a crowne / Of sundry flowres'. Her imprisonment in the pirates' cave is also Proserpine's descent into the underworld: 'she thought her self in hell, / Where with such damned fiends she should in darknesse dwell' (x. 43). Also her imprisonment means, or rather *is*, light imprisoned by darkness. In this connexion Spenser exploits the brilliant chiaroscuro effects of the darkness, the candle-light, and Pastorella's blazing beauty. She appears to the merchants

> decayd and mard,
> And eke but hardly seene by candle-light.
> Yet like a Diamond of rich regard,

In doubtfull shadow of the darkesome night,
With starrie beames about her shining bright.   (xi. 13)

Again, she appears 'like the faire Morning clad in misty fog' (xi. 3).
Her imprisonment is also seen as life imprisoned by death: 'shut
vp in deadly shade', her beauty fades 'like to a flowre, that feeles
no heate of sunne, / Which may her feeble leaues with comfort
glade' (x. 44). When she is wounded,

> Her louely light was dimmed and decayd,
> With cloud of death vpon her eyes displayd;
> Yet did the cloud make euen that dimmed light
> Seeme much more louely in that darknesse layd,
> And twixt the twinckling of her eye-lids bright,
> To sparke out litle beames, like starres in foggie night.
>
> (xi. 21)

What before has been signified by the imprisonment of Amoret
and the flight of Florimell is seen in the fiction itself.

Her rescue by Calidore is presented in extravagantly romantic
terms, his breaking down the door of the cave and slaughtering
the pirates until their dead carcasses fill the entrance. Her rescue
is at the same time her resurrection to life, and therefore the
restoration of beauty, life, and light to the world. Calidore brings
her 'to the ioyous light': 'so her vneath at last he did reuiue, /
That long had lyen dead, and made againe aliue' (xi. 50). When
she is restored to her parents, the purple mould upon her breast,
which 'like a rose her silken leaues did faire vnfold' (xii. 7) is
unfolded. Her mother 'rent vp her brest, and bosome open layd, /
In which that rose she plainely saw displayd' (xii. 19). In her
poignant lines: 'and liuest thou my daughter now againe? / And
art thou yet aliue, whom dead I long did faine?' the restoration of
Pastorella to life is rendered literally. In contrast, for example, to
the Red Cross Knight's 'death' before Orgoglio which is to be
interpreted anagogically as his spiritual death, Pastorella's death
need not be interpreted: we see it. It is literal while being most a
fiction.

This fiction yields to the closing episode of the book, where
Calidore engages and quells the Blatant Beast. Again the fiction
is perfect in its kind. Calidore's act of defeating the beast by
throwing his shield on him, could not be simpler, yet in the context of the whole poem where the shield has dominated so many
battles, it could not be more significant. That Beast itself realizes

completely the Dragon figure of earlier books combined with that symbol of the enemy whom no force can defeat. To see how completely the meanings are contained in the fiction itself, we need only recall the Witch's Monster whom Satyrane subdues with Florimell's broken girdle: in this earlier image, the monster who feeds on woman's flesh, who devours Florimell's horse, and who is bound by her girdle, may be understood and interpreted in terms of the larger action which contains it. But no one, nor any number, of allegorical meanings may exhaust the significance of this beast. Yet it is not that indefinite monster—indefinite in meaning then—whom Arthur wounds in Book I, nor that horrific Dragon whom the Red Cross Knight slays. It is very real with its monstrous tongues, and the poet turns its destruction to a direct application in the closing stanzas when he recognizes that his verse cannot escape its 'venemous despite'. And through this sudden turn at the end where the poet speaks of his own verse, the fiction and the whole poem are suddenly distanced and realized as a work completed as a fiction:

> Ne may this homely verse, of many meanest,
>   Hope to escape his venemous despite,
> More then my former writs, all were they clearest
> From blamefull blot, and free from all that wite,
> With which some wicked tongues did it backebite,
>   And bring into a mighty Peres displeasure,
>   That neuer so deserued to endite.
> Therfore do you my rimes keep better measure,
> And seeke to please, that now is counted wisemens threasure.

Suddenly, almost violently, we are brought into the real world of here and now and out of the poem's world. Yet the beast we have met there, is seen here; at least its effects are seen in those wicked tongues who attack the poem. That last line is the most bitter that Spenser ever wrote: since he cannot hope that his writings will escape attack, he will seek only to please: even wise men find *that* is their treasure in a world infected by the Blatant Beast. The haughtiness with which Spenser, in the letter to Ralegh, had scorned the use of these days where nothing is esteemed unless it is delightful and pleasing to common sense, yields now to pessimism. That line brings his fiction to an end.

VI

The Golden World

The waies, through which my weary steps I guyde,
 In this delightfull land of Faery,
 Are so exceeding spacious and wyde,
 And sprinckled with such sweet variety,
 Of all that pleasant is to eare or eye,
 That I nigh rauisht with rare thoughts delight,
 My tedious trauell doe forget thereby;
 And when I gin to feele decay of might,
 It strength to me supplies, and chears my dulled spright.

(VI, Pr. 1)

T HAT 'rare thoughts delight' which ravishes the poet when he
contemplates the 'sweet variety' of the ways 'in this delightfull
land of Faery' defines our way of reading in order that we may
follow him. That faery land itself is built of 'the brightnesse of
braue and glorious words'. Our first and surely our final impression on reading the poem is that language is being manipulated.
Spenser's faery land is the most deliberate artifact in our language.
In another way, however, it is a product entirely of the Elizabethan age, at least of the 1580's and early 1590's. The primacy of
its fiction results from the Protestant emphasis upon the literal
sense of Scripture, the clear light of the Word itself. Thus Tyndale's
insistence upon Scripture's literal sense might serve as a text for
our reading Spenser's poem:

They [the Roman Catholic theologians] divide the scripture into
four senses, the literal, tropological, allegorical, and anagogical. The
literal sense is become nothing at all: for the pope hath taken it clean
away, and hath made it his possession. . . . Thou shalt understand,
therefore, that the scripture hath but one sense, which is the literal
sense. And that literal sense is the root and ground of all, and the
anchor that never faileth, whereunto if thou cleave, thou canst never
err or go out of the way. And if thou leave the literal sense, thou canst
not but go out of the way.[1]

[1] *Obedience of a Christian Man*, in *Doctrinal Treatises* (Parker Society, 1848), pp.
303–4.

The supremacy of Spenser's fiction results from the Elizabethan love of artifice; in ornament and pageantry everywhere we find that joy in appearance. Here our text might be any page of Sidney's *Arcadia,* and to open the book at random:

The earth it selfe (woont to be a buriall of men) was nowe (as it were) buried with men: so was the face thereof hidden with deade bodies, to whome Death had come masked in diverse manners. In one place lay disinherited heades, dispossessed of their naturall seignories: in an other, whole bodies to see to, but that their harts wont to be bound all over so close, were nowe with deadly violence opened: in others, fowler deaths had ouglily displayed their trayling guttes. There lay armes, whose fingers yet mooved, as if they woulde feele for him that made them feele: and legges, which contrarie to common nature, by being discharged of their burthen, were growne heavier.[1]

Since the writer is Sidney we know that there is the pressure of actual experience in what he writes of war; yet no modern reader can fail to be astonished at how artificial conceits actualize such experience. The integrity of Spenser's fiction results from Elizabethan critical theory with its stress upon art, imitation, and exercise. Here our central text, as we have shown earlier, is Sidney's *Apology* with its central doctrine that 'in Poesie, looking for fiction, [readers] shal vse the narration but as an imaginatiue groundplot of a profitable inuention'.[2] From this ethos of religion, life, and critical theory Spenser wrote an allegory in which the reader must focus upon the literal level. When he speaks of the 'rare thoughts delight' which sustains him in writing his fiction, he stresses the *delight* of the sweet variety in the delightful land of faery. Delight is primary for him, as it must be for the reader; and yet, to spell out the phrase, it is delight awakened by *thoughts* which are *rare.*

In this chapter I shall consider the quality of delight which the sweet variety of faery land evokes; and treat in more general terms than in the previous chapters, the poet's use of words, how they are organized into a fiction which becomes a continued allegory, and how the whole poem becomes a golden world.

Spenser's dolphin-like playing with words, his joy in them for their own sake, which sustains him through more than 35,000 lines of poetry, is open to every reader who is willing to share this primitive and sophisticated pleasure. While the poem was still in

---

[1] ed. Feuillerat, p. 388.   [2] *Apol.,* p. 39.

manuscript, Abraham Fraunce quoted a stanza from the Palmer's sermon on 'wrath, gealosie, griefe, loue do thus expell' (II. iv. 35) as an example of the grace and delicacy which proceeds from its rhetorical figures.[1] There is the record of Keats reading the poem 'as a young horse would through a spring meadow—ramping' and singling out the image of 'sea-shouldring Whales' (II. xii. 23).[2] The poem may be opened at random to find effective single lines. For example, when Artegall becomes Radigund's slave, dressed in woman's attire and forced to domestic chores, all the delight and laughter aroused by his effeminate state is contained in the closing line of this stanza:

> But they were forst through penurie and pyne,
> To doe those workes, to them appointed dew:
> For nought was giuen them to sup or dyne,
> But what their hands could earne by twisting linnen twyne.
>
> (V. v. 22)

That last phrase holds up and then releases the reader's response as the punch line of a good story. Spenser's love of words leads to an elaboration which seems excessive until we learn the language of his allegory. Where Chaucer writes succinctly of April's showers which 'bathed every veyne in swich licour / Of which vertu engendred is the flour', Spenser speaks of fountains endued with virtues by great Dame Nature

> from whose fruitfull pap
> Their welheads spring, and are with moisture deawd;
> Which feedes each liuing plant with liquid sap,
> And filles with flowres faire *Floraes* painted lap. (II. ii .6)

His imitation is expanded with phrases such as 'great Dame Nature', 'faire *Floraes* painted lap' which become deeply significant, as we have seen, to our understanding the allegory of the book. Often, of course, his effects depend upon a rhetorical idiom which is lost to our ear, no matter how laboriously we read the Elizabethan rhetorical manuals. We may never cry with E. K. upon discovering 'a gallant exclamation moralized with great wisedom and passionate wyth great affection'. But some of the comic effects come through, as when Glauce explains to the love-stricken Britomart why love afflicts her at night:

[1] *The Arcadian Rhetorike* (1588), ed. E. Seaton (Oxford, 1950), p. 60.
[2] Charles and Mary Cowden Clarke, *Recollections of Writers* (London, 1878), p. 126.

The time, that mortall men their weary cares
   Do lay away, and all wilde beastes do rest,
   And euery riuer eke his course forbeares,
   Then doth this wicked euill thee infest,
   And riue with thousand throbs thy thrilled brest;
   Like an huge *Aetn'* of deepe engulfed griefe,
   Sorrow is heaped in thy hollow chest,
   Whence forth it breakes in sighes and anguish rife,
As smoke and sulphure mingled with confused strife.

                             (III. ii. 32)

We hear the voice of a garrulous old nurse: the nursery tale opening, the absurd folk belief in the power of night to stop rivers,
the monstrous comparison of Britomart's chest (!) to Mount
Aetna, her sighs being compared to smoke and sulphur. The line
'and riue with thousand throbs thy thrilled brest' merits a place
in Bottom's lamentable comedy. But the full effects are open only
to his contemporary reader who would know, almost instinctively,
how absurd her simile is, and how fitting is Spenser's reference
later to Britomart's 'huge sea of sorrow, and tempestuous griefe'
and her 'mist of griefe' (III. iv. 8, 13). Without that rhetorical
training we have lost the 'ioy of liuing speach' through which
Spenser's characters define themselves. It is this, and perhaps the
dramatic form which has attuned our ears to the individual rather
than the typical. Still, we may know Amavia's loving state in
the poignantly rendered line, 'my Lord my loue; my deare Lord,
my deare loue' (II. i. 50). We understand the violence of Terwin's
despair in the rising climax of his cry: 'for Gods deare loue, Sir
knight, do me not stay' (I. ix. 25). (That violence is enforced by
his reference to God's dear love which he does not know, though
perhaps he is fleeing for it.) Or the clear accents of grief in Una's
lament upon hearing the news of her knight's fall:

   Tempestuous fortune hath spent all her spight,
   And thrilling sorrow throwne his vtmost dart;
   Thy sad tongue cannot tell more heauy plight,
   Then that I feele, and harbour in mine hart:
   Who hath endur'd the whole, can beare each part.
   If death it be, it is not the first wound,
   That launched hath my brest with bleeding smart.

                             (I. vii. 25)

The steady rhythm of the first two lines is suddenly broken with

the heavy tolling stress of 'thy sád tóngue'; but the overflow of
grief is checked by the steady rhythmic pattern of the next where
she recalls almost impersonally her role as wisdom. But with the
word *death*: 'If DEATH it be', her grief destroys the pattern in the
short-breathed accents of the rest of the line:

Íf déath it bé, ít ís nót the fírst wóund

until with the heavy stress of the last phrase she lapses into
despair.

The imagery of Spenser's line points both to itself for the
delight it offers, and to the context through which we understand
its significance. I refer to that kind of imagery in which movement
reveals sense, as in the line: 'and on the rocke the waues breaking
aloft' (II. xii. 33) where the line breaks at the word to indicate
sense, or from the same stanza: 'the whiles sweet *Zephirus* lowd
whisteled / His treble, a straunge kinde of harmony' where the
second line itself achieves a strange kind of harmony. Or such a
line as 'and *Vna* wandring in woods and forrests' (I. ii. 9) where
the broken line suggests her wandering. When Talus is described as

Immoueable, resistlesse, without end   (v. i. 12)

the line itself, without any accent being as immovable as Talus,
shows us Artegall's unswerving justice. When Terwin is seen in his
despair,

He answerd nought at all, but adding new
Feare to his first amazment, staring wide
With stony eyes, and hartlesse hollow hew,
Astonisht stood . . .   (I. ix. 24)

Here the run-on of the first line bears all the force upon *feare*; the
comma after 'amazment' leads to the slow movement of the next
line, until with 'stood', the line shows his arrested motion. The
rhythm of the line here creates the image. When Orgoglio raises
his club to slay the fallen Red Cross Knight,

His heauie hand he heaued vp on hye   (I. vii. 14)

the alliteration, and the heavy stress upon *he he-aued*, shows the
power of that hand, and the three short syllables at the end show
it rising for the final blow. Or the imagery of a line may be

extended to consolidate the entire significance of an episode. Aesculapius's cave is described in one line:

> Deepe, darke, vneasie, dolefull, comfortlesse　(I. v. 36)

Each word is separated by its comma into a block of rhythm: the alliteration of the first two heavily-stressed words, the lightly-stressed 'vneasie' which is a bridge to the echoing pause on 'dolefull' until the whole weight falls on the final word, 'comfort-lesse'. The trailing accents of this word contain all the meaning of his present state of one eternally damned in hell, beyond all hope of redemption. A similar effect is gained in the line which describes the Red Cross Knight's fallen state:

> Disarmd, disgrast, and inwardly dismayde.　(I. vii. 11)

The iambic pattern is broken both by the alliteration which gives stress to the initial syllable, and by the allegorical weight of 'arms' and 'grace'; each word in its ominous implications becomes a separate image which focuses the significance of his fall into one line. It is not possible to separate delight in the style from the understanding which it brings from the whole context. In Sidney's fine phrase, which he wastes in another connexion, his style is 'such as caried riches of Knowledge upon the streame of Delight'. When Arthur's shield is unveiled in his battle against Orgoglio,

> Such blazing brightnesse through the aier threw　(I. viii. 19)

where the echo of *through* and *threw* shows light bursting. But more than this image, the line gathers those earlier references to light which we have traced in Book I: the knight's glistering armour, the glittering house of Pride, Duessa's borrowed light, and Una's blazing brightness.

Through our awareness of the larger meaning given by the context, what might become clichés in another writer, stock phrases dulled by repetition, become alive with significance. When the wrathful Cymochles is soon overcome by Phaedria's charm, Spenser moralizes:

> So easie was to quench his flamed mind
> With one sweet drop of sensuall delight,
> So easie is, t'appease the stormie wind
> Of malice in the calme of pleasant womankind.
>
> > (II. vi. 8)

The typical Spenserian effects, the alliteration in the third line, the internal echo of *easie* and app*ease*, the echoing phrases in 'so easie was . . . so easie is' may seem to deaden the language itself. Yet he earns the language which he uses. Cymochles' *flamed* mind has already been shown in the wrath which Atin 'kindled' in his mind (II. vi. 2), and later when he throws off the sleep which 'quench[ed] the brond of his conceiued ire' (27). The *calm* of pleasant womankind is literally realized in Phaedria's idle lake. Here Phaedria's drop of sensual delight quenches Cymochles' flamed mind: at the end of the canto, all the waters in the Idle Lake cannot quench Pyrochles' flaming body. Spenser exploits this metaphor further when we see those few drops which trill down Acrasia's breasts arouse desire,

> And her faire eyes sweet smyling in delight,
> Moystened their fierie beames, with which she thrild
> Fraile harts, yet quenched not.[1]   (II. xii. 78)

Everywhere in his poem the metaphorical possibilities which lie latent in our language are explored. Its repeated epithets and phrases, such as 'wrathfull', 'goodly', 'gloomy', or 'foul', are justified within a context where every psychological, moral, and ethical state is contained. Lust which is described as greedy or beastly or brutish may be shorn of meaning in another writer, but in Spenser such phrases focus meanings gathered throughout the poem into such images as the stripped Duessa, Acrasia's beasts, the Witch's Monster, Lust itself, or again Corflambo. He may refer to 'dreadfull darkness' or 'ioyous day' because we see Night herself and also Una unveiled. These 'stock' phrases are repeated because Spenser uses his language of allegory consistently throughout his poem. Even sleep, a state which we might expect to be neutral at some time, and in the later books which treat of lovers to be a time of joy, remains ominous throughout: either it is 'deadly' or a prelude to harm. There is the one exception, of course, where we expect it to be: in his Arcadia, Meliboee tells how 'all the night in siluer sleepe I spend' (VI. ix. 22). Through this language the whole poem is held upon the level of metaphor, being

---

[1] There is, as we might expect, exact physical theory behind Spenser's use of the images of fire and water throughout the book, and here given its final statement. Acrasia is Circe who, according to Comes, is the mixture of the elements which is caused by heat and moisture. See C. W. Lemmi, 'Symbolism of the Classical Episodes in *The Faerie Queene*', *P.Q.* viii (1929), 270–87. Of course, the connexion here only enforces the *sterility* of nature, which is Spenser's point.

itself a continued metaphor. Consequently, our understanding of any one episode reaches out to embrace the whole poem. Literally, and in a degree to which no other poem reaches, its meaning is the missing part of the context which is the rest of the poem. Out of this context his language becomes dead; and this is its particular virtue. To quote a stanza which we have considered earlier, Scudamour's vision of Amoret:

> Thus sate they all a round in seemely rate:
> And in the midst of them a goodly mayd,
> Euen in the lap of *Womanhood* there sate,
> The which was all in lilly white arayd,
> With siluer streames amongst the linnen stray'd;
> Like to the Morne, when first her shyning face
> Hath to the gloomy world it selfe bewray'd,
> That same was fayrest *Amoret* in place,
> Shyning with beauties light, and heauenly vertues grace.
>
> (IV. X. 52)

There are no immediate effects of concentration, tension, or ambiguity in the style; no direct feelings are evoked, but rather almost matter-of-fact reporting. This is what he saw. There is no complexity which would be involved if Amoret were love of something: she is simply love itself. But within the poem this stanza is, as we have seen, immensely significant. Each detail is alive with meaning. Even the simile, 'like to the Morne', which seems ordinary enough to be used anywhere, is used in this form only once before, when Britomart first appears to Artegall 'like to the ruddie morne' (IV. vi. 19). Spenser uses it here because Amoret *is* the morning, that love which is the source of all joy, life and light. The detail of the feminine virtues sitting 'all a round in seemely rate' takes the reader back to the monstrous order of the sins driven by Lucifera, and to the disorder of the ladies who serve Alma in her Castle, and forward to Calidore's vision of the hundred naked maidens 'raunged in a ring' who surround Colin's damsel. Even without consciously recalling these other episodes, this detail, like all others, strikes the reader as inevitable, necessary, and meaningful.

Being so rooted in the reality of the poem, this language defies translation into other terms. It must remain metaphor. When Timias languishes for Belphoebe's love, she refuses to yield 'that sweet Cordiall, which can restore / A loue-sick hart',

That dainty Rose, the daughter of her Morne,
    More deare then life she tendered, whose flowre
    The girlond of her honour did adorne:
    Ne suffred she the Middayes scorching powre,
    Ne the sharp Northerne wind thereon to showre,
    But lapped vp her silken leaues most chaire,
    When so the froward skye began to lowre:
    But soone as calmed was the Christall aire,
She did it faire dispred, and let to florish faire.

(III. v. 51)

Her virginity, in other words, we may want to add : but we cannot,
even though the metaphor is the most traditional that Spenser
could use. We cannot, because after the opening phrase, 'that
dainty Rose', the metaphor belongs to the poem: the simple
meaning of *virgo intacta* becomes an emblem of human nature in
its state of innocence when the stanza is succeeded by the description of the Garden of Adonis where we see all life in the image of
the flower. We cannot translate this metaphor any more than we
can Shakespeare's in *The Winter's Tale* where Perdita distributes
flowers to her maidens, 'and yours, and yours, / That weare vpon
your Virgin-branches yet / Your Maiden-heads growing' (IV. iv.
114–16). Through this image of Belphoebe tending her dainty
Rose, we are brought from that vision of Nature's sterility seen
in the Bower of Bliss where we hear the cry, 'gather the Rose of
loue' and where we see Acrasia upon a bed of roses—all dead
flowers—to Nature's fertility which cannot be destroyed. The
poem itself translates this image in the story of Florimell who
endures despite her rape, and later in the story of Pastorella whose
rose is finally unfolded. Through translating itself in this way,
the whole poem becomes a continued metaphor.

Even the allegorical reference which turns us from the reality
of the poem to another world of reality becomes absorbed within
the metaphor of the poem. In the letter to Ralegh Spenser tells us
that Una's armour is the armour of a Christian man specified by
Saint Paul in Ephesians. The poem itself tells us as much and more
in its opening lines :

A Gentle Knight was pricking on the plaine,
    Y cladd in mightie armes and siluer shielde,
    Wherein old dints of deepe wounds did remaine,
    The cruell markes of many' a bloudy fielde;

Yet armes till that time did he neuer wield:
His angry steede did chide his foming bitt,
As much disdayning to the curbe to yield:
Full iolly knight he seemd, and faire did sitt,
As one for knightly giusts and fierce encounters fitt.
But on his brest a bloudie Crosse he bore. . . .

The breaking of the iambic pattern with the stress upon 'old dints' and 'deepe wounds' and again with the stress upon 'that time' and 'he neuer' points up the allegorical significance and contains it within the poem. We know that with their old dints these are no ordinary arms, and that the knight who has never worn them before is no ordinary knight. He may seem to be a 'full iolly knight' BUT he wears the cross—the 1590 edition had the weaker 'And'—and the full stress upon that word together with the alliteration reveals that he is a knight in the medieval sense, one who serves Christ. 'Gentel men with ihesu' is Langland's term.[1] The armour of a Christian man which is defined in these opening stanzas is expounded in the unfolding allegory of Book I where, as we have seen, the glistering armour opposes the powers of darkness until in that climactic battle it defeats the brazen armour of the Dragon.

                          The weapon bright
Taking aduantage of his open iaw,
Ran through his mouth with so importune might . . .

The arms, rather than the man himself, win that final victory. This allegory of the armour is continued in the later books. In Book II, for example, Guyon's armour, without the horse and spear, is defensive; but worse than this, not only can it not defend him against his inner foes, its power in his shield and Arthur's sword opposes his rescue from his foes. In Book III, again, Britomart upon her horse wields the enchanted lance with which she unhorses all her enemies; but when her horse is wounded by Artegall's sword, she is defeated. Within this allegory there are elaborate patternings in battles where each blow is fraught with special significance: as the wounding in the head in Book II where the offence of intemperance is against reason, or the wounding in the thigh in Book III where the wound is concupiscence, or

[1] *Piers Plowman*, xix. 40.

the hewing of the shield in Book V as the symbol of political dominance. Or in Book IV, to choose an episode which we have slighted, in Cambel's battle with the three brothers there is careful patterning in the three equal stages: the first section of eight stanzas (iii. 6–13) shows their 'equall worth, / And equall armes': the wound in the thigh is met with the wound in the shoulder, the wound in the head with the wound in the windpipe, and the weapon which Priamond wields to kill Cambel is returned to kill him. The second section of eight stanzas (14–21) describes the battle not through blows but through images as the contest between two tigers, and a vulture with a heron. The final section of sixteen stanzas (22–37) describes the double battle against Cambel until at the end the two Champions are joined in friendship. Other allegorical references, such as the horse upon which the knight rides, are also absorbed within the metaphor of the whole poem. Since the horse is traditionally linked with the passional element in man, and therefore with the body, we see Guyon journey without his horse, and subdue Pyrochles after he severs his horse's head. Later we see Britomart wield her enchanted lance while she rides her horse, but defeated when Artegall wounds her horse's hind quarters. Or Florimell's translation to the underworld is preceded by the Monster devouring her horse.

But all terms within the poem, not only the overtly allegorical ones, belong to the continued metaphor. We have traced how the Red Cross Knight's fall before Orgoglio is displayed as a passage through the four elements: from the fire of the boiling sun, to the cooling wind (air), to the poisoned water, to the fall to the ground (earth). His ascent comes when he is taken from the earth by Arthur, is baptized by the Well of Life, and passes through the purgatory of fire and wind in the belching flames of the Dragon. In Book II Spenser develops the symbolism of water in Guyon's passage over the water and his victory over the two ducking maidens. But in Book III we see Timias wounded while he passes through the water; and the allegory of the book is worked out in the contrast between Guyon passing *over* the water and Florimell imprisoned *under* the water. The resolution of the book is achieved when Britomart passes through the fire which surrounds the house of Busyrane and defeats the god whose power is revealed in the wind which closes the doors that imprison Amoret. The resolution of Book IV comes when Florimell is released from the power of

Neptune. But commentary upon these matters may be, and should be, endless.

Even similes may develop into patterns which belong to the metaphor of the poem, and assist our understanding. To offer one example which seems extraneous because it is the one definite influence upon the poem of the poet's long stay in Ireland, the attack of flies or gnats. When the Red Cross Knight confronts Error, her monsters swarm about his legs but cannot hurt him:

> As gentle Shepheard in sweete euen-tide,
>> When ruddy *Phœbus* gins to welke in west,
>> High on an hill, his flocke to vewen wide,
>> Markes which do byte their hasty supper best;
>> A cloud of combrous gnattes do him molest,
>> All striuing to infixe their feeble stings,
>> That from their noyance he no where can rest,
>> But with his clownish hands their tender wings
> He brusheth oft, and oft doth mar their murmurings.
>
> (I. i. 23)

Since Una tells the knight that the place breeds dreadful doubts, we link the brood, and therefore the flies, with doubtful thoughts. In the second part of the canto we see Archimago served by sprights who are compared to 'little flyes / Fluttring about his euer damned hed' (38): that is, he is seen as Satan, Lord of the Flies, and the wicked spright who abuses the knight's fancy—it is '*his* irkesome spright' (55)—is that evil thought which leads him to doubt Una's truth. This connexion is made clear in Book II where, in the Castle of Alma, the head is filled with flies:

> And all the chamber filled was with flyes,
>> Which buzzed all about, and made such sound,
>> That they encombred all mens eares and eyes,
>> Like many swarmes of Bees assembled round,
>> After their hiues with honny do abound:
>> All those were idle thoughts and fantasies,
>> Deuices, dreames, opinions vnsound,
>> Shewes, visions, sooth-sayes, and prophesies;
> And all that fained is, as leasings, tales, and lies.
>
> (II. ix. 51)

Inevitably, Maleger's besieging forces are compared to a swarm of gnats:

As when a swarme of Gnats at euentide
   Out of the fennes of Allan do arise,
   Their murmuring small trompets sounden wide,
   Whiles in the aire their clustring army flies,
   That as a cloud doth seeme to dim the skies;
   Ne man nor beast may rest, or take repast,
   For their sharpe wounds, and noyous iniuries,
   Till the fierce Northerne wind with blustring blast
   Doth blow them quite away, and in the *Ocean* cast.

(II. ix. 16)

Arthur is that northern wind which blows them away when he
casts Maleger into the lake. The same image is found in Book V
where the vulgar crowd attacks Burbon 'as a swarme / Of flyes
vpon a birchen bough doth cluster' (xi. 58) until Talus drives
them into the sea. By this repetition the image establishes itself
within the metaphor of the poem. Consequently, when Spenser
uses it in Book VI it gathers all its allegorical significance within
the fiction itself. When Calidore is attacked by the thieves who
hold Pastorella captive, the battle is described mainly through this
one image:

How many flyes in whottest sommers day
   Do seize vpon some beast, whose flesh is bare,
   That all the place with swarmes do ouerlay,
   And with their litle stings right felly fare,
   So many theeues about him swarming are.   (xi. 48)

The image is most literal—for the first time we see the stings in
the bare flesh—while it renders the allegorical significances of the
vulgar mob stirred up by evil thoughts, and that satanic power
which seeks to separate a lover from his desire.

Besides such patterns of similes there are those larger metaphors
which organize each book, and these we have traced earlier. In
Book I there is the opposition of light and darkness for the body
of the knight. Mankind in its fallen state no longer holds the
world in its subjection and having lost rule over the West is
enclosed in the brazen body of the Dragon, shut off from the life-
giving powers of the Tree and Well of Life. Once the Dragon is
slain we are free to begin the pilgrimage. In Book II the organiz-
ing metaphor is that of the besieged body. The Dragon figure is
Maleger, and once he is slain, mankind may see how Temperance
may hold the world again in subjection. In Books III and IV the

central image is the body wounded by concupiscence, and this is the Dragon figure which must be slain. Through the power of chastity we see how love is released, and then how love restores the wounded body. When the body is restored by love, the masculine and feminine may be joined in the bond of marriage: this figure of the perfected human state, the hermaphroditic state of marriage, is the unifying metaphor of Book V. Since this is a social relationship, one achieved within society, the Dragon figure becomes the evil powers in the world. Once the true marriage is achieved by Britomart and Artegall, Arthur overthrows the evil marriage of Adicia and the Souldan, Duessa's efforts to destroy social bonds are revealed in Mercilla's court, Arthur overthrows Gerioneo's destroying alliance with the widow Belge, Artegall unites Burbon and Flourdelis in marriage, and finally he 'marries' Irena to her people. In effect, mankind seeks to regain that lost rule over the West. In Book VI all these images are consolidated. That opposition of light and darkness which is definitively rendered in the Pastorella episode appears throughout the book; the image of the besieged body is seen in the forces of Crudor and Turpine which attack the lovers' state; the body wounded by concupiscence is seen in the afflicted Serena; the true marriage state is seen in the relationship of Colin to his damsel and in Calidore's courtship of Pastorella, while all the worldly powers which oppose virtue and love are seen in the Blatant Beast. Its image is the opposition of man's natural goodness and his natural depravity. The one is expressed in Calidore, in Timias, and the Salvage Man, and of course in Arthur; the other is expressed in the cruelty of Crudor, the unredeemable baseness of Turpine, and the savage lawlessness of the brigands. This image is the simplest in the poem, and yet the most profound. In this way the separate images build into the total image which is the whole poem, an image which is unified because the entire narrative level is rendered into metaphor.

To see the whole poem as an image is to glimpse at least some of that 'sweet variety' whose 'rare thoughts delight' sustained the poet over some sixteen years of labour. We have seen how Book I defines the scope of the whole poem, and how Book VI resolves its entire action. Its unity may be seen also in its relation to the whole life of man: the adventure of the Red Cross Knight shows that pattern into which human life is born; Temperance defines that primary virtue through which man first establishes an equation with the external world; Acrasia is that mother-figure whom the child must destroy in order to enter manhood; Chastity is that virtue whereby the adolescent keeps his integrity, Amoret's release being the preparation for marriage which is shown in Book IV; Friendship shows the mature man establishing social relationships, the chief one being marriage; Justice is the concern of middle age when the right social relationships are consolidated into the just state; and Courtesy is that maturing of human virtue in the complete man. If Book VII treats Mutability, it would show how old age and death bring the completion of one cycle and the beginning of another. Such unity would be readily seen by Spenser's Elizabethan reader who read the *Aeneid*, for example, as an allegory of human life. Yet the poem is not an allegory of human life: rather, our life is an allegory of the poem which reveals our life as it should be. Here there is no question that Spenser wrote with the faith that his poem would fashion Elizabeth's courtiers in virtuous discipline. At the end of Book IV when the marriage of the Medway and the Thames heralds the bursting of the waters which precedes the rebirth of England, and the return of Spring in the person of Florimell completes the natural cycle, Plato's Great Year stands poised to turn down into another cycle. At this point Spenser turns the poem to the fallen world, to show how England may achieve its redemption. With Book V it becomes clear what Spenser was about when he was exhorted by Piers:

> sing of bloody Mars, of wars, of giusts,
> Turne thee to those, that weld the awful crowne.
> To doubted Knights, whose woundlesse armour rusts,
> And helmes vnbruzed wexen dayly browne.

and so planned an heroical poem

> to restraine
> The lust of lawlesse youth with good aduice:
> Or pricke them forth with pleasaunce of thy vaine,
> Whereto thou list their trayned willes entice.
>
> (*Oct.* 39–42, 21–24)

He plans to move England's courtiers to all virtuous action; and in a dedicatory sonnet he urges them to read his books:

if their deeper sence be inly wayd,
And the dim vele, with which from comune vew
Their fairer parts are hid, aside be layd.
Perhaps not vaine they may appeare to you.

('To Burleigh')

In the persons of Britomart and Artegall, the British heroine and
hero, he shows them everything they should do. The fifth book
would be the poem's climax, where there is no passivity or idleness at the end but all virtuous action. Here is all that must be
done to build Jerusalem 'in England's green & pleasant Land'.
If only the nobility will understand his allegory, it will become a
light through which they may vanquish the powers of darkness.
Yet such is only one special end or working of the poem.

If we keep the poem as metaphor, we may see that it treats as
extensively and profoundly as any poem has done, man's relation
to nature: not only psychologically, but ethically and meta-
physically. Its moral centre—and it may be Spenser's own faith
for all we know—is given in these lines:

all the sorrow in the world is lesse,
Then vertues might, and values confidence,
For who nill bide the burden of distresse,
Must not here thinke to liue: for life is wretchednesse.

(III. xi. 14)

The simultaneous awareness of the power of virtue and the
wretchedness of life drives the poem into metaphor. Consequently
its central visions are always twofold: Una is veiled, woman's
beauty is combined with the serpent's tail in Error and Duessa,
the glorious Lucifera as the fallen Faery Queen, Florimell and the
false Florimell, Amoret bound, Venus with the snake wound
around her feet, Isis and the crocodile. By exploring these visions
the poem moves towards an image of man seen perfected in
Arthur and also the image of Nature. As Arthur appears in the
various knights, Nature appears in her various forms, from that
original vision of the Faery Queen and the primary vision of Una
to Belphoebe, Amoret, Florimell, Britomart, Colin's damsel surrounded by the graces and maidens, until Nature herself appears
in the Mutability Cantos. We see this unfallen Nature in opposition
to fallen Nature, her counterpart in the twofold vision. Since this
nature is both without and within man, we see unfallen man in the

images of virtue at one with nature opposed to fallen man in the
images of vice. Once we see that opposition upon all levels,
Nature is redeemed, and therefore man. It is in this sense that
Spenser delivers in his poem a golden world.

Spenser's poem was answerable to its great Idea through the
medium of fiction, and the decline of fiction brings that eclipse
which we noted at the beginning of this study. The general history of the decline of allegory in the seventeenth century has been
traced elsewhere,[1] and I may round out this study of Spenser's
allegory by noting some of its effects upon his kind of fiction.
Mainly, it is the triumph of that first enemy Du Bartas, now in
English guise in Sylvester's translation of the *Divine Weeks*. At
one point the translator appeals to God

> That I by this may wain our wanton ILE
> From *Ovids* heirs, and their un-hallowed spell
> Heer charming senses, chaining soules in Hell.
> Let this provoke our modern Wits to sacre
> Their wondrous gifts to honour thee, their Maker:
> That our mysterious ELFINE Oracle,
> Deep, morall, grave, Inventions miracle . . .
> May change their subject, and advance their wings
> Up to these higher and more holy things.[2]

Sidney's right poet is supplanted by the divine poet, fiction by
truth. Jonson believes that Spenser's fiction could lead England
back to the golden age,[3] but Cowley who records that the '*Eternal
Word*, hast call'd forth Me / Th' *Apostle*, to . . . teach that *Truth
is truest Poesie*' believes that the heroical poem must be baptized
in Jordan before it can bring about 'the accomplishment of the
Kingdom of Christ'.[4] One R. R. records

> Foole that I was, I thought in younger times,
> That all the *Muses* had their graces sow'n
> In *Chaucers*, *Spencers*, and sweet *Daniels* Rimes
> (So, good seems best, where better is unknown)

until he reads Du Bartas and prefers 'his *Fruits* before their
Winter-shaken *Leaves*'; and to those who do not agree with him,

[1] See Douglas Bush, *Mythology and the Renaissance Tradition in English Poetry* (Minneapolis, 1932), esp. pp. 240 ff.
[2] Du Bartas, *His Diuine Weekes*, trans. Sylvester (London, 1633), pp. 81, 82.
[3] 'The Golden Age Restor'd', in Herford and Simpson, vii.
[4] *Davideis*, i. 39–42, in *Poems*, ed. A. R. Waller (Cambridge, 1905), p. 243, and Preface to *Works* (1668), in Waller, p. 13.

most unfairly he adds 'let *Gryll* be *Gryll*'.[1] But the real difference is not that of their end but of their means. Spenser's fiction maintains its integrity while being consonant with God's Truth, but the defenders of divine poetry rejected the element of fiction. George Wither writes: 'can we be delighted to heare a Heathen *Poet* sing a fabulous story of *Hercules*, their great Champion (whose valour neuer benefitted vs) how hee went downe to hell, and by force brought thence the Lady *Proserpina*, whom the Prince of that infernall Region had rauished? And can we not take as great pleasure to heare the diuine *Muse* of this heauenly *Poet*, sing in a true Historie, how for the benefit of all men (euen for vs) Christ our farre more victorious Captaine descended into the lowest depths, for the saluation of our soules; and hauing subdued death, and hell, deliuered that faire Ladie the Church from being rauished by the Prince of Darkenesse?'[2] Spenser writes that he uses the historical fiction of Arthur for the delight and profit it gives the reader, and through his fiction shows Arthur imitating Christ.

With fiction supplanted, the heroical tradition ends.

[1] *Diuine Weekes*, B7ʳ.
[2] *A Preparation to the Psalter*, 1619 (Spenser Society, 1884), p. 77. See L. B. Campbell, 'The Christian Muse', *Huntington Library Bulletin*, viii (1935), 32.

Index

PRINTED IN GREAT BRITAIN
AT THE UNIVERSITY PRESS, OXFORD
BY VIVIAN RIDLER
PRINTER TO THE UNIVERSITY